Treating Dissociative and Personality Disorders

Treating Dissociative and Personality Disorders draws on major theorists and the very latest research to help formulate and introduce the Relational/ Multi-Motivational Therapeutic Approach (REMOTA), a new model for treating such patients within a clinical psychoanalytic setting.

It forms the clinical reverberation of the common factors model, promoting a perspective of integration of different theories and approaches and introduces the question of the relationship between traumatic structure and personality disorders. REMOTA constitutes an integrative and comparative new approach that will be indispensable for combining relational clinical knowing and motivational system theories, which identify the universal invariants that govern human relatedness, starting from evolutionism and infant research.

Supported by her contributors, Antonella Ivaldi provides an overview of existing theories and evidence for their effectiveness in practice, setting out her own theory in detail through rich and compelling case histories. The narratives in this book show how it is possible to integrate different contributions within a multidimensional aetiopathogenic treatment model, which considers the mind as a manifestation of the relationship between body and world.

From a conceptual perspective, according to which consciousness emerges and develops in the interpersonal dimension, this book shows how it becomes possible to understand, in the therapeutic space, what stands in the way of sound personal functioning, and how to create the conditions for improving this at different levels of functional complexity.

Treating Dissociative and Personality Disorders will be highly useful in addressing the particular clusters of symptoms presented by patients, stimulating therapists of different backgrounds to explore the complexity of human nature. It will appeal to psychoanalysts and psychotherapists, especially those in training, clinicians of different backgrounds interested in comparative psychotherapy, as well as social workers and graduate and postgraduate students.

Antonella Ivaldi is a training analyst at the psychotherapy postgraduate program of LUMSA University, the Institute of Relational Psychoanalysis and Self Psychology (ISIPSÉ), and the School of Cognitive Psychotherapy. She is also Member of the International Association for Relational Psychoanalysis & Psychotherapy, the International Association for Psychoanalytic Self Psychology and the Italian Society of Cognitive and Behavioural Therapy.

'Relationship, theory, and clinical acuity all come together in the wonderful synthesis that is central to Antonella's presentation and personhood. Using rich clinical examples, she demonstrates how her use of motivational theory enables her to navigate the challenges of treating difficult patients.'
– **Joseph D. Lichtenberg**, Psychiatrist and Psychoanalyst, Founder and training analyst at the Washington Institute for Contemporary Psychotherapy and Psychoanalysis, Past President of the International Association for Psychoanalytic Self Psychology and Editor in chief of Psychoanalytic Inquiry.

'To my knowledge, Ivaldi's work is the first attempt at a comparison of two different theories that focuses more on the lived experience of a dynamic psychotherapist – both in her formative encounters with senior professionals and in her exploration of clinical realities – than on abstract theorizing.'
– **Giovanni Liotti**, Psychiatrist and Psychotherapist, teaching at the APC postgraduate School of Psychotherapy in Rome, Past President of the Italian Society of Behavioural and Cognitive Therapy (SITCC).

'Ivaldi's book expresses all the determination, but also the creativity, of a passionate clinician. When the writing seems heavily theoretical, it melts in the clinical dimension; and when it is likely to become fervently clinical, it turns to the dialogue with the theoretical dimension. It is a useful and complete book, capable of holding together different approaches. The relational breath of Ivaldi's multidimensional model hosts a brilliant and critical exchange with Lichtenberg's and Liotti's motivational theories. When we read the clinical histories written by Ivaldi we find ourselves not only thinking about clinical cases described by a sensitive colleague: It is as if the voices and behaviors of our "real" patients are coming to life.'
– **Vittorio Lingiardi**, Psychiatrist and Psychoanalyst, Director of the postgraduate school of Clinical Psychology and Full Professor of Dynamic Psychology, Faculty of Medicine and Psychology, Sapienza University of Rome.

'This book is an intriguing and very important attempt by Antonella Ivaldi to create a new approach to dissociative and personality disorders. In a very sophisticated and yet clear and expressive way, she uses motivational theories of different approaches to create a unique theory and a unique treatment.'

– **Gianni Nebbiosi**, Psychoanalyst, founding member and President of ISIPSé, Vice President of IARPP and member of the IAPSP International Council.

'This is an important and creative contribution to the psychotherapy integration movement. It brings together two different yet overlapping perspectives in the treatment of some of the most difficult – and painfully suffering – patients we work with. It does not gloss over differences, yet creatively seeks commonalities and complementarities. Moreover, by adding group work to the work with individuals it still further extends the reach of the integration and contributes valuably to the effort to relieve human suffering.'

– **Paul L. Wachtel**, Ph.D, Distinguished Professor, Doctoral program in clinical psychology, City College of NY and CUNY Graduate Center.

'Today there are so many psychotherapy books that it is really difficult to get oriented. This book by Antonella Ivaldi is surely worth reading: it goes right to the heart of crucial issues of contemporary psychotherapy. It deals with theory of motivation and with the possibility of integrating different therapeutic approaches. And what is most fascinating is that while it shows the importance of theory, it never loses sight of the nuances of clinical encounter. In this book the patient seems even more "real", when seen through the lens of theory.'

– **Paolo Migone**, M.D., Editor, Psicoterapia e Scienze Umane.

'Antonella Ivaldi's Relational/Multi-Motivational Therapeutic Approach (REMOTA) is an important text for clinicians seeking to impact severely traumatized individuals whose intersubjective possibilities have been severely compromised. In bridging two major multi-motivational systems theorists, Lichtenberg and Liotti, Ivaldi further extends the terrain to include data from multiple sources - infant and attachment research, neuroscience, trauma theory, the treatment of dissociative disorders, individual and group therapies. With beautifully illustrated clinical sensitivity, with vibrancy and fluidity, and with a dialogic touch, Ivaldi continuously questions and postulates afresh the strengths and limitations always intrinsic to this complex field of mind and soul.'

– **Hazel Ipp, Ph.D.**, Joint Editor-in-Chief, Psychoanalytic Dialogues: The International Journal of Relational Perspectives, Past-President of IARPP.

'This fascinating and inspiring book edited by Antonella Ivaldi has many clinical and scientific merits, the main of which is its successful attempt to harmoniously integrate theories and methods originating from different perspectives in a new multidimensional aetiopathogenic treatment model for patients with personality and dissociative disorders. Thanks to a series of well-described and enlightening clinical cases, Antonella Ivaldi convincingly guides the reader thorough her innovative model in which individual and group psychotherapy are efficaciously combined. Using the therapeutic relationship in a complex way, she builds a bridge between contemporary psychoanalysis and cognitive-evolutionary model.

This really is a brilliant book, which I strongly recommend.'

– **Rita B. Ardito**, Ph.D., President of the Italian Society of Behavioural and Cognitive Therapy

PSYCHOANALYTIC INQUIRY BOOK SERIES
JOSEPH D. LICHTENBERG

Like its counterpart, *Psychoanalytic Inquiry: A Topical Journal for Mental Health Professionals*, the Psychoanalytic Inquiry Book Series presents a diversity of subjects within a diversity of approaches to those subjects. Under the editorship of Joseph Lichtenberg, in collaboration with Melvin Bornstein and the editorial board of *Psychoanalytic Inquiry*, the volumes in this series strike a balance between research, theory, and clinical application. We are honoured to have published the works of various innovators in psychoanalysis, such as Frank Lachmann, James Fosshage, Robert Stolorow, Donna Orange, Louis Sander, Léon Wurmser, James Grotstein, Joseph Jones, Doris Brothers, Fredric Busch, and Joseph Lichtenberg, among others.

The series includes books and monographs on mainline psychoanalytic topics, such as sexuality, narcissism, trauma, homosexuality, jealousy, envy, and varied aspects of analytic process and technique. In our efforts to broaden the field of analytic interest, the series has incorporated and embraced innovative discoveries in infant research, self psychology, intersubjectivity, motivational systems, affects as process, responses to cancer, borderline states, contextualism, postmodernism, attachment research and theory, medication, and mentalization. As further investigations in psychoanalysis come to fruition, we seek to present them in readable, easily comprehensible writing.

After 25 years, the core vision of this series remains the investigation, analysis and discussion of developments on the cutting edge of the psychoanalytic field, inspired by a boundless spirit of inquiry.

For a full list of all the titles available in the Psychoanalytic Enquiry Book Series, please visit the Routledge website.

Vol. 53
Attachment Across Clinical and Cultural Perspectives: A Relational Psychoanalytic Approach
Sonia Gojman-de-Millan, Christian Herreman & L. Alan Sroufe (eds.)

Vol. 52
The Muse: Psychoanalytic Explorations of Creative Inspiration
Adele Tutter (ed.)

Treating Dissociative and Personality Disorders

A motivational systems approach to theory and treatment

Edited by
Antonella Ivaldi

LONDON AND NEW YORK

First published 2016
by Routledge
2 Park Square, Milton Park, Abingdon, Oxon OX14 4RN

and by Routledge
711 Third Avenue, New York, NY 10017

Routledge is an imprint of the Taylor & Francis Group, an informa business

© 2016 selection and editorial matter, Antonella Ivaldi; individual chapters, the contributors

The right of the editor to be identified as the author of the editorial material, and of the authors for their individual chapters, has been asserted in accordance with sections 77 and 78 of the Copyright, Designs and Patents Act 1988.

All rights reserved. No part of this book may be reprinted or reproduced or utilised in any form or by any electronic, mechanical, or other means, now known or hereafter invented, including photocopying and recording, or in any information storage or retrieval system, without permission in writing from the publishers.

Trademark notice: Product or corporate names may be trademarks or registered trademarks, and are used only for identification and explanation without intent to infringe.

British Library Cataloguing in Publication Data
A catalogue record for this book is available from the British Library

Library of Congress Cataloging in Publication Data
Names: Ivaldi, Antonella, editor.
Title: Treating dissociative and personality disorders : a motivational systems approach to theory and treatment / edited by Antonella Ivaldi.
Description: Milton Park, Abingdon, Oxon ; New York, NY : Routledge, 2016. | Includes bibliographical references and index.
Identifiers: LCCN 2015047617| ISBN 9780415641371 (hbk) | ISBN 9780415641401 (pbk) | ISBN 9781315637297 (ebk)
Subjects: LCSH: Dissociative disorders – Treatment. | Personality disorders – Treatment.
Classification: LCC RC553.D5 T74 2016 | DDC 616.85/23 – dc23
LC record available at http://lccn.loc.gov/2015047617

ISBN: 978-0-415-64137-1 (hbk)
ISBN: 978-0-415-64140-1 (pbk)
ISBN: 978-1-315-63729-7 (ebk)

Typeset in Times New Roman
by Florence Production Ltd, Stoodleigh, Devon

Contents

List of Contributors	xii
Foreword Giovanni Liotti	xiii
Foreword Joseph D. Lichtenberg	xv
Acknowledgements	xvi

	Introduction	1
	ANTONELLA IVALDI	
1	**Theorizing about theory**	5
	JOSEPH D. LICHTENBERG	
2	**Theoretical foundations**	11
	ANTONELLA IVALDI	

Where this model fits among other theoretical perspectives in psychotherapy 11
Motivational systems theories 24
A comparison of the two theories: a personal synthesis 30

3	**The therapeutic relationship from the theoretical perspective of motivational systems**	38
	JOSEPH D. LICHTENBERG AND GIOVANNI LIOTTI	

Introduction – Antonella Ivaldi 38
Motivational systems and the problems of patients with narcissistic, borderline, and dissociative disorders Joseph D. Lichtenberg 39

*The debate between Joseph Lichtenberg and Giovanni
Liotti. From infant research to evolutionism: two
motivational perspectives in dialogue*
Giovanni Liotti and Joseph D. Lichtennerg 50

4   **Complex trauma theories and psychopathology:
    the difficult patient**   63
    ANTONELLA IVALDI

    *Who is the difficult patient? 63
    Trauma and dissociation 68
    Psychophysiology of trauma 88*

5   **Personality disorders: diagnosis and treatment**   102
    MARIANGELA LANFREDI AND ANTONELLA IVALDI

    *Empirically supported psychological approaches to the
       treatment of personality disorders 106
    Why do different treatment models prove to be equally
       effective? A hypothesis based on motivational theories 111*

6   **The relational/multi-motivational therapeutic
    approach (REMOTA)**   115
    ANTONELLA IVALDI

    FIRST PART   115
    *The structure of the dual setting REMOTA: a simple
       structure for a complex process 119
    The therapeutic relationship and its complexity 120
    How the therapist trains for the complexity of the
       relationship 127
    The first phase of treatment: individual therapy 135
    Setting and relationship: negotiating the therapeutic
       alliance 137
    The metacontext: therapy in the real context of the
       patient's life 148
    Working with emotions 156
    Empathy: a complex process? 158
    The body in therapy: the use of non-verbal communication
       in the relationship 167*

SECOND PART 171
The group: methodological considerations 171
Is affiliation an inborn motivation? 174
Being in a relationship using two session rooms 176
The therapeutic relationship and the group 181
Why does the integration of the individual and the group
 setting improve working conditions? A biopsychosocial
 hypothesis based on evolution theory 187
Conclusion 193

7   **Some methodological considerations on outcome
    research in psychotherapy and results of a naturalistic
    study in the treatment of patients with severe axis I/II
    comorbidity disorders**   197
    GIOVANNI FASSONE

Some food for thought 197
The Gold Standard for research on outcomes in medicine
 and psychotherapy: is all that glitters gold? 199
Some problems with RCTs in psychotherapy 201
Conclusion 205
Results from a controlled naturalistic study in the
 treatment of severe comorbid axis I/II patients 207

8   **Group psychotherapy: addressing impediments to
    engaging the affiliative motivational system**   217
    ROSEMARY SEGALLA

Functioning in groups 220
Affiliation and group membership 221
Aspects of affiliation in group therapy 223
Impediments to the activation of the affiliative motivational
 system 225
From individual to group: a case 228
Summary 237

References   239
Index   257

Contributors

Giovanni Fassone, MD, PhD, is a professor at the School of Cognitive Psychotherapy and teaching member of the Scientific-Didactic Commission of the Italian Society of Cognitive-Behavioral Psychotherapy (SITCC).

Mariangela Lanfredi, PhD, is a researcher in the Unit of Psychiatry at the Saint John of God Clinical Research Centre in Brescia, Italy and an ordinary member of the Italian Society of Behavioral and Cognitive Therapy (SITCC).

Joseph D. Lichtenberg, MD, is Editor-in-Chief of Psychoanalytic Inquiry, Director Emeritus of the Institute of Contemporary Psychotherapy and Psychoanalysis, past President of the International Council for Psychoanalytic Self Psychology, and a member of the Program Committee of the American Psychoanalytic Association.

Giovanni Liotti, Psychiatrist and Psychotherapist. Teaches 'Clinical Applications of Attachment Theory' at the APC postgraduate School of Psychotherapy in Rome, Italy. Past President of the Italian Society of Behavioural and Cognitive Therapy (SITCC).

Rosemary Segalla, PhD, CGP, FAGPA, is on the faculty of the Group Psychotherapy Training Program of the Washington School of Psychiatry, Washington, DC. She is co-founder and Director Emeritus of the Institute of Contemporary Psychotherapy and Psychoanalysis, Washington and also member of the International Association of Psychoanalytic Self Psychology governing council.

Foreword

Giovanni Liotti

The continuously shifting different motives that underpin any affectively significant and durable exchange between human beings are a key focus of interest for psychotherapists in general and psychoanalysts in particular. In contemporary clinical practice, it is likely that the majority of psychoanalysts and even a wider proportion of dynamic psychotherapists of any orientation do not rely any more on the classical theory that reduces these motives to two basic instinctual drives, sex (libido) and destructive aggression (mortido). Multi-motivational approaches to human relatedness – considering attachment, intersubjectivity and other systems of motives together with sex and aggression – are emerging substitutes for the classical dual drives theory. Two multi-motivational theories – the psychoanalytic one advanced by Joseph Lichtenberg and a cognitive-evolutionary one – provide comprehensive conceptual backgrounds both for the study of the multiple primary systems that regulate human relationships and for the applications to clinical practice of the emerging multifarious view of the basic underpinnings of relational experiences and behaviour.

In this book, Antonella Ivaldi provides the lively picture of a clinical practice influenced by both these multi-motivational theories. She does so by narrating not only her experience of the clinical exchange with difficult patients with a history of chronic childhood traumatization, but also her lived dialogues with Joseph Lichtenberg and with myself as a supporter of the cognitive-evolutionary theory of motivation. To my knowledge Antonella Ivaldi's is the first attempt at a comparison of two different theories that focuses more on the lived experience of a dynamic psychotherapist – both in her formative encounters with senior professionals and in her exploration of clinical realities – than on abstract theorizing. Going through the pages of this book, readers not only can learn which are the basic tenets of the two multi-motivational theories, the number and types of motivational systems considered by each and their similarities and differences, but they can also figure out the mental processes of a clinician who is engaged, during her practice, in dialogic thinking between herself, two of her professional mentors and each of her difficult patients. In dialogic thinking there is not room for defending the superiority of one's own preferred theory, because the focus of attention is in the exchange of ideas and experiences as a source of intellectual riches that vanish when one is too strongly defending one side of the dialogue and striving to prove the other side wrong. In dialogic thinking, one is always hoping that the inner or outer interlocutor, rather than the self, is right. One hopes so because she or he is aware that this is the only way both to support the robustness of one's preferred theory and to expand it by amending it of mistakes. When dialogic thinking between the different theories of two interlocutors is going on in the mind of a third party that is remembering the personal encounters with the proponents of the two theoretical positions, as is the case with Ivaldi, it may rise to the apex we call open-mindedness and versatility. In her book, Ivaldi is not interested in arguing which one of the two theories is to be preferred because of its scientific rigor, its width of scope or its clinical usefulness. Rather, she is interested in sharing with colleagues her enthusiasm for the perspectives opened up by the continuous comparison of the two theories in her professional life. The final result of putting this comparison in the pages of a book is not only deeply informative, but also quite refreshing reading for any clinician.

Foreword

Joseph D. Lichtenberg

Antonella Ivaldi has written a book about relationships. Read her sensitive human interchange with Angie for an introduction to her clinical relationally-focused sensitivity. She describes for the reader the depth of the connection she has made to her two principal mentors – of whom I have the honor and satisfaction of being one. In the spirit of her book, Antonella tells not only about Liotti and Lichtenberg as two theoreticians whose concepts converge, differ, and overlap, but also about her personal attachment to each of us. Relationship, theory, and clinical acuity all come together in the wonderful synthesis that is central to Antonella's presentation and personhood. Many components of the book cover new ground in the treatment of very troubled patients in an easy-to-read and informative manner. Particularly rich is the discussion of the place in day-to-day therapy of theory, especially a well-formulated theory of motivation. Using rich clinical examples, she demonstrates how her use of motivational theory enables her to navigate the challenges of treating difficult patients.

Antonella in her writing, and Giovanni and I in our debate, carefully avoid polarizing stances, instead keeping issues open for what can be gained from each. This dialogic perspective enables her to use two theories and two treatment methods – individual and group. The combination facilitates her sensitivity to both a patient's and therapist's ever-shifting motivations. Antonella's empathy and willingness to be an involved presence radiates throughout the pages giving the presentation a liveliness reflective of its author.

Acknowledgements

It is a pleasure for me to thank Silvia Guglielmi, who, with great sensitivity and ability, has translated my chapters.

A warm thank you to Joe Lichtenberg who believed in me.

I wish to thank the following publishers and authors for allowing me to use in my book previously published material:

Raffaello Cortina Editore for Table 2.1 and Figure 4.1

Eastern Group Psychotherapy Society and GROUP Journal for Tables 7.1 and 7.2

Giovanni Liotti for Franco Angeli Editore

Maurizio Ceccarelli for Curcu & Genovese Editore

Introduction

Antonella Ivaldi

When I thought about writing this book, I wondered whether it would really be worthwhile to outline a new treatment model for patients with personality and dissociative disorders, since many are already available, all of them authoritative and of proven effectiveness (Linehan, 1993; Bateman and Fonagy, 2006; Kernberg, 1984; Young, 2003).

It is however interesting to try to understand why treatment models originating from such different theoretical approaches are all equally effective with patients belonging to the same diagnostic category. All these models are based on integrated teamwork involving different settings and psychotherapeutic skills.

Is it possible to explain this on the basis of a meta-theory on human relatedness, such as the multi-motivational theory? In an attempt to answer this question, I will focus on the theoretical contributions offered by infant research (Tronik, 1989; Lyons-Ruth and Jacobvitz, 1999; Beebe and Lachmann, 2002; Stern, 2004), neurosciences (MacLean, 1973; Edelman, 1989; Damasio, 1994; LeDoux, 1996; Panksepp, 1998; Schore, 1994) and motivational theories (Lichtenberg, 1989; Liotti, 1994/2005).

I will refer to the theories of complex trauma in order to better understand the 'difficult patients' for whom my approach is designed. I will then briefly describe the evidence-based treatments used with these patients.

Finally, I will introduce my method, which is a simple yet original synthesis of these different perspectives and the result of many years dedicated to working with difficult patients.

Since 1998, I have been using a model that attributes a central role to motivational systems theories, both from Lichtenberg's psychoanalytic perspective and from Liotti's cognitive-evolutionary[1] vantage point.

Motivational systems theories have been revolutionary inasmuch as they have provided an important alternative to Freud's dual instincts theory (life and death), as well as a meta-theory that is open to many therapeutic approaches, which I believe can be integrated. Developments in neurosciences and infant research suggest that it is indeed possible to know and to better define phenomena belonging to the intersubjective and relational spheres, which for many years have not been investigated scientifically.

For a long time in psychoanalysis mental phenomena could only be interpreted on the basis of very suggestive hypotheses: from the classical Freudian approach to developments leaning ever more towards a relational outlook (Aron, 1996).

Thanks to evolutionism and infant research, we have been able to better orient ourselves in the sphere of our emotions and to introduce a theory on human motivations that can help us to categorize mental and relational phenomena, largely comforted by the results observed in neurobiological studies.

This motivational theory has the merit of doing away with the drives theory as it applied to the human mind, providing strong support and even more scientific value to the revolution that was initiated during the seventies in psychology (Bateson, 1972 and the Palo Alto school) and in psychoanalysis (Greenberg and Mitchell, 1983) by the relational and intersubjective schools of thought (Benjamin, 1990; Stolorow and Atwood, 1992).

The combined individual and group therapy model that I will present refers primarily to attachment theory (Bowlby, 1969) and to interpersonal motivational systems theories. It also refers to how they are applied in clinical work based on the cognitive-evolutionary model (Gilbert, 1989; Liotti, 1994/2005) and in clinical work based on contemporary psychoanalysis (Lichtenberg, 1989). Particular importance is given to the awareness of self-with-other in the process of personality development, from the relational and intersubjective prespective.

My background is diverse. After completing my initial training in transactional analysis some thirty years ago, I started using the group setting in private clinical outpatient practice. Over the years, I trained in various areas: systemic family therapy, cognitivism, Gestalt therapy, group analysis. Through my work I came into contact with the world of psychoanalysis. Years ago, I collaborated with the Institute of Child and Adolescent Neuropsychiatry ('La Sapienza' University of Rome), and, more recently, with the Institute of Self Psychology and Relational Psychoanalysis of Rome (ISIPSÉ), where I got my postgraduate degree.

I never stopped using the group in my work and I learned more about group psychodynamics through various experiences. I have shifted from focusing on individuals in a group (Berne, 1968) to working with a group conceived as a whole (Bion, 1959). The ongoing dialectic between individuals and the group is one of the particular elements of the working model that took shape in the course of my experience. Even before approaching evolutionary cognitivism and collaborating on a clinical and research project, I followed my patients in my own private practice. I worked with the same patients in individual as well as group therapy.

Although at first I had not conceptualized anything about this practice, I felt it was useful with 'difficult' patients with whom it was harder to have a constructive therapeutic relationship. I felt like a pioneer and was rather worried about what other group therapists would say about these unorthodox experiments.

I thought that what they would probably criticize most was the fact that the same therapist would move from the individual therapy room to the group therapy room together with the patients, raising issues about boundaries, transference, and much more. I accidentally discovered that Rosemary Segalla has been using the same combination of individual and group setting for years.

The years from 1996 to 1999 were crucial in my professional experience. Contact with Giovanni Liotti and evolutionism, and later with Joseph Lichtenberg and his theory, was instrumental in helping me to understand what I already found useful. Attachment theory and the theory of interpersonal motivational systems developed in the realms of psychoanalysis and cognitivism, respectively, allowed me to explain why combining the individual and group settings can be so useful. When I eventually encountered Bateman and Fonagy (2006) and their model based on mentalization, as well as selfpsychologists and relational analysts, I was glad to see that the experience I had gathered over the years was similar to that of many others.

Note

1 The cognitive-evolutionary perspective is a complex theory, based on the principles of evolutionism, which looks at motivation. It has used, and continues to use, ethological observation and the contributions of neurosciences, in elaborating the pivotal concept of motivational systems which, when referred to the intersubjective sphere, is known as the interpersonal motivational systems.

Chapter 1

Theorizing about theory

Joseph D. Lichtenberg

Is a theory necessary to practice psychoanalysis? Why not approach each event in the therapy of individuals, couples, or groups with an 'open mind' guided only by the observable phenomenon that emerges. To answer: an 'open mind' is a myth. Open mindedness is a valuable cultivated attitude. Humans (and higher animals) process experience by making implicit and explicit inferences about the affects, intentions, actions, and goals of others and themselves. Being human we can't not make inferences. And having a theory, however simple or complex, is a prerequisite for forming an inference. Sometimes, actually very often, we make our inferences, assumptions, conjectures, hypotheses, estimates, assessments, and appraisals so rapidly that we are not aware we have made them, and generally are not aware of the theory we are using. We hit the brake to avoid a pedestrian who started across the street before we 'know' we have made an assessment and constructed an action response or that we have based our action on a conception of safe driving practices. We feel the 'Oh my God' relief after the moment in which the inference, action, and goal have played out. The phenomena in psychoanalysis we recognize as transference involve assumptions patients make about their analysts – our theory tells us that affectively strong past events trigger dispositions to form expectations of repetitions. And transferences involve the inferences that analysts draw about an implicit or explicit attribution a patient is making about them – our theory alerts us to the subtlety of metaphoric references to the analyst protectively encased in speech and gesture. Additionally, analysts time their interpretations of transference based on inferences, often implicit, about when the patient might be receptive – our theory tells us that affect, speech and gesture patterns provide clues to openness or turn off to information or influence.

A clinical example: His face animated, Mr. T. enters and immediately begins to talk about a phone conversation with his parents. His tone conveys his usual skepticism about their 'foolishness' in reference to his troubled dependant older brother. But he adds how come his parents assume all information goes from his brother to them or him to them. Why would they believe that he and his brother would not exchange information?

I infer he is in an animated state, eager to tell me the latest evidence that supports his chronic attitude of skepticism. My posture changes (out of my awareness) to a higher degree of alertness. As I listen, I contrast his current state with his affectless state in the last session when he had droned on and on and I could barely stay awake. His reactions to the phone call are a familiar theme with some new details that hold my interest, but my level of interest peaks when I hear him ask 'how come' his parents do not assume he and his brother have a relationship that does not centre on them. The content of the question is not what 'grabs' me – it is the fact that he is asking a question! Two sessions before I had challenged him on his lack of curiosity about both an unexpected sexual pattern he had followed in college, and later a variant of the pattern kept secret from his wife and from me for a long time into his treatment. I had conjectured that the subsequent affectless session that followed was an aversive response to my challenge and the shame my comment probably triggered. Now I conjectured that he had absorbed my challenge and was ready to explore a peripherally related aspect of the problem. With his curiosity now available implicitly, I inferred he would be open to my expanding my comments. As the session progressed, his further receptivity confirmed my positive expectation.

What place did theory occupy as I did my work as a psychoanalyst with Mr. T? As a psychoanalyst I have a theory that every mind state involves motives and emotions. My theory holds that different emotions or emotional attitudes are commonly associated with different intentions and goals. For example, persistent preoccupation with parents indicates unresolved attachment intentions and skepticism represents the negative aspect of an ambivalent attachment. Interest and curiosity are associated with the problem solving aspects of exploratory intentions. An analytic session characterized by avoidant dissociated affects or 'deadness' indicates the presence of an aversive intention of withdrawal and may further indicate a rupture in the transference–countertransference dyad. Each of these theory constructs guided my witnessing, my recognizing, my empathic listening and my self-reflection as I acted as a participant observer/interpreter during the session and when I reviewed it in my mind afterward.

If a theory is necessary for psychoanalysis, what particular qualities recommend a motivational systems theory? Central to Freud's considerations were theories that explained what motivates human behaviour in general and what goes awry in the psychoneuroses and other mental illnesses. Libidinal and aggressive instinctual drives (or Eros and the death instinct) provided an explanation for the symptomatic neuroses and war trauma respectively. Levels of awareness, a dynamic unconscious, executive functions, a defensive organization, values, moral guides, and ideals had to be accounted for. An internal world of self and object representations and modes of regulating the drives and affects became a later focus. The principle of adaptation moved the explanation from an exclusive intrapsychic focus to a greater account of interactions with the animate and inanimate environment. Differing analytic theories described a holding environment, object relations, interpersonal relationships, attachment theory, a self–selfobject matrix, intersubjectivity, and the relational perspective. With the shift of emphasis from intrapsychic dynamics to an interactive perspective, clinical theory took on a new vocabulary pointing to other dynamics. The analyst is brought more directly into the interplay of transference and countertransference, in concepts such as providing a container function, in the recognition of enactments as both negative and positive, and in attachment seeking. Even more contemporary concepts point to implicit relational knowing, a selfobject experience of vitalization and/or soothing, new relational experience, and the building of a dyadic realm of safety and positive ambiance (a 'third').

I argue that a theory of motivational systems includes and integrates the seminal elements of these shifts in theory and therapeutic approach (Lichtenberg, Lachmann, and Fosshage, 1992, 1996, 2002, 2011; Lichtenberg and Kindler, 1994; Lichtenberg, 1989, 2005). Additionally, motivational system further integrates modern non-linear systems and complexity theory, and a contemporary non-linear development theory integrated with findings derived from neuroscience.

When does 'theory' enter the process of inference making? A theory is the necessary template out of which an inference is selected. Both template and inference may remain implicit or be brought into awareness. Humans are continuously processing information and using a simple or complex template (theory) to draw the inferences needed for navigating their procedural, social, conceptual, and affective experiential worlds. Social operational theories may be simple and personal. An example would be an experience Tom, an elementary school age child, described: 'When I came home from school, my mother was cranky, not her usual glad to see me. When I left for school she was in a happy mood so I figured something had upset her and it wasn't me.' Tom drew his inferences from a series of templates he had formed from prior experience. First, when a person has a change of emotional state, the change is the result of some occurrence, and second, when the shift is from a positive affect to a negative affect the occurrence was disturbing. In inferring (concluding) that he was not the responsible source, Tom drew on a theory (belief) that his mother was very fond of him and he was solidly in her good graces. His operant theory (reasoning) was that when a person is in the good graces of a person fond of him, he is not apt to be a negative factor unless evidence is revealed to the contrary. Were he to scan his mind and remember that he had left his room a mess or failed to take out the garbage as promised and/or he saw his mother looking in the direction of his room or the garbage, he would have an instantaneous shift in inference – based on a simple cause–effect theory. From this example and countless others from ordinary daily life, I aver that as humans we form templates, maps, or schemas from which we draw ad hoc theories to orient ourselves about every lived experience and use these theories to form the inferences that guide our expectations and choices.

A reexamination of empathy offers a further example. The conventional view of empathy is that it is a mode of perception by which we place ourselves as much as possible into the state of mind of another person. As we listen to our patient empathically we sense her state of mind, her emotions, her thoughts and her perspective including us. This delineation is correct but incomplete. We don't just sense into another's state of mind, we also make inferences about what we believe we perceive. We infer the patient's intentions and goals as well as the context that is most relevant to those intentions and goals. In addition we also implicitly 'theorize' about past and present determining influences and make predictions about what associations will come next – where the session, the patient and we are going next. This places empathy in our broader clinical theory.

Each valued psychoanalytic theory – Freudian, Kleinian, Winnicottian, Jungian, Laconian, Sullivanian, ego psychological, Mahlerian, Kohutian, intersubjective, evolutionary, and attachment – has tended to privilege one or another group of affects, intentions, and goals. With awareness and respect for these many theories, motivational systems theory attempts to offer a flexible inclusive integrated account of the diversity of human emotions, intentions, and goals. A point of departure for motivational systems theory is the continuous interplay between each individual and the human and inanimate environment in which he and she develop and live from birth (and before) to the end of life. No single motivational system is privileged as more significant for human functioning and survival, rather intentions and goals continuously shift in their dominance as mental states and contexts fluctuate. In this way the theory is concordant with the shifting associations and themes representing implicit and explicit motivations in each clinical session. Each system self-organizes based on a principal or paramount grouping of affects, intentions, and goals we indicate by the designations we have chosen: a system for the regulation of physiological requirements, for attachment to individuals, for affiliation with groups, for caregiving, for exploration and the assertion of preferences, to react to aversive experience via antagonism and/or withdrawal, and for sensual excitement and sexual excitement. Beyond the verbal designators that epitomize the needs and motives of each of the seven systems, world pictures and event stories in each system help analysts to evoke an infant and older child's dyadic and triadic experience, a school aged child's peer and widening experience, and an adolescent and adult's more complex intentions and goals. A therapist attempting to infer unfolding motivational themes utilizes the affective/metaphoric power of the picture-stories that animate the more abstract system verbal designators. Word and imagistic picture-stories provide the orienting sensitivity for analysts to feel themselves empathically into the mind state of analysands. The necessary knowledge is of *what* to observe. I believe that the pictures and stories derived from motivational systems theory contribute to the necessary knowledge of *what* to observe for optimal therapeutically productive inferences. Analyst and analysand sharing on-target word pictures and metaphoric connections derived from motivational systems theory builds a sense of intimacy, a mutual sense of understanding and being understood, a co-created positive affective state the dyad can share, and an easily re-created sense of safety and trust after disruptions. These positive effects of the use of motivational systems theory (or any effective theory) are the *sine qua non* of successful analysis.

Chapter 2
Theoretical foundations

Antonella Ivaldi

Where this model fits among other theoretical perspectives in psychotherapy

Dear Angie,
Reading the book that you picked for me was very moving. I think that you have uncommon intuitive skills and a likewise unique sensitivity. Your gift came at a difficult and painful moment in my life and it was like receiving a warm embrace. As I read it, I felt ever more grateful to you for what you were communicating to me. It is an honour for me to be compared to Dr Semmelweiss, not just for his undeniable value, but especially for his great ability to love – as Celine says, to be moved. While reading, I thought that you were communicating to me something very intimate and important about yourself, Angie. What is Dr Angie like? I wondered. Does she not conduct her work with love? And is it not true that her insights are extremely helpful to the people who turn to her? And in your case, those people are children, so your sensitivity is all the more valuable.

And what is Angie like as a woman? She is thoughtful with everyone she meets, is never false, is willing to expose herself, sometimes too much and in a dangerous way; she gives herself completely, selflessly.

So why does she suffer so much? What is wrong? Dear Angie, you have done a lot for me with this book and I want you to know how much I care about you. And that is why I am going to tell you something that you may not want to hear but that you will appreciate later on, I am sure. As I said, you are incapable of being false; however, at times you are unable to be authentic, essentially because your state of consciousness is altered. I mean to say that sometimes you are not clear-headed, self-aware, enough to understand and handle your emotions well. One might say that you appear to be 'possessed' by your emotions, or rather, by your emotional chaos. That is why you seek help. We have been exploring together the roots of your problem for some time now, and of course we can carry on this work and complete it.

However, there is an aspect that cannot be disregarded in your therapy. I am referring to your self-destructive behaviour. Dear Angie, in order to reach significant results in your treatment we have to address this aspect at the behavioural level. In other words, you must use your will power to change some bad habits, some behaviours that prevent you from making faster progress in your therapy and that continue to have harmful consequences, which you and I have to deal with constantly, diverting our attention from deeper and more significant interventions that would get to the core of your distress.

Dear Angie, you have to stop drinking! You must follow the drug therapy with perseverance and get help from your psychiatrist, from me and from those who are close to you and can help. This will require commitment on your part, and at times it will be very painful, but you have no other choice if you really want to make it. I am quite convinced of what I am saying and I hope you will think it over. If you should not accept these conditions, I am afraid that this therapy would not be very effective and, at any rate, it would not proceed as it should.

With great affection,
A.

Every now and then someone still comes up to me and says that, in order to practice psychotherapy, I must surely be trained to keep the necessary 'emotional detachment'. This letter is a good example of the quality of the relationship that is established with patients who suffer from a personality disorder, or from disorders that do not fit into one single diagnostic category and present a particularly complicated polysymptomatic clinical picture.

In order to work with such patients, therapists must have undergone extensive training: indeed, they must be capable of carefully monitoring the emotional course of the relationship and must be flexible enough to tap into all of the patient's resources, life, and therapeutic context. The 'emotional detachment' many people evoke when they talk about our work is not possible, since in our effort to understand the other we are guided precisely by our emotions. Rather, a psychotherapist and psychoanalyst must explore those very emotions at the time they are experienced, in order to engage in a joint reflection with the patient regarding what is happening in the relationship.

The point is, how are we to explore? We inevitably need theoretical foundations that we can refer to when we go about exploring and explaining phenomena. In psychological and clinical work, I believe it is indispensable to reflect on the need for and the choice of a theory which, in attempting to explain how the mind works, helps to identify the disorder, how it is expressed and how it can be treated. This has direct clinical consequences: if the main tool used in psychotherapy is the relationship and the means of communication are emotions, a theory that tries to explain how humans function necessarily informs us about the meaning of our emotions, which channel our intentions and mental life, and about the nature of the relationship we are living.

On the need for theories

Many fascinating developments have characterized psychiatry and psychology, since their inception and up until today. Influenced by the advances in scientific and philosophical thinking, every development has been the result of the culture that characterized the historical period during which it came into being (Ellenberger, 1970). By and by, sickness and healing have been interpreted on the basis of the knowledge available, sometimes of the 'trends' of the moment, of the opportunities afforded by the economic and political systems in force. Psychopathology too appears to be influenced by the historical context within which it evolves and changes, and indeed is a reflection of the dysfunctional aspects of the systems within which it arises and matures; the knowledge available is not always capable of accounting for the phenomena that occur, so it is necessary to constantly explore and innovate the theories we refer to.

Borderline personality disorder is an example of such a phenomenon, inasmuch as it is one of the disorders that have most contributed to triggering the crisis that has overcome all classical treatment models, from psychoanalysis to cognitivism. We know how much scientific attention it has received and how many models of proven effectiveness have been developed in recent years (an overview is provided in Chapter 5).

I believe that as pathological forms evolve, they challenge the theories and treatment methods of the moment and, by so doing, they have the beneficial effect of preventing the consolidation of dogmas, thereby rescuing us clinicians from rigid thinking and from deluding ourselves into believing that we possess the 'truth'.

Categories are indispensable to guide us but at the same time they are limited and are not always sufficient when it comes to explaining phenomena. The process of knowing is the result of the ongoing dialogue between models and theories, based, in some cases, on sound scientific grounds and on the experience that is needed to constantly verify such theories.

We have to categorize and simplify the more complex phenomena in order to study and understand them, and this is useful to knowing, but we must never forget that we are working to approach a reality that is much more complex. In psychotherapeutic work, this awareness is fundamental for it allows to develop the humbleness we need in our constant quest for meaning with the other; it is one of the important components of empathy without which we cannot even approach the other.

Humility is not to be understood as 'false modesty', but rather as the awareness of one's human limitations and, therefore, of the importance of the other, of the difficulty people have in understanding each other, and at the same time of the need for such understanding.

So clinicians benefit from theories, but they learn early on that experience is irreducible and requires a sense of adventure and flexibility. Only this way is it possible to grasp the uniqueness of every human and therapeutic experience, thereby favouring the treatment process.

On the value of research

Every treatment model is based on a theory that identifies what should be regarded as the 'sound' functioning to be restored, that is what we are genetically and naturally predisposed for. The validity of theories and clinical practice can be verified by means of research programs. In mental health, it has been – and continues to be – hard to lend scientific evidence credibility to the theories. This is partly due to the particular nature of this work, which has always positioned itself somewhere between science, art, and philosophy, so that it is difficult to identify the most effective therapeutic factors of psychotherapy. No doubt, psychotherapy develops through the relationship between therapist and patient, which represents the intimate, in some respects inviolable space where change should take place. It is very difficult to conduct research in clinical work on this topic. Research has evolved mainly within the sphere of cognitivism, which has traditionally attempted to render psychotherapeutic practice measurable and verifiable, as opposed to the classical psychoanalytic approach. This necessarily involves oversimplifying experience and does not spare clinicians the effort of having to play it by ear in the therapeutic relationship, in which they will unwittingly experience something that is unknown and unmeasurable, the so-called 'aspecific factor'. However, failing to regard as fundamental the effort to review and lend scientific credence to theories and treatment models – as was indeed the case for a long time – would be tantamount to failing to take into consideration the ethical commitment of offering useful and effective therapies to our patients (Popper, 1959). Psychotherapeutic research is going forward also in the area of psychoanalysis (Luborsky *et al.*, 1998, 2004; Bucci, 2005; Dazzi and De Coro, 1998; Dazzi *et al.*, 2003; Dazzi *et al.*, 2006; Lingiardi *et al.*, 2005; Lingiardi *et al.*, 2006) and we are coming ever closer to a knowledge that cuts across theories and models which originally differed significantly.

In psychology, some theories are hard to verify also on account of the historical split between mind and body, which in the Western world has often given rise to a pointless and harmful rift between organicists and non-organicists, medicine and psychology. For a long time, the compartmentalization of knowledge and the excessive rigidity of the areas of application prevented doctors and psychologists from conducting profitable exploration, disregarding the complex and unique machine that is the human being. In some cases, this has slowed down the knowing process and has not permitted to make the best use of the therapeutic resources available, mostly to the detriment of patients.

More and more, contemporary scientific and philosophical culture seems to promote a holistic view of man and of human phenomena. The tendency towards an ever-increasing multidisciplinarity is allowing us to move towards a vision in which mind and body are no longer separate entities. One need only consider the crucial role that new diagnostic and radiological technologies (such as functional MRI) have played in significant discoveries of the way our mind works, such as the discovery of mirror neurons (Rizzolatti *et al.*, 2001; Gallese *et al.*, 2009; Ammaniti and Gallese, 2014), and how biology, neurology, physiology, psychology, and sociology have become intercommunicating fields supporting extremely original studies and theories, like Stephen Porges's polyvagal theory (2011).

These discoveries are changing the therapeutic models adopted in psychology, medicine and culture in general.

The book proceeds in this direction. The intent is to consider some important contributions, in the various interconnected disciplines, and to try to determine the consistency between etiopathogenesis and psychotherapy, bearing in mind the cultural context in which they developed, while maintaining a dialectical balance between some reference theories and the need to continue exploring, stepping away from rigid stances.

On the mind-body issue

> One of the temptations of having a mind is to try using it alone to solve the mystery of its own nature. Philosophers have attempted this since time immemorial. Psychologists fall back on it, as do we all from time to time. But as a general method to explore the matter of the mind, it just won't do.
>
> (Edelman, 1992: 31)

A recurring and invariant theme in all cultures is the problematic nature of the concept of the *mind-body* binomial, in relation to which many different theories have developed – implicitly and explicitly – in various areas.

In Western philosophy various paradigms corresponding to the different formalizations of the problem have succeeded one another (Ceccarelli, 1998, 2005):

- *the dualist paradigm,* according to which human nature consists of two different and separate entities: the body and the mind. The distinction between Plato's *sensible world* and *intelligible world* and Descartes' *res Cogitans* and *res Extensa* are examples of this;
- *the monist paradigm,* which upholds that the two entities flow into each other; according to Hobbes' materialist view, only the body exists, while Berkeley (idealist monism) maintains that there is only the mind.

The *multidimensional relational paradigm,* according to which human nature is determined by the relationship between mind and body, is indeed an expression of this relationship. A similar view can be found in

Kant, who focuses on the relationship between *a priori categories* and *a posteriori categories,* as well as in the phenomenological-existentialist approach. For Brentano *intentionality* lies in the knowledge with which the mind – without emerging from itself – opens up to the world; Buber believes that man is *I-world* and *I-you* relationship; Merleau-Ponty posits that man and the world are inseparable, *perception* is primordial, inborn, and structural openness to the world of life.

But it is the Darwinian approach, in its processing of the relationship between living matter and environment – *variation-selection-heredity* – that provides a method for studying the body in relation to the environment and represents the link between biology, psychology, and sociology (Lorenz, 1941; Popper, 1990).

Different epistemologies, which justify different theories, correspond to the different paradigms.

A dualist epistemology underpins the interdisciplinary approach, which reinforces the separation between different areas of knowledge on man, like neurobiology, psychology, and sociology.

In two-dimensional biological theories, the body, the brain is considered to be the *instrument* of the mind (Eccles, 1989).

An example of a psychological two-dimensional theory is the classical psychodynamic model, which regards the body as the energetic component of mental representation.

Monist epistemology is one-dimensional and focuses on the body (biological reductionism) or the mind (psychological and sociological reductionism). According to *one-dimensional biological theories*, the laws of physics and chemistry are sufficient for understanding living matter (for example Gall's theory of phrenology).

One-dimensional psychological theories instead do not consider the material structure. In this direction, in psychology, *functionalism* (Putnam, 1975; Dennett, 1991) has influenced different areas of cognitivism and of the systemic-relational approach.

Relational epistemology (Morin, 1990, 1991) upholds man's unitariness and complexity, hence the need for a complex systemic approach based on multidisciplinary knowledge, which encompasses the different variables through an open and ongoing dialogue.

> At 'the brain of the matter' is the most complicated arrangement in the known universe. To understand it will take us from philosophy

to embryology, in a curious but necessary leap. When we have taken it, we will be in a position to return to philosophy via biology in the next two parts.

(Edelman, 1992: 31)

Multidisciplinary theories – both biological and psychological – are based on the assumption that the mind is a manifestation of the relationship – seen in its historical-temporal dimension – between the body and the world.

Some examples of biological multidimensional theories are those of Jackson (1932), Luria (1976), MacLean (1973), Edelman (1992), Damasio (1994).

Instead, examples of psychological multidimensional theories can be found in the work of Vygotskij (1962) and Donald (1991), in Bowlby's attachment theory (1969), and the motivational theories of Liotti (1994/2005, 2001) and Lichtenberg (1989).

The multidimensional relational paradigm is at the basis of the model proposed in this book. Such a paradigm is currently inspiring many contemporary scholars, belonging to different schools of thought and with different clinical approaches. It is sufficient it to consider the new research and theories on trauma and the lively debate on *body-oriented* therapies, which we will come back to in the next chapter.

Ceccarelli (1998, 2005) summarizes the core concept of the relational theory of the mind as follows: the mind consists of the representation of the relationship between body and mind. This representation is sustained by a multiplicity of inborn tendencies to interact with the environment, which are philogenetically inherited. The inborn tendencies are hierarchically organized in relation to representational complexity in the course of the individual's ontogenic development.

The relational turn

Our century has been characterized by significant cultural shifts. Since the forties, the systemic theories of first- and second-order cybernetics, quantum physics, Gestalt theory, with the concept of *field*, have greatly influenced the way in which mental health and illness are understood. The Palo Alto School and the Mental Research Institute, with their leading exponents (Bateson, 1972; Watzlawick *et al.*, 1967), and the phenomenological philosophical current (Husserl, 1913) were, in my view, the starting point of what was later referred to as the 'relational turn' (Lingiardi *et al.*, 2011) in psychoanalysis as well as in psychotherapy. Regarding the single individual necessarily as part of a system of relations has led to a new understanding of humans, their development and their functioning as indissolubly bound to relatedness. The idea that it is *impossible to not communicate* and that *the observer influences the observed* have challenged the assumption of the analyst's neutrality, typical of the classical psychoanalytic setting. Attachment theory and the work of John Bowlby (1988) have further contributed to confirming man's intrinsically relational nature. One of Bowlby's merits was that of adopting a scientific approach also in the field of psychology, advocating research in order to validate the hypotheses he formulated on the basis of direct clinical observation and referring constantly evolutionism. His work inspired studies on attachment (Stern, 1985; Main and Hesse, 1990; Main and Solomon, 1990; Lyons-Ruth and Jacobvitz, 1999; Lyons-Ruth *et al.*, 2003; Lyons-Ruth *et al.*, 2005) and influenced Infant Research (Sander, 1962; Stern, 1971; Trevarthen, 1974; Meltzoff and Moore, 1977; Tronick *et al.*, 1978; Meltzoff, 1990; Beebe and Lachmann, 2002), which have greatly contributed to a better understanding of what favours sound human development and have promoted a greater interdisciplinarity between clinical psychology and neurosciences (MacLean, 1982; Edelman, 1989; Damasio, 1994; Panksepp, 1998; Schore, 1994, 2003a, 2003b). In the wake of attachment theory, two lines of research and studies on human motivations that regulate our mental life developed simultaneously in psychoanalysis, through the work of Lichtenberg (1989), and in cognitivism, through that of Gilbert (1989) and Liotti (1989). Not just attachment, therefore, but also other motivations based on evolved disposition, constitute the fabric of relationality, a sort of universal code. The child's actions are no longer driven by the pleasure principle but by the fulfilment of needs to build up and preserve the integrity and coherence of the sense of self and of consciousness.

We will come back to motivational theories in the next section, since they constitute the main theoretical framework to which I refer in this book and in my clinical work. Now, however, I would like to dwell a little longer on the significant contributions to the development of a relational and intersubjective approach in psychoanalysis.

The brief overview that follows does not do justice to the complex innovative process of the relational movement. Other authors have borne witness to the most significant stages of this cultural revolution, including Lewis Aron in *A Meeting of Minds* (1996), and Vittorio Lingiardi *et al.* in *La Svolta Relazionale* (2011).

In 1998, with the publication of Mitchell's book *Relational Concepts in Psychoanalysis,* relational psychoanalysis officially came into being; a group of American clinicians and theoreticians influenced by the British models of *object relations*, the *interpersonal theory* and the cultural movements of *postmodernism* and *feminism* joined the movement.

Like all approaches, relational psychoanalysis was the result of a long process of change featuring various important stages, which were characterized by the original and creative contributions of numerous authors. Such contributions were not always accepted lightheartedly by the psychoanalytic community, since they were critical of the classical theory. The time frame we will be referring to is the post-war period, which was particularly rich in innovative contributions in various areas.

During the fifties and sixties, while ego psychology (Heinz Hartmann, David Rapaport, Jacob Arlow) dominated the American psychoanalytic community, Harry Stack Sullivan, in the attempt to extend psychoanalytic treatment to schizophrenic patients, modified the sense of the clinical dialogue and introduced interpersonal psychiatry. Sullivan was one of the main inspirers of the relational movement.

The interpersonalistic approach emphasized the therapeutic potential of interaction in the *hic et nunc* of the analytic dyad, in which *parataxic distortions* emerged, that is states and behaviours influenced by previous self-with-other representations. From this perspective, the therapeutic relationship became the space in which the patient could express illusions or distortions and externalize them, and in which, with the help of an experienced observer of such dynamics (the analyst), the patient could distinguish between past and present, heightening his or her awareness. One of the pivotal instruments of the interpersonalist model was confrontation. The interpersonal field in the *hic et nunc* thus constituted the scenario and instrument of treatment.

In those years, in England, some authors, who are also regarded as being among the principal inspirers of the relational model, created with their conceptualizations a nexus between the interpersonalist theories and the Freudian theory (Fairbairn, 1952; Balint, 1952; Winnicott, 1965). Fairbairn in particular, at the theoretical level, gave a strongly relational sense to the motivational framework of psychoanalytic theory, stating that pleasure was not the aim of the drive but a means towards an end, which is the relationship with the other. The sense of object relations changed substantially; drives and object relations were regarded as coexistent and, according to this view, the child, who needs others from the moment it is born, orients itself towards them throughout the course of its development.

Greenberg and Mitchell, with their book *Object Relations in Psychoanalytic Theory* (1983), searched for a possible nexus between *interpersonal relations* and *internal object relations*, trying to reconcile different – and at times incompatible – theoretical and practical approaches based on a common and critical assumption: the relational nature of the human mind.

During the 1990s, the process was further enriched by the contribution of Infant Research (Beebe and Lachmann, 2002; Beebe, 2000; Stern, 1971, 1985, 2004; Lichtenberg, Lachmann and Fosshage, 1992; Lichtenberg, 1981, 1983, 1989), focusing attention on the level of implicit communication, both in development and in the consulting room. Emphasis was placed on *how* the relationship cures. Similarly to what was observed in the mother–child interaction, one began to speak of the therapeutic relationship in terms of rhythm and attunement, rupture and reparation, beyond words. The therapeutic alliance became a fundamental instrument by means of which to exercise one's capacity for self- and hetero-regulation, while processing implicit traumatic experiences.

More and more, the analyst's subjectivity has been regarded as an important variable and the relationship as a 'clinical exchange' (Lachmann, Fosshage and Lichtenberg, 1992), emphasizing the concept of reciprocity.

From the intersubjective perspective, the *clinical exchange* became a permanent condition of *mutuality* through which the two subjects, the patient and analyst, *co-construct* a relational reality. The focus shifted towards what happens in the *intersubjective field* and the analyst became even less of an observer and more of a co-actor. The intersubjective current incorporated by the relational movement, however, flowed into various arteries distinguished by slightly different views on the core concepts. A fundamental contribution was offered by Benjamin (2002), who used feminist critique to suggest rethinking development, recognizing a mother's right to her own subjectivity. In classical psychoanalysis, the mother was regarded as an object. Her role was reduced almost exclusively to her mechanical capacity to fulfil the needs and therefore ease the tensions of the child; the mother–child relationship seemed to be based almost exclusively on a physiological dependence. The object relations perspective and feminism that drew inspiration from it, instead, rediscovered the mother's role, shedding light on new aspects of the mother–child relationship which show that both are autonomous subjects capable of responding in a personal way. There must be mutual recognition between mother and child, in spite of their different roles and positions in the relationship. Jessica Benjamin is interested in understanding how reciprocity evolves in the course of development as well as in the analytic relationship. Feminism gave a very significant contribution to relational psychoanalysis, for it provided a basis for a critique of some basic principles of the Freudian theory, thus contributing to the evolution of psychoanalysis, in line with the most fertile cultural movements of the time. Jessica Benjamin's thinking proceeded very much in keeping with the developments of infant research, especially the ideas of Stern (1985), according to whom intersubjectivity, which assumes the value of a motivational system in every respect, serves precisely to develop an ever greater recognition of the mother on the part of the child. In other developmental researchers, these insights interweaved with studies in neurosciences and evolution and gave rise to concepts like mentalization, that is, the ability to be in a relationship distinguishing between oneself and the other in terms of emotions and intentions (Bateman and Fonagy, 2006).

The intersubjective conception of Stolorow and Atwood (1992), Orange *et al.* (1997) and Orange (1995) originated from Kohut's self psychology (1971, 1977), especially with regard to the empathic approach to the relational experience, and then became radicalized on a contextualist position: there is no innate self, the self develops and is maintained in intersubjective contexts.

In this intersubjective current there was no room for an evolutionary perspective; the basic assumptions were those of existentialist philosophy regarding human nature. An interesting concept introduced by this current was the *myth of the isolated mind*, which the authors found traces of also in the relational movement.

Postmodernism, constructivism and phenomenological thought constitute the philosophical framework within which the relational movement developed.

There is no one truth to which the analyst refers; rather, the theories, with their differences, constitute a point of departure. They are hypotheses to be verified or invalidated through the direct experience of the analytic relationship, which is unique to every patient and can never be reproduced in the same form. It is therefore possible to offer different explanations of phenomena, all of which are potentially viable, based on the experience that is shared and co-constructed with the patient (Hoffman, 1992).

This position elicits interesting reflections on the possible search for universal invariants – such as motivational systems – that govern the mental functioning of our species, and therefore on the intent to formulate theories that take into account both the universal and the personal elements as constituents of the intersubjective experience. The relational paradigm in psychoanalysis differs from the relational paradigm mentioned previously (see p. 16) in relation to the developments of Western philosophy, for it does not refer to evolutionism, phylogenesis, and neurobiology.

This view, instead, is more in keeping with motivational theories, as we will see in the next section. Over the years, relational psychoanalysis has become ever more open to the latest developments in neurosciences, although there are still some criticalities in relation to one of its basic assumptions; in other words, there are no universally accepted objective explanations which the analyst can refer to as if they were certainties. As I see it, these positions are only apparently incompatible in clinical practice; in this respect, paradoxically, I feel very much a relational psychoanalyst. I think we would need another evolution – like the one brought about by relational psychoanalysis – in the direction of a psychotherapy/psychoanalysis that integrates knowledge as far as possible, overcoming barriers and focusing to a greater extent on clinical work. In my experience, for years I have managed to reconcile the relational psychoanalysis model, which pays close attention to the experience of the here and now and the uniqueness of the relationship that is created with every individual person, and a phylogenetic and hierarchical view of human mental functioning (Panksepp, 1998; Jackson, 1932; Janet, 1889, 1898; Ey, 1975; Ey et al., 1978). According to such a view, there are invariants that are genetically transmitted, influenced, and modified by the history of the evolution of species; these invariants constitute a universal foundation, that is, *values*, as Edelman (1989, 1992) calls them. Values define the limit of human relational possibilities. From this perspective, the focus of a caretaking relationship becomes exploring the personal ways in which individuals, within their specific relational context, develop and use the genetically predisposed mental functions that the entire human species is endowed with (Lichtenberg, 1989; Gilbert, 1989; Liotti, 1989).

Motivational systems theories

Interpersonal motivational systems are inborn goals, evolutionistically selected values that generate functional systems for regulating social behaviour during interaction with the interpersonal environment (Edelman, 1989; Panksepp, 1998).

By introducing attachment theory and referring to Darwin (1872), Bowlby (1969) set off a revolutionary process of investigation into inborn motivational systems which, like attachment, regulate our physical and mental activities at different levels of functioning of our nervous system. This evolutionary approach to human phenomena and the rules that govern them challenged the Freudian paradigm, which is based on the life and death instinct, proposing the human tendency toward seeking the most adaptive response to difficulties and obstacles – both natural and not – that stand in the way of life and species survival. This transition marked a fundamental change in the understanding of health and sickness and, consequently, of possible treatment.

In 1989, Joseph Lichtenberg, a psychoanalyst, and Paul Gilbert, a cognitivist, each published a book on inborn motivations that regulate human relatedness. Within the sphere of behavioural cognitivism, Giovanni Liotti (1994/2005) then further developed Gilbert's work formulating what he referred to as the cognitive-evolutionary motivational theory. Thus, motivational theories developed in different areas and with different characteristics, all referring to John Bowlby's work. The event was highly significant in psychology and psychiatry because it provided important indications on the functioning that all human beings are genetically predisposed for, above and beyond the culture to which they belong and their differences in terms of race and temperament. The fact of considering some invariants of human functioning allows us to reflect on what instead varies from one individual or experience to another, on what we regard as unique and unrepeatable. Such a dialectic is extremely valuable in clinical work because it allows us to explore the complexity of the relational experience and of mutual functioning starting from what we have in common. What better base to make us feel on a par and cooperative? Everyone now agrees that cooperation and therapeutic alliance are at the heart of the analyst's/psychotherapist's work (Safran and Muran, 2000; Lingiardi, 2000; Lingiardi *et al.*, 2014); but how one works on the alliance, that is on and through the therapeutic relationship, depends on one's reference theory. In this sense, the study of inborn motivations provides the clinician with very interesting indications, for it presents itself as a relational theory which, however, distances itself from the radical constructivism of some intersubjective and relational movements. We will come back to the therapeutic alliance – a rather important and complex topic – more than once in the book, and we will discuss it in greater depth when we look at the treatment model.

The cognitive-evolutionary motivational theory: Giovanni Liotti's contribution

I discovered the motivational theory in 1995 when, in the course of my training, I met Giovanni Liotti. He and Vittorio Filippo Guidano had published a book entitled *Cognitive Processes and Emotional Disorders* (1983) in which they developed a new theoretical and methodological approach focused on human relatedness in the cognitive-developmental field, where this aspect had not received much attention up until that time.

Giovanni Liotti (1993), who later diverged from Vittorio Filippo Guidano, further explored and developed Gilbert's work (1989) and, in 1988, established together with a group of like-minded colleagues the Association for Research on the Psychopathology of the Attachment System (ARPAS) – to which I have the honour of being affiliated – and developed a research current on inborn motivations known as Assessment of Interpersonal Motivation in Transcripts – AIMIT (Liotti and Monticelli, 2008).

The work of Bowlby and evolutionism are at the heart of Liotti's theory and render the motivational theory compatible and integrable with the biological multidimensional theories (see p. 18) of Jackson (1932), MacLean (1973), Edelman (1989, 1992), and Damasio (1994, 1998), all of which confirm the hierarchical functioning of the mind, tracing back its corresponding levels to the phylogenetic development of our brain.

MacLean (1985) identified three phylogenetic levels of functioning: the *reptilian complex* (*protoreptilian, R-complex*), the *limbic system* (*paleomammalian complex*), and the *neocortex* (*neomammalian complex*). Each presents distinct structural and chemical features that distinguish it from the others and, at the same time, are interconnected and interact with the other two, working in an integrated fashion while maintaining some degree of functional autonomy.

The cognitive-evolutionary motivational theory distinguishes motivational systems that correspond to the different levels of functioning indicated by MacLean.

In the *reptilian brain* we find *homeostatic motivational systems,* which are the oldest, such as the ones that regulate human body homeostasis, the defence against environmental hazards (fight-or-flight), the tendency toward exploration, sexuality not involving the development of a bond, and territorial defence, which are present in all vertebrates. In the *limbic brain, interpersonal motivational systems* (IMS) underpin some fundamental functions that govern relatedness: the inborn tendency toward seeking care and protective proximity (*attachment*), providing care (*caregiving*), competing for social rank (*dominance-subordination*), and forming of the sexual pair (*sexuality*). These motivational systems are present in all mammals and are manifested with similar behaviours. In higher mammals, another motivational system was formed, the *egalitarian cooperative system*, which is highly developed in human beings, to which, according to evolutionary cognitivism (Liotti, 2001), two subsystems can be referred: *social play* and *affiliation* which, however, are still in the process of being investigated.

Table 2.1 summarizes the goals of each IMS and the emotions that correspond to the state of need and to the fulfilment of the need that relates to each motivation.

Epistemic motivational systems are active in the *neocortex*. This third level, which belongs to the human species, involves the cognitive sphere of *intersubjectivity* and of the *construction of meanings,* an emergent feature that presides over the other two groups of motivational systems and governs their activity, integrating information according to different combinations and complex syntheses which are then expressed in social interactions.

Intersubjectivity develops progressively through a series of being-with-the-other experiences, over a long period of time that goes from roughly nine months to four years of age. During this considerable lapse of time, the child builds up what has been referred to as the *Theory of the Mind* referred to by Fonagy and Bateman as 'mentalization' that is the ability to intuit, explain, or interpret his or her own actions and those of others in terms of beliefs, intentions, needs, and desires. This is the most complex and philogenetically-recent level of functioning, and it is the one that should be activated first, automatically, coordinating the activities of the lower levels (limbic and reptilian). When neocortical functioning is hindered, the

Table 2.1

IMS	Emotions that signal the need – goal	Emotions that signal that the need – goal has been met
Attachment system	Fear (caused by separation) and Anger (protest)	Comfort
	Sadness (caused by loss)	Joy
	Desperation	Confidence
	Emotional detachment	Trust
Agonistic system	Fear (of being judged)	Anger (elicited by defiance)
	Shame	Triumph, power
	Humiliation	Pride
	Sadness	Contempt
	Envy	Superiority
Caregiving system	Anxious concern	Protective tenderness
	Sympathy	Joy
	Guilt	
Cooperative system	Guilt	Empathy
	Remorse	Mutual loyalty
	Isolation	Sharing
	Distrust	Trust
	Hatred	Joy
Sexual system	Modesty	Erotic desire
	Fear (of rejection)	Erotic pleasure
	Jealousy	Erotic mutuality

Translated from G. Liotti (2001) *Le opere della coscienza*, p. 53

lower levels, which are less evolved and insufficient to cope with the complexity of our relational life, are automatically triggered, thereby generating phenomena of alteration of consciousness, deficits of mentalization and mastery.

Joseph Lichtenberg's motivational theory

My work with human motivations came to an important turning point in 2006, when I met Joseph Lichtenberg. I had already read about his theory, but meeting and talking to him was very enriching for me, both humanly and professionally. Lichtenberg, who comes from the psychoanalytic tradition, proposes a model that is focused primarily on the intersubjective context within which individuals express themselves.

His scientific frame of reference is primarily infant research. He is familiar with and considers the developments in neuroscience, but does not dwell on the hierarchical functioning of the brain as identified by evolutionism, and the motivational systems he refers to in his theory do not correspond to the specific levels of functioning associated with the phylogenetic development process.

His motivational theory is the synthesis of an original combination of empirical data from infant research and the theoretical paradigm of self psychology: the cohesion and confidence of the self are a superordinate motivation.

Every system contributes to self-regulation in mutually regulated interactions with the child's caretakers. In healthy development, the different motivations alternate and integrate one another smoothly and harmoniously, according to the emergent need and intersubjective context, while in critical or traumatic development conditions the regulation system tenses and the aversive system, with its antagonism and withdrawal, ususally prevails.

Lichtenberg's motivational theory includes the systems listed below.

The system of mental regulation of physiological requirements

The sense of self is based on the possibility for the infant to perceive its own internal state, which is associated with essential physiological requirements (hunger, sleep-wakefulness, excretion, physiological evacuation) and on the recognition of these needs by the caregiver, who develops response models that remain in the infant's implicit memory and influence subsequent regulations.

Clearly, the physiological regulation system and the attachment system are separate but they are inevitably intertwined with each other. One determines the other's functioning. If natural attunement is established between the child and its caregiver, the infant will become familiar with its bodily needs – a physiological self – and will develop a sound attachment; vice versa, only in a sound attachment relationship can an empathic and safe environment arise in which the infant may express its own physiological needs and begin the functional process of recognizing and distinguishing between itself and the other.

The attachment-affiliation system

According to Lichtenberg, this motivational system, in a broad sense, has to do with the possibility of establishing bonds as one learns in the course of development – through repeated affective attunement – to 'be with', identifying and distinguishing oneself more and more from the other.

Affiliation is regarded as an extension to the *attachment motivational system*. The infant is born into a family and social context, which it perceives at first primarily through the attachment relationship with its caregiver; it later experiences a growing sense of belonging to the group – first the family and then the social group. The sense of belonging and its critical features become especially important during adolescence.

The exploratory-assertive system

The child comes into contact with the environment and learns to cope with its challenges. In the beginning, exploration is mediated by the caregiver, but as development progresses, it becomes ever more autonomous. Exploring the environment and overcoming its challenges allows the infant to develop the personal capacity and confidence to express itself and learn by trial and error.

The aversive system

In Lichtenberg's theory this system corresponds to the fight-or-flight model. It responds to the need to react to antagonism and, in the small child, it serves the function of signalling to the parent that needs relative to other motivational systems have not been met. It has a strong adaptive relevance inasmuch as it gives the self the ability to repair and overcome obstacles.

The sensual–sexual system

This system includes two aspects that correspond to different affective states but are correlated with each other. Sensual pleasure is consequent to the decline in the internal tension caused by a state of need and involves all the senses. Sexual pleasure, instead, involves an increase in physical stimulation, producing rising tension up to orgasm. Both aspects contribute to the development of a wilful self, capable of desiring.

In a recent revision of his theory (Lichtenberg, Lachmann, Fosshage, 2011), Lichtenberg defined affiliation as a separate system and added the *caregiving system*, which he previously regarded as a natural and implicit offshoot of the attachment system.

A comparison of the two theories: a personal synthesis

In thirty-two years of clinical work, I have met few people who have had a profound impact on my life and work. Giovanni Liotti and Joseph Lichtenberg are surely among those few and have represented a milestone in my growth process. They are men of extraordinary intellectual skills, endowed with great courage and creativity. My encounter with them has been professional as well as – and especially – personal, and I am extremely grateful to both.

From Liotti I have learned to appreciate the value of evolutionism. He has taught me to look for the *invariants of relationality* with a humble spirit, never losing sight of their limits, but always convinced of their importance with a view to overcoming a relativistic stance that can lead to a dangerous non-scientific validation of any clinical action. I felt drawn by his passion, his courage. I developed a deep bond with him, based on our interest in and investigation of the scientific side of our work – vital elements that combine and interweave life, affects and profession. I have greatly appreciated his ability to make choices that were sometimes difficult, avoiding compromises in the name of freedom of thought and action; his courage to take firm stances and willingness to be held personally accountable for his ideas and principles; his devotion and commitment to learning and to developing an interdisciplinary knowing, harmoniously blending scientific approach and poetry.

Joseph Lichtenberg embodies the historic tendency of psychoanalytic tradition that has never ceased to place the relationship in the foreground. He has had the ability and courage to formulate a motivational theory that represents an alternative to dogmatic conceptual assumptions, which are not always functional, and yet are prevalent, in psychoanalysis. He has helped me to discover the *craft*: presence, the ability to be with the other, to perform sophisticated acts of empathy and synthesis. He has taught me to strengthen the 'sense of me', implicitly, through our friendship,

Theoretical foundations 31

generously stressing our commonalities, attunements, showing enthusiasm in exploration, and encouraging my projects. I owe this book to him.

He continuously combines theoretical assumptions and clinical practice and has an extraordinary ability to observe and empathize in his work as well as in his life. In clinical work, he uses techniques and tools both known and invented, creating harmony and innovation. When I met him I was immediately struck by his lively gaze, which is so much like that of a child – curious, as if he were yet to discover the world. I thought to myself that vitality is ageless and that an authentic encounter with people is indeed possible and should be sought as a precious and contagious value.

Theories make sense only when the people who formulate them convey a sense of harmony, and both of these authors have their own personal harmony. Only from this perspective can I attempt to comment on their thought.

The differences between their theories depend mostly on the method employed to explore and conceptualize. As we have seen, Liotti refers to evolutionary epistemology. The method followed by ethnologists to identify interpersonal motivational systems is based on the specificity of (nonverbal) communication signals, which in all species mediate the corresponding motivational activation (the separation cry, which takes different forms in different species, is the invariant sign of the attachment motivational system, just as frowning in a certain way and grinding one's teeth are specific signs of agonistic activation, and so forth). The invariance of these signals allows evolutionism to identify them and to assume that they are inborn.

Lichtenberg neglects this invariance and focuses more on the subjective experience of motivation. He bases his research on infant observation, connecting it constantly with the clinical experience, which is characterized by a prevalently empathic approach.

According to him, *cohesion* and *self-confidence* are superordinate motivations that correpond to *intersubjectivity*, which Liotti believes is the motivation specific to neocortical structures.

Reference to *biological multidimensional theories* in the cognitive-evolutionary theory, especially in the work of Paul MacLean (1982), further marks the difference with Lichtenberg's theory.

The *system of mental regulation of physiological requirements*, for instance, would correspond to homeostatic motivations, which, in Liotti's neuro-psychological approach, are not regarded as interpersonal motivations but rather as phylogenetically-motivated behaviours, present also in animals whose brain system is limited to the functions of the *reptilian brain*. From an evolutionary perspective, homeostatic motivations should be studied independently from the subjective experience of their satisfaction. The subjective experience, instead, is determined by the neocortex, whose functioning no doubt differs from that of the underlying structures (*R-complex* and *limbic system*). Therefore, according to evolutionary neuropsychology, homeostatic motivational systems and the systems that participate in the construction of subjective experience are distinct and independent from one another. The neocortical systems can use the results of the former, among the great deal of information treated by their functional processes.

So in his theory Lichtenberg does not refer to a hierarchical functioning of the mind, and his *system of mental regulation of physiological requirements* seems to connect homeostatic motivations with the attachment motivation and with the neocortical motivations of an early intersubjectivity; according to his theory, the functions that regulate fundamental physiological needs constitute the ground on which the attachment relationship and the child's early sense of self and of self-with-other develop.

The same applies to the *exploratory-assertive system,* which would correspond to the fullest expression of neocortical activities according to the cognitive-evolutionary theory.

In fact, in the reptilian brain a motivation for the exploration of the world (exploring to procure food or to mark one's territory) is present, but the neocortex adds an intersubjective dimension to primitive exploratory activity, allowing expanding of the knowledge already acquired by means of the nervous structures of the R-complex and the limbic system. '*The structures of the neocortex make it possible to develop the language of symbolization and of consciousness, which have to do with the sense of self and with self-assertion, self-understanding, and self-mastery*' (Liotti, 1995, p. 111).

The differences pointed out would make sense prevalently from a conceptual-categorical point of view, rather than from a clinical one. In a highly intuitive and creative way, Lichtenberg constantly refers to the intersubjective dimension and to the complexity of our functioning, which is constantly co-regulated within the relationship. Although Liotti shares the relational perspective, he is careful to underline how the various motivational systems correspond to the various levels, marked by phylogenesis, attributing the superordinate value of intersubjectivity to the neocortical function, with the intent, I believe, to simplify the complexity in order to better explore its mechanisms.

The other motivational systems identified by Lichtenberg would correspond to the motivations that regulate the social behaviour of members of the same species and are based in the limbic system, according to evolutionary neurobiology. The two approaches differ somewhat also in relation to these motivational systems.

The *attachment system* is a common basis in the two theories, but Liotti defines it as a state of need activated by specific signals of distress, pain, fear, and insecurity, while Lichtenberg has a broader view of this motivation, which he regards as a basis for developing the more general ability to 'be with', to attune onself and to create bonds, distinguishing oneself from the other, which Liotti attributes to the more sophisticated functions of the neocortex.

The *affiliation system* present in Lichtenberg was recently introduced also in Liotti's theory; however, according to the latter, it would be an extension of the cooperative motivational system, whereas Lichtenberg posits that the nature of affiliation is on a par with that of attachment: the sense of familiarity and reliability that characterizes the attachment bond is similar to the sense of belonging to one's family or context of growth. The critical point for both authors is always the same: in order to name an inborn motivation, the ethologist needs to identify activation signals and, in the case of affiliation, Liotti proposes the closest signal, which is the same one that inspired the identification of the *egalitarian-cooperative system* – the finger pointing to an object, which stimulates joint attention (Tomasello, 1999). Lichtenberg's concept of affiliation, instead, is based on the results of infant research, particularly on the studies of Cowan and MacHale (1996), MacHale (1997), MacHale and Fivaz-Depeursinge (1999).

During the 1980s, these researchers of the Lausanne group studied the possible configurations of what is defined as the 'primary triangle'[1] (mother-father-child), introducing a new method for studying the origin of triangularity, that is the infant's ability to develop a sense of the 'fabric of relations' that it is part of since – or even before – birth.

The infant refers primarily to its attachment figure, but at the same time it comes into contact with other significant family members who are connected with one another through peculiar relational weaves. The infant will absorb values and mentalitites that will become part of it and will make it perceive a sense of affiliation that is implicit to that context.

During adolescence, the pull of the peer group will stimulate a very powerful affiliation that will accompany adolescents through the conflictual stage of growth and will allow them to further develop their identity and distinguish themselves from others, first and foremost from the attachment figures. I also work with group dynamics in a broad sense (families, therapeutic groups, work groups, etc.) and my clinical experience is very much in keeping with Lichtenberg's notion of *affiliation*.

This topic will be taken up again later, when discussing the treatment model, in which the social aspect is very important.

In an early version of his model, Lichtenberg did not regard *caregiving* as a separate motivational system, which instead is the case in the cognitive-evolutionary theory; however, in his recent revision he refers to it as an inborn motivation. This motivation is especially important in the presence of a disorganized attachment style. In these cases, the infant tries to make up for the serious shortcomings of the development context by activating the caregiving motivation *vis à vis* the caretaker instead of the attachment motivation, reorganizing – albeit pathologically – its functioning and relationships on the basis of other conditions. We will look at *controlling strategies* (Lyons-Ruth and Jacobvitz, 1999) in Chapters 3 and 4.

The *agonistic system* of ethologists corresponds to forms of subjective experience that are partially included in Lichtenberg's *aversive motivational system*. According to Liotti, the *agonistic system* signals a competitive activation aimed to establish positions of dominance and submission in relationships, in addition to using parameters useful for evaluating/judging oneself or others based on performance, merits, and demerits, in relation to the expectations of the context to which one belongs. The cognitive-evolutionary perspective allows to distinguish between agonistic rage (aimed at establishing dominance/sumbission) and attachment rage (aimed at seeking help and reassurance) (see Table 2.1). This is particularly useful in clinical work. In Lichtenberg such a distinction does not emerge; the *aversive system* has the purpose of signalling a distress that can be caused by various unmet needs in general.

On the contrary, Lichtenberg attributes greater importance to the aversive motivation for the development of a sense of mastery and assertiveness in the child. In his theory, this motivation favours the development of the sense of a *secure-agentic* self, capable of negotiating in relationships. I believe this is an added value with respect to the agonistic sense of assertiveness as a way of dominating over the other or conquering rank.

This aspect too has significant repercussions in clinical work, as is shown by the clinical stories of Sister Mary and Veronica narrated by Lichtenberg, and by the debate that follows (see Chapter 3).

The *sexual system* of ethologists has to do especially with experiences that Lichtenberg studies as the *sensual-sexual system*. The two authors depart from the Freudian paradigm and basically agree that sexuality is one of the motivations while not the main one. From an evolutionary perspective, sexuality is essential for the survival of species and the need to form a couple in higher mammals, in which the growth of cubs requires more time than in other species and therefore greater resources for caring for the offspring. Furthermore, sexuality intertwines with other IMS that lend a different meaning to it in relationships; consider the love bond, for instance, in which sexuality, attachment, and cooperation are all involved at the same time. Sexuality can sometimes be used pathologically instead of the attachment motivation in relationships with abusive and highly disorganized caregivers.

Cognitive-evolutionary research is in its infancy so I hope that it will further investigate this motivation, which I believe has not been explored much.

In his theory, Lichtenberg places next to *sexuality* (a motivation aimed at seeking pleasure through an escalation of orgasmic excitement) *sensuality*, which he regards as a motivation that aims to reduce tensions and excitement by satisfying all sensual needs and reaching a state of contentment and security.

There is no conceptual compatibility between the two theories with regard to the motivational value of the pursuit of pleasure and the opposite expression of aversion. Lichtenberg considers the pursuit of pleasure as a motivational system in itself and places it alongside the pursuit of sexual pleasure. From an evolutionary perspective, instead, the pursuit of pleasure is not, in itself, at the basis of a primary motivational system. Rather, sensual pleasure is experienced when the specific goal of each motivational system is reached, such as, for instance, the sense of reassurance produced by the parent's embrace (attachment), tenderness deriving from caregiving behaviour, or the sense of triumph determined by agonistic success.

Likewise, according to Liotti there is no motivational system aimed at repelling or averting unpleasant experiences. Just as pleasure marks the success of each IMS, regret and aversion are an indication of the failure of a given IMS and take on a qualitatively different role, depending on the system involved, such as for instance sadness for loneliness (attachment), humiliation for defeat (agonism), and so forth.

Finally, *cooperation,* the last motivation studied by ethologists, which Liotti includes among the inborn interpersonal motivations, is characterized by the ability to recognize the other who is equal to us in intentionality; it is active in the child as of nine months of age, which is when, according to Tomasello (1999), intersubjectivity originates.[2]

Lichtenberg believes that *cooperation* is the result of negotiations and attunements with the other, for the purpose of reaching agreement and closeness in a relationship characterized by mutual recognition and differentiation.

I do not consider these two positions incompatible. Is it reasonable to imagine that there is an inborn tendency to cooperate which, during the various stages of development, is expressed in an ever more complex and sophisticated way? I believe it is.

With reference to Edelman's (1989) and MacLean's (1982) theories on the hierarchical functioning of the mind, we can suppose that each motivation finds a more primitive or a more evolved expression depending on the activated levels of functioning.

The cooperative motivation, for instance, can be limited to sharing attention on an object or joining forces in order to achieve a common goal (such as in team play), but it can also be the result of more complex mental endeavours: mutual exploration, negotiation/conflict over differences, mutual recognition. The purpose of this more complex activity would be to construct and maintain an *us* entity that allows us to feel the joy of sharing and the sense of safety that comes from closeness, both of which are definitely superordinate motivational values that have to do with the sophisticated neocortical intersubjectivity (Ivaldi, 2008).

Notes

1 The 'primary triangle', as it is conceived, emerges within a theoretical frame that associates the systems theory with the ethological-microanalytic paradigm, as well as with the studies of infant research (Sander, 1987; Trevarthen, 1979, 1980) and of Stern (1985) on 'affective attunement'. The Lausanne group starts from the systemic consideration that 'everything is an emergent property' and that, consequently, the triad must be observed as a whole. The innovation consists in having developed a research method that can go beyond the observation of the mother–child dyad.

2 According to Tomasello (1999), the ability to consider conspecifics as equal intentional agents begins to develop at around nine months of age. Various experimental studies conducted by Sander, (1969, 1976), Meltzoff and Moore, (1977), Meltzoff, (1990), Stern (1985), Tronick (1989), and Bebee *et al.*, (1985), instead, have shown that mutual interaction is possible as of the infant's early months of life. Trevarthen (1979) distinguishes between two different forms of intersubjectivity: *primary* and *secondary intersubjectivity*. A first, rudimentary form of mind theory can be traced to as early as the second month of life, when the infant interacts through the '*innate proto conversational readiness*', while he identifies a second, more evolved form at nine months, when the gestures of showing, holding out, and pointing to an object begin to be aimed at sharing attention on an object or an action with the mother (Beebe *et al.*, 2008).

Chapter 3

The therapeutic relationship from the theoretical perspective of motivational systems

Joseph D. Lichtenberg and Giovanni Liotti

Introduction

Antonella Ivaldi

From the proceedings of the international conference 'Personalities and relationships: a polyphonic game among different psychological themes' held at La Sapienza University of Rome in 2007

Over the years, the discourse between the theories of Lichtenberg and Liotti has raised stimulating points for reflection and, in some instances, has resulted in their influencing each other. I am happy to have offered my own contribution – however small – to this process by organizing an international conference on personality disorders and the therapeutic relationship, which was held at La Sapienza University of Rome in 2007. The highlight of this conference was a debate between the two authors on the topic of motivational theories.

I have decided to dedicate a chapter of this book to the conference session that featured this dialogue, which has been transcribed faithfully from a video recording of the event.

Through the stories of two patients, Joseph Lichtenberg briefly describes his motivational theory, particularly with reference to personality disorders; he illustrates some theoretical concepts and, at the same time, shows how the therapeutic relationship works in clinical practice based on his model.

Some highlights of the debate between Lichtenberg and Liotti then follow, giving the reader an opportunity to follow a highly significant dialogue between theory and clinical practice.

Motivational systems and the problems of patients with narcissistic, borderline, and dissociative disorders

Joseph D. Lichtenberg

A motivational systems theory provides a schema or template that helps therapists and researchers to understand a full range of human experience. The proposed systems must be broad enough to capture a wide range of disparate experiences and focused enough to appreciate any discrete motivational thrust. I conceptualize five motivational systems. Each system develops in infancy in response to a specific human need and the caretakers' response to that need: the need for psychic regulation of physiological requirements, the need for attachment and affiliation, the need for exploration and the assertion of preferences, the need to react aversively through antagonism and/or withdrawal, and the need for sensual enjoyment and sexual excitement. No one system is paramount. Developments in each system affect developments in the others. At any moment one system will be dominant, another active, and another dormant.

What do I mean by a motivational *system*? Each system self-organizes and self-stabilizes during infancy and childhood. Each system exists at all times in dialectic tension with each of the other systems and with alternate motivational thrusts that occur within the system. Throughout the life cycle, the dialectic tension in each system leads to small or large degrees of hierarchical change and reorganization. Each system exists in a complex relationship with other systems: those systems that are within the boundaries of the sense of self, and those systems – dyadic, triadic, extended family and social and cultural groups – that reside outside the experiential self. The five motivational systems are non-linear, that is, they are predictable only in broad outline while unpredictable in specifics for any person. Each person's experience is variable as to the context in which an experience occurs, the expectations the person brings to the experience, and the inferences the person draws from the experience.

Motivational systems theory allows us to view development and clinical experience within perspectives of both moment-to-moment and longer-term shifts in motivational-affective-cognitive dominance. My focus on the original formulation of the five systems was on conceptualizing moment-to-moment shifts in motivational dominance occurring in infants in coordination with the necessary recognition and response by the caretaker, in other words, a developmental approach. The other pole of my original formulation was to account for the shifts in motivational-affective-cognitive dominance noted in any treatment session – a clinical process approach. Today, my focus will be on the use of the schema or template to help in understanding those human misadventures we call personality disorders, specifically narcissistic, borderline, and dissociative experiences playing out in an analytic treatment.

Motivational systems receive and integrate information in order to regulate affect, perception, and attentional focus, cognition and behaviour. To my way of thinking, affect and communication – to self and to others – are key to all the rest. Consequently, the regulation of affect and internal and external communication are what is disrupted in personality disorders (usually from infancy on), and what are central to success or failure in treatment. The affects most dysregulated in these disorders are those of the aversive motivational system: anger, fear, shame/guilt, and sadness. The dysregulation is manifest in the disruptive effect on cognition and action of *affect states* of rage, panic, paralyzing shame, humiliation, embarrassment and guilt, and depression/mania.

Before I launch into clinical material, I will offer you an orientation to my view of the narcissistic, borderline, and dissociative disorders. Healthy ranges of pride/shame evolve from secure base attachment experiences and the positive qualities of mirroring, twinship, and idealization. Patients with narcissistic personality disorders have great difficulty regulating their self-worth within those healthy ranges. Instead, when self-worth is at issue, these patients are vulnerable to wide swings from grandiose entitled self-centredness or submissive hero-worship to painful inadequacy and/or disillusion. They are also vulnerable to experience criticism or even non-critical minor empathic failures as narcissistic injuries, triggering rage and a desire for vengeance. Everything I have just characterized as the problems of narcissistic disorder patients is also true of borderline patients, only more so. With borderline patients, dysregulation impairs not only the attachment and aversive systems but commonly involves the physiological, exploratory, and/or sensual-sexual systems as well. In the attachment/relational area, borderline patients struggle not only with problems of self-worth but also with problems of basic security. They employ strategies of preoccupation characterized by themes of domination-submission and/or strategies of avoidant standoffish isolation. For dissociative patients, everything I have characterized as the problems of narcissistic and borderline patients is also true, except these patients enter an altered state of consciousness in which feelings and awareness are attenuated or obliterated and connection between states de-linked. I will return to the dissociative strategy of regulation later.

A clinical example: Sister Mary

Sister Mary, a heavyset nun schoolteacher dressed in ordinary clothes, began her four times a week analysis stating, 'This is the ugliest room I have ever been in. You must be some fucking idiot to have a couch as uncomfortable as this!' She persisted in this vein until the middle of the second hour when she paused for the first time giving me a chance to say, 'I clearly hear that you are very, very angry about something. As yet I do not know what it is.' She answered, 'Well at least you do not take it personally,' and we began.

The Aversive System: Our first of many crises centred on her claim that I was punishing her with the 'silent treatment'. Not only was this 'abuse' occurring if I did not speak but equally so when I did speak since my voice was like sandpaper. In time we unraveled a source of this abusive attachment experience in her mother's rejection of her from birth and on her being called a big greedy baby like the father's family rather than having a small delicate refined body and appetite like her mother's family. With the slightest provocation, Sister Mary's mother would say to Mary's younger sisters in a stage whisper, 'We do not talk to her. We just ignore her.'

The Physiological System: Sister Mary was very skilled at treating other people as a pariah. Students in her class who crossed her were given the silent treatment. When she entered my office her nose in the air, eyes averted and a haughty look on her face, I knew I was in for it. A retired elderly nun who lived in the group house was a special target for Sister Mary's sadism. Sister Mary suffered from dysregulated eating and sleep. She rarely experienced clear-cut indicators to herself of hunger or satiety. At regular meals she ate only tiny portions, but gorged herself with stealth raids on private caches of food. To help get to sleep she drank alcohol nightly. For Sister Mary, the retired nun was a potential source of exposing her eating and drinking habits. Consequently she tormented her with practical jokes and haughty snubs.

The Sensual-Sexual System: Sister Mary's problems with sensual-sexual motivations made a dramatic entry. Sister Mary was adviser to a young adult who was considering joining their order. The young woman, Grace, became very attached and dependent. With a mixture of defiance and shame, Sister Mary revealed that they embraced often and fondled one another. Included in my attempts to understand and interpret Sister Mary's motivation were expressions of my concern about appearances and exposure. Sister Mary was generally so rebellious about rules that my concerns about risk went unappreciated and unheeded. She reported in a glow that she had had a wonderful weekend. Grace had come and agreed to stay over. They undressed and fondled all over and satisfied themselves lovingly. In a voice that revealed my mixture of disapproval, concern, and alarm, I said she was involving herself sexually against her own commitment as a spiritual adviser. Even more of a problem, she was sexually enticing a young woman who had placed her trust in her. Sister Mary became outraged, telling me that everything I said was further proof of my dirty mind. She insisted that their embracing was an expression of love. It provided her with a badly needed affirmation that she was worthy of love, and that another woman was appreciating her large body, so depreciated by her mother. She roared, 'This was love, not sex!' Without reflection, I roared back, 'When you and another person get in bed naked and masturbate one another that is sex! Whatever else is involved, it is sex!' A silence followed that seemed both an expression of exhaustion after the intensity of emotion, but also to involve reflection on both our parts as we regained our composure. What followed was unexpected. Sister Mary explained to Grace that they could not continue. It was not good for either. Grace needed to look elsewhere for a loving relationship (which she subsequently did). I remained puzzled by Sister Mary's compliance since it was so divergent from her usual overt or covert rejection of authority. Later, as we were considering her relations with men, she described an episode from her early teen years. A neighbour boy and she had formed a crush on one another and, somewhat flamboyantly, were publicly affectionate. Word of their flirtation got back to her parents. One morning before going to work, her father yanked her out of bed, told her what he had heard, and called her a little whore. He raised his hand in a gesture he called the 'right hand of the law' and forbade her to have anything further to do with the boy. Terrified and cowed, she agreed. She could defy her mother and find creative ways to get around her, but not her father. She was genuinely fond of her father, whose good opinion of her she desperately wanted to retain, and she genuinely feared his wrath. Using our interchange about Grace and the memory of her father's emotion-laden insistence, we could understand her acceptance of my eruption. Further, we could begin to recognize that when she responded to rules and prohibitions with defiance, she associated the authority with her mother. If she responded with acceptance, she linked the authority with her father. This helped to explain why the onset of her depressive symptomatology occurred after the breakup of the in-house convent system. Sister Mary had chosen a life of regularity and consistency within the convent of her order. To her, the convent's strict regimen was like her father's strict but benign authority. Once forced to leave the convent and live without the regularity and consistency of its rules she felt she had lost the only secure base of attachment she knew.

The Exploratory-Assertive System: Following this understanding of her relationship with her father, Sister Mary was more willing to reflect on her harsh techniques of disciplining children. She started to appreciate the wounding effect of her silent ostracism and the panic she inspired by her austere 'right hand of the law' terrorizing. Her ability to handle her class in the more effective and competent way began to allow her to have more pride in her ability to teach and inspire her students.

The Aversive System – Transference and Countertransference: The ups and downs of Sister Mary's provocative behaviour with authorities and her frequent public denunciations of me led the leaders of her order to question the efficacy of the treatment and their financial support. Her anger was now shifted off me and directed to those who threatened her as she tenaciously held to her need and desire to continue. I helped by arranging a consultation with the psychiatric adviser to the diocese. He reported that she was making significant progress and advised that her outpatient treatment, while she served a professional function, was much less expensive than repeated short or long hospitalizations. Continued support was authorized, and Sister Mary now redirected her belligerence to me. I dealt with the attacks and devaluing much as I had before, trying to recognize the source in any occurrence between us or any carryover from the many exigencies of her daily life.

In the past, my approach had been both stabilizing and effective in adding to our understanding, but now progress was stalled. The devaluing intensified, and I was at a loss to relate it to anything I was doing. Sister Mary also became increasingly desperate and arranged for a consultation with the referring therapist. She returned saying he reassured her that of course her attacks bothered me. This comment opened my eyes to my contribution to our enactment. It was not what I was doing that had us at an impasse; it was what I was not doing. I was not letting her know that I was really troubled by her criticisms and personal attacks. I was depriving her of the satisfaction of knowing that her attacks got through my professional armour and caused me pain. In the beginning of the treatment, by her acknowledgment, my 'not taking it personally' had been central to her feeling safe. Now she not only wanted me to take it personally, she *had* to have me take it personally. Unless I was distressed, she couldn't believe I knew that attacks on her she had told me about really hurt her. Looking inward, I realized that I was reliving a response from childhood when an intimate member of my family who had been under the pressure of terrible pain from an illness had become angry and critical. I developed a strategy of absorbing the attacks with minimal emotional responses of retaliation while discounting much of the exaggeration in the content. This ability to deflect attacks without impairing my attention, what might be called becoming thick-skinned, had been useful in my early work with Sister Mary but had now become a distinct constraint on our progress. With the memory from my childhood available to me, we began to build a model scene of the meaning to us of my withholding from her the recognition of the power of her protests. I needed to recognize that the goal of her angry protests was not only to alert me to her distress but also to wound, to get under my skin. We could examine how I was contributing to her increasingly desperate need to be heard and how this led to her increasing the amplitude of her attacks. From the work with the model scene informing each of our contributions, Sister Mary came to recognize how desperately she needed the empowering quality of anger to convey and cope with her lifelong feelings of shame and powerlessness, and I learned the great significance of recognizing and acknowledging an ouch!

Second clinical example: Veronica

Veronica was on her way home from graduate school during a holiday when her car broke down. With trepidation she called her father, who, as she expected whenever anything made him anxious, railed at her,

'How can you be so stupid that you can't look after your car properly?' Shattered, she went into her dissociative robot fog state, which lasted through the whole vacation period. She arranged to see a counsellor who had helped her through high school and college. The contact had been intermittent depending on the severity of Veronica's bulimia. Her treatment could never be called psychotherapy but for Veronica and her family, the more acceptable euphemism of counseling. On this occasion the level of concern of both therapist and Veronica rose to the point where a more consistent treatment was agreed to and she was referred to me.

The fog having lifted, Veronica struck me as an attractive, vibrant, almost hypomanic, ambitious, resourceful, bright young woman. From her prior therapy, she had formed a picture of her family. Her father, a successful industrialist, dominated the family. He was easily made anxious whenever anything threatened his control and had frequent temper outbursts. Her mother, who possessively doted on Veronica, was completely submissive to her husband's demands. She could be childlike in her dependence on Veronica. During her adolescence, Veronica's mother lived vicariously through her social and athletic accomplishments and was often intrusive with flurries of gifts and demands.

An understanding of the attachment disruption that contributed to Veronica's fog states unfolded over a period of time. As described in the D-category paradigm proposed by Hesse and Main (1990), Veronica's father was both frightened and frightening, as well as shaming and seductive. In the middle of the night if a thunder and lightning storm occurred, he would awaken the whole family in a state of great anxiety insisting they all go to the basement and hover together. As Veronica got older, she no longer believed in her father's reasons for panic at storms but could not help but be caught up in his frightened state. Her father's frighting side lay in his raging and screaming. In caricature-like style of an adult temper tantrum, at his club he would break up golf clubs and slam tennis rackets. Veronica could disavow her embarrassment at her father's public displays of temper when it did not involve her. However, his screaming at her at home in front of her friends or the sound of his voice criticizing her heard above the cheers and hoots of other parents during athletic events would resonate in her ears for hours. As soon as she could be alone she would walk outside, smoke, look at nature and enter a dissociative state. Her mother, ever alert to Veronica's not being her smiling effervescent self, would cajole her to forgive her father, forget what he had done since 'he did not mean it'. Veronica was sent to calm him so peace would be restored and he would not take out his anger on her mother.

A symptom that presented early in the treatment was nighttime panics. She could not calm herself enough to get to sleep. She used alcohol and cigarettes to produce a fog state, finally getting to sleep, only to be disturbed by upsetting dreams of disasters. At different times in her treatment, I phoned Veronica nightly and would let her know where I could be reached on weekends.

Her family visited and for several days enjoyed the sights of Washington. Then on returning to their hotel, she became confused momentarily about directions. Veronica pulled the car over to the curb. Her father said something, she didn't remember quite what, and she froze. In robot fashion Veronica got them back to the hotel. Her mother stood helplessly by assuring her that her father loved her. Subsequently, believing her concentration was adversely affected, Veronica worried that she was losing her credibility at work and had a full return of insomnia, drinking nightly, and disaster nightmares. After work, she was holing up in her apartment, not contacting friends and even foregoing the athletic events that had sustained her in the past. The car experience I believed had triggered a serious traumatic dissociative state of altered consciousness. I phoned nightly and we increased the frequency of meetings. I urged Veronica to re-enter her trancelike state in the car while with me. She filled in detail after detail as we relived the experience together. Furthermore, we were more successful than before in relating the content of the persistent nightmares to the traumatic effect of daytime experiences. We were able to integrate our understanding of the recent experience in the car with the original car breakdown.

The next crisis again involved a car. Veronica came in completely distraught and told me she had to go home for a holiday because her mother had sent her tickets saying, 'Your father misses you so much.' On inquiry Veronica said she could neither refuse nor could she go. The principal horror was that father would insist they go to visit his mother. On the long drive, he would be tense about seeing his mother whom neither he nor anyone in the family liked. Something always happened on the road and he would start screaming at mother or her and she'd be frozen while trapped in the car for hours. What should she do? As usual I was no help. I suggested she had to choose between not going home when Veronica interrupted, 'I have to, I cannot just not see them. They are my family.'

I continued, 'or negotiate a plan that would make it safe for you'. Veronica, interested, asked, 'Like what?' I responded, 'Like not doing what you do not want, and picking out things you do want, like seeing your friends.' The effect of this exchange was like glass shattering. Veronica emerged from her fog with a burst of purposeful agency. She called her parents who accepted her parameters and the visit went well. She also changed jobs, going to a company where she would work under two successful women she liked.

Veronica became sexually and emotionally involved with a series of narcissistic, prancing star-men who treated her badly and frequently disappointed her. Somewhat to both of our surprise Dick, the last of the series, not only dropped her but also refused to even make eye contact or acknowledge her presence when they met in professional settings. Veronica went into an emotional funk characterized by insomnia, anxiety, anger at me, and an intense, almost delusional insistence that Dick must come back, must call her. Nothing I could say or offer helped. Reiterating what we knew of her father's coming to her room to make up and charm her with pet names after their disagreements fell flat. Something in Veronica's tone, a little girl voice as she insisted he must come back, triggered my conjecture that Veronica was dealing with a vulnerability other than the Oedipal configuration with her father, a vulnerability derived from an earlier or at least different source. Veronica's stock portrayal of her mother was that she was always seeking Veronica out for company and solace, for stories to brag about to her friends and to shower Veronica with gifts and clothing as though she were a Barbie doll. This view was well substantiated by current experiences. Spontaneously I asked Veronica about her mother's diabetes. She responded that when she was small her mother had great difficulty getting her diabetes under control and that her father's outbursts would make it worse. Veronica responded to this line of inquiry with interest and an affective shift. Together we developed the picture of Veronica's mother having episodes of physiologically induced discontinuities that were inexplicable to the little girl. The he of 'he must come back, he must call' served to obscure the symbolic condensation of the abandoner – she (of the need for a secure base attachment) and he (of Oedipal desire) must return to re-establish sustaining affective connection.

An unexpected sequence of events followed. On a driving trip with her family through the Southwest, Veronica, rather than ineffectually ridiculing her father with other family members, directly confronted him. She declared that his temper outbursts, harangues, and road rage behaviours were unacceptable. If he did not agree to stop she would fly back to Washington. Despite the absence of support from other family members, Veronica remained firm and they completed the trip.

On her return, Veronica switched employment to a prestigious position that required retraining and working in a competitive environment. Now 'having found her voice' through challenging her father, she was more effective at work, despite brief periods of depressive anxiety when she was 'out of favour'. While she poured out torrents of anger to and at me, her actual behavioural strategy was to be compliant and submissive when challenged and sulky and avoidant otherwise. Veronica reported a vivid dream that upset her. She suddenly saw a tornado approaching. No, two tornadoes. She was terrified but saw a building that she was able to find a way to get under and take refuge and then woke up. We had long before identified the tornado as a reference to her father's temper and to his fear of actual tornadoes cowering in the basement during storms. As Veronica described the building under which she took refuge, we both recognized it as standing for my office, which is on a lower floor of my house. Veronica generally did not like to acknowledge openly the protection she felt from me. But she asked, 'Two tornados?' I answered, 'The second one is you. You have a temper like your father. You have as much power as he but you do not know yet how to harness it to get what you want.' Not long after this session, Veronica conceptualized a project at work that required much diligence and skilled interpersonal maneuvering. The success of the project was reported in newspapers and won her awards.

Not long after our interpretive work with her tornado dream, Veronica met and married a quiet young professional who is caring and very supportive of her. They have one child with another on the way. Veronica has continued to work professionally at a very high level having completed a second major project that has earned her a sequence of honors. She has had no further serious episodes of fog state dissociation. She continues to struggle with severe impatience when others' slow tempo or lack of ambition interferes with her up-tempo requirements for action and success. Rather than a fog state, these frustrations now trigger rage responses in which she is the entitled attacking tornado while at the same time having increasing reflective awareness of the negative impact of her raging on herself and others.

Veronica's experience illustrates a serious disturbance in the organization of the aversive motivational system as a consequence of moments of traumatic disruptions in the attachment system. Not only was her mother a poor source of strength to model on, she also failed to be a source of protection. Not only was her father a poor source of a model for a romantic partner who could be respectful and sensitive, but he was also a source of fear, fright, shaming, and seduction. I believe Veronica's dissociative episodes reflect a D-category experience of moments of early traumatic disorganization and detachment. Both Dr. Liotti and I independently suggested that the detachment noticeable within the first year of life might well be the precursor of the later use of dissociative strategies for dealing with affect states that would be painfully disruptive. Dr. Liotti tracked this hypothesis and has provided strong evidence in support of it. I lack evidence to confirm or disconfirm that Veronica had detachment/dissociative episodes within the first year. I do know that subsequently there were sufficient repeated traumatic episodes centring on her father's frightened and frightening behaviour and her mother's diabetic and emotional absences along with her possessive intrusive clinging dependence on her daughter.

Discussion

A member of the audience might say, 'You have described two interesting cases but I do not yet see how motivational systems theory would help me with my clinical work. Is the theory just another abstraction like id, ego, and superego? If not, how do I use it?' My answer begins with my placing (along with Kohut) the empathic mode of perception at the centre of my clinical endeavour. My goal is to sense into the state of mind of my patient. As close as I can, I want to sense my patient's feelings, thoughts, intentions, goals, and values from within his or her perspective. To accomplish my empathic entry, I can benefit from a schema or template that orients me to particular organizations of self with other. Freud suggested many schemas that we all use: the triadic romantic desire and rivalry of 4- to 6-year-old children with their parents, the way in which a narrative of a present experience may contain a pattern that reflects the significance of a past experience, the way in which a narrative about someone past or present may reveal the patient's current experience of the analyst. If I can gauge from the patient's communications (words, gestures, facial expressions, body movements, odours, stomach gurgles, silences, and behaviours) the patterning characteristic of a particular set of motivations, then I can quickly orient myself within a context that brings me closer to my patient's perspective. Each of the 'stories' in the narrative of Sister Mary and Veronica are examples of schemas recognizable in each motivational system. Now of course there are hitches. To use motivational systems theory, a therapist must learn about the development and dynamics of each system. Which emotions are most prominent in the system? What interactive and intersubjective relational elements are characteristic of the system? What symbolic forms – linguistic, imagistic, gestural, enactive, and dream-organized – provide an entry into the narrative of that system as a set of human experiences from which expectations are formed and inferences drawn? And there is a further hitch. First a therapist learns and gains mastery over the dynamics of each system and how to recognize from the narrative flow and total intersubjective communication when one or the other is dominant. But then therapists should not use that knowledge in a formalistic or ritualistic way. Rather, therapists must hold all knowledge of the systems in the 'back' of their mind to be free to respond with spontaneity and personal authenticity. I propose that we not learn our *craft* to build in the linear form of a carpenter, but in the creative style needed to probe both the graspable and the difficult to fathom in a spirit of inquiry.

The debate between Joseph Lichtenberg and Giovanni Liotti. From infant research to evolutionism: two motivational perspectives in dialogue

Giovanni Liotti and Joseph D. Lichtenberg

I had something in mind before listening to Professor Lichtenberg: I wanted to try to discuss how basic research can support a motivational theory that has come into being independently of basic research. After listening to Joseph Lichtenberg's contribution, I have a clearer sense of how to go about this. I will talk about what basic research on attachment offers in support of the theories that Professor Lichtenberg argued prior to and independently of this research. There has always been a sort of divorce between clinicians and researchers. That is a shame because they could potentially converge significantly, especially in the area of developmental psychology.

I will focus on some contributions of attachment research, particularly with reference to disorganized attachment, a construct on which research has offered sound and reliable contributions. Professor Lichtenberg mentioned the 'frightened and frightening parent'. This expression does not refer merely to a violent, harsh, abusive parent; in fact, it has been shown that similar psychopathological effects can be caused by a parent who does not beat a child but is terribly vulnerable, entirely inept and incompetent. I believe that this research datum is enlightening for clinicians and could correct much of the literature currently available on trauma and its consequences. A very vulnerable and not very loving parent can be traumatic. Since we all refer to the disorganization of attachment, what does research tell us about what comes after? What happens to a 12-month-old baby as a result of a traumatic attachment relationship as we have just described it? We will dwell on the early research results relating to children who are classified as disorganized at age one and are subsequently re-examined between three and six years of age. There are five longitudinal studies that span from the first year of life up to age 19 or 26. These individuals are monitored over time and in the course of their development. You can have a video tracking the childhood of a disorganized child and then you can see what that child, who has become an adult, says in the Adult Attachment Interview and determine whether or not there is continuity in that person's life, in between the two observations. I do not think that results like these have been reached in any area of psychological research. In the vast majority of cases, the child develops a controlling strategy towards the parent with whom a disorganized internal working model was previously active and the disorganization appears to have vanished. If you think about it, were that not the case, all children with disorganized attachment, at around age two or three, would have to be taken to the paediatrician or child neuropsychiatrist for a severly impaired coherence of conduct. But that does not happen! At around two and a half years of age, with the parents' unwitting collaboration, the child begins to find a way out of disorganization by resorting to so-called 'controlling' strategies. What controlling strategies have been identified? One is the *controlling-punitive strategy*: a person who, when in need of help, acts as if he or she wants to dominate you, attacking you for the purpose of humiliating you, making you feel like you count for nothing. This may seem to make no sense, and yet it has a very deep and significant sense. How can you understand such a phenomenon without a multi-motivational theory? If it were not possible to use a motivational system different from the careseeking system – a ready-to-use system? When attachment is severely impaired, such a phenomenon is very frequently observed. Almost half of the children with disorganized attachment become '*controlling punitive*', while others become '*controlling caregiving*'. The latter seem to use another motivational system instead of, or in support of, the attachment system, which should be dominant but is not: they begin to take care of the parent who appears to be vulnerable. These are not necessarily the only controlling strategies and a child does not necessarily develop just one of them; however, it appears that one prevails over the others. It is possible that, with the help of a seductive parent, as Veronica's father might have been, a child may develop a *sexualized* controlling strategy, that is, use sexuality; in this sense, we might recall how psychoanalysis came into being, particularly the Oedipus complex, considering the developmental age that we are referring to. Starting from a disorganized attachment, the sexual system can be used to substitute for the impaired attachment system. There may also be a *controlling-submissive* strategy to substitute for the attachment functions: it is sometimes necessary to reassure a parent, acknowledging his or her superiority, dominance, right to shame us. This could serve to preserve an impaired attachment relationship and would explain some patients' self-attacking attitudes. Once again, I would like to point out that talking about multi-motivational theories is not only useful but indeed indispensable. For instance, they can help us therapists to understand what map our patients are using to get their bearings in their relationship with us, starting from the world of their needs.

Let us go back to the motivational structure that I was proposing and that is backed up by research, namely the situation in which there is a system that substitutes for the impaired functions of another system that should be dominant: attachment. In the *controlling-caregiving* strategy attachment should be dominant, but there is another system that comes into play to manage the relationship: the caregiving system. In the controlling strategies, therefore, the caregiving system and the system that aims to dominate/humiliate the other compensate for the impaired functions of the attachment system.

But what happens if the attachment system is powerfully stimulated? What happens to the controlling strategy and its vicarious function? What happens is that the controlling strategy collapses and chaos sets in; the disorganized world manifests itself, for instance, with dramatic narratives laden with contradictory emotions that appear to make no sense. Sometimes in the interviews, during which the interviewer strongly stimulates the attachment system, altered states of consciousness arise. The strong alertness that causes someone to seek care causes the controlling strategy to collapse, allowing a disorganized world to emerge. In other words, disorganization, which is kept at bay by means of the controlling strategy, surfaces dramatically. This could happen to our patients when they experience a traumatic life event, or when the attachment system is activated by something that is not overtly traumatic, such as for instance separating from one's family to get married, or even just the wish to separate. At any rate, the attachment system is activated and could supersede the defensive capacities of the controlling strategies. In this sense, it would be useful to explore under what conditions a patient displayed symptoms. We would expect to find conditions in which the patient's attachment motivational system was strongly activated.

Allow me to offer a clinical example to show how subtle the strategies that invalidate a motivational system which compensates for another system can be. Diana is a young married woman, a very self-giving physician who leads a fulfilling professional and personal life. In her life, she has often experienced temporary dysphoria and dysthymia, which she has always tried to treat by herself. When she was still a medical student, she managed to identify the right antidepressants and to self-prescribe them without seeking help. This self-giving young woman, who does not seek help for her recurring bouts of neurotic depression, at one point experiences strong dissociative phenomena: a particular type of depersonalization that verges on body dysmorphic disorder, on account of which she is forced to ask for help. This is very difficult for her, because she cannot accept the therapeutic relationship: 'The therapeutic relationship scares me, it upsets me.' Diana experiences her body like Kafka's cockroach: she feels that she is morphing, becoming hideous. She is convinced that if she goes out in the street people will look at her strangely, she will somehow induce disgust; she knows this is not true, but it is how she feels. She senses her body becoming grotesquely transformed, and the more absurd it seems to her, the more it makes her fear that she is going crazy. This had never happened to her before. She has sudden memory lapses, lacunar amnesias, which she realizes are not ordinary slips. Also, in the process of falling asleep she experiences panic. Diana describes the typical fears – which Veronica also displays – that are reported by patients who have been victims of incest and sexual abuse in childhood: a huge and overpowering, dark male figure walking ominously into the room, regarded as a hallucination which occurs only when one is in the process of falling asleep or is just about to wake up. Now, this patient endured terrible incestuous experiences during her childhood, which she has never forgotten. Throughout her life Diana has always had a very clear recollection of her trauma. Diana's trauma can be summarized as follows: a mother suffering from major depression and probably from bipolar disorder, who was institutionalized more than once for psychiatric reasons. Diana presumably develops a disorganized attachment (incidentally, there are research data proving that major unipolar or bipolar depression in the mother is a risk factor for the development of disorganized attachment). As a child, Diana probably developed a caregiving strategy, her few memories indicate that this was her choice, and her professional vocation seems to confirm it: she is a good, self-giving doctor. Diana began to look after her mother as early as she could (some children begin at age 3) and her father probably accepted that she was the real woman of the house, so eventually he took her to bed with him. This went on for three or four endless years, during which she was her father's sexual partner. Diana wanted to spare her sister, who was four years younger than her, from this atrocious situation. Diana was sure that she was protecting her little sister, so she took care of her in any way she could, shielding her from their father's unsound attentions. These caregiving controlling strategies prevented her from having dissociative phenomena. She managed to not 'be dissociated'; naturally, it was hard for her to give up her own pleasure, for indeed if you are a child and you have to take care of someone else, you cannot go out to play. As I always say, in jest, if you become your father's or your mother's parent, you become your own grandparent, which is not exactly a cheerful prospect for a child! So it is understandable that Diana managed to hold out for many years and did not have any dissociative disorder until she was 33, or at least until her sister told her that she had found a boyfriend and needed to see a psychotherapist because she had been repeatedly abused by their father. Diana thus discovered that her capacity for caretaking was limited, the strategy collapsed and the dissociative symptoms emerged. In this case, dissociation does not appear as a result of the resurgence of traumatic memories, for indeed Diana had never forgotten the traumatic events.

This is an example that shows the purpose of motivational systems. How can you explain a clinical picture like Diana's without considering motivational systems, which are in dynamic tension and can either hold out or collapse?

I will try to conclude by saying that multi-motivational theory allows us to review and reconsider some classical notions of psychopathology and psychotherapy, like for example defensive apparatuses. Can a motivational system be used as a defensive strategy, for instance towards another system that carries with it unbearable pain? It probably can! But I believe that Professor Lichtenberg's work goes much further than this.

Finally, I wish to highlight a point of divergence. I mentioned a system which I regard as a primary system: the caregiving system. It is not the same as attachment, nor is it the same as affiliation. These systems use different brain mediators: if you give children oxytocin, they no longer want to be cuddled, but if you administer oxytocin intranasally to adults, they feel like cuddling and babies seem wonderful to them. If instead the brain is not soaked in oxytocin, babies may appear as monsters. Oxytocin is the substance that sustains the need to take care of the other, which is a primary need. Furthermore, I would add another system to the ones mentioned so far: the egalitarian-cooperative system, which is probably primary. Tomasello, an evolutionary anthropologist, collected a series of extraordinary data which lead us to conclude that probably the one single motivation that sustains the human ability to produce culture is the motivation to perceive the other as equal to oneself, associated with the capacity for cooperating with the other on a par. According to Tomasello, from the very beginning of life, the human being, probably on account of a variant of the genome of anthropomorphous apes that led to *homo sapiens*, can perceive the other as 'equal to him in intentionality'. Only the human infant has the following experience: 'You are different, you are bigger, you are a man, you are a woman, I am a child, I see that, I understand that, I am not stupid – but you are the same as me in your intentions, so I too can point to an object to share attention and you can explore this experience and share it with me.' Obviously, in order to do this, the attachment system must not be activated, the caregiving system must not be activated – the sexual system can be active perhaps, as the life of a couple shows.

In conclusion, I believe that we can add two systems to the ones described by Professor Lichtenberg: the caregiving system and the egalitarian-cooperative system.

Joseph Lichtenberg

My original point was to take up certain supposed givens about childhood and the schemas that apply to adults that were laid down through psychoanalysis and ego psychology. My original purpose was to challenge that with facts. So instead of building a theory from top down – that is from the adult reconstructing childhood, from an observation of what adults were like in order to understand what childhood must have been like – I wanted to build a theory from the bottom up, that is from careful observation of neonates, infants, toddlers and then older children. I then applied the results to the theoretical constructs that I had learned as a psychoanalyst. Of course this was not always popular with some people, but at any rate I think that eventually careful observation and research wins out. So that was my starting point.

Now, let me give a cross point to Professor Liotti's point: he emphasized, for example, that evolution would make it absolutely necessary that there be a kind of caregiving, and he says that, biologically, we actually have substances in the brain that serve to promote this, so that there is a genetic base, an evolutionary base giving a genetic base, and so on. So there should be a caregiving system which then, in a sense, is utilized to serve another purpose in certain children who often grow up to be preoccupied adults.

My knowledge of research utilizes a research at the National Institute of Health that studied 2-year-olds and observed that 2-year-olds are altruistic in response to someone's pain, so you have then the very foundation of caregiving by a child. A 2-year-old child can try to comfort an upset mother by handing the mother the child's bottle, 'This makes me comfortable when I am unhappy, here is my bottle Mommy, you use it, you get comfortable,' or by patting the Mommy like this, '... Mommy, Mommy ...'. All children across the spectrum have this as an emerging property at around two years of age. This pattern is then utilized by certain insecure children to promote their own security by looking after the caregiver in order for the caregiver to be repaired enough to look after them. I see this as no disagreement, so to speak; it stands that what evolution has built into us is the most important way to formulate who we have become, and I say I use that as one factor, but I also see other factors that I do not think have to be limited to the evolutionary concept, I just use that as one example. I have more but I will stop.

Giovanni Liotti

I am sure that Professor Lichtenberg has much more to say. In actual fact, the early methods yielded comparable, not equal results. Comparable, and that is extraordinary. When I first discovered Professor Lichtenberg's theories I was astonished by the results, which were so similar to the ones produced by an evolutionary-ethological approach. A perspective that is close to the world of neuroscience and very close to the original framing of Bowlby's theory, attachment theory, which is the prototype of the evolutionary perspective. Incidentally, as you may know, at the end of his life Bowlby wrote a book, a biography of Darwin, his hero, and he did so because he hoped that this would help people to understand that his was an evolutionary perspective. As we were pursuing attachment theory and formulating a set of ideas, Lichtenberg's book came out. In spite of some dissimilarities, these radically different theoretical perspectives that know very little about each other but are both based on a fundamental common principle – the method of empirical observation – appeared to converge. That said, what did I admire about Lichtenberg's work, which I still admire and is missing in our work? The deep contact with human experience as it develops during interactions with others over the years, ever since childhood. The great complexity of this approach, which is obviously lacking if you adopt a perspective that seeks to identify the ethological signals of every motivational system – the *separation cry* for attachment, gentle and constant contact for caregiving, a pointed finger to share attention for cooperation, seductive poses for sexuality. That is how ethologists think and work: they look for and identify the invariant signals in the various animal species, which are the same in humans, such as for instance the chick's cry and the baby's cry; they have the same formal structure – high-pitched and acute tones. No species asks for care in a low tone, it is an invariant! Another invariant consists in having five phalanxes at the end of a limb instead of four. All species have five, and that is, I repeat, how evolutionists proceed. It is extraordinary that this way of proceeding leads to the same conclusions as a method based on empathy and child observation, that is, the identification of interpersonal motivational systems. Apart from some slight differences that can surely be found in each theory, this to me is proof that presumably there is something 'true' – forgive me for using this outdated word – at the root of these theories. Of course they remain theories, but they are not just 'one of the many' out there. When you reach the same conclusions from different perspectives, that is a strong indicator that such perspectives point to something 'true'. So I completely agree that in each of the two theoretical systems it is possible to reformulate what is observed in the other. But I would venture to say that I am not at all sure they are two different theoretical systems; rather, I believe they are two angles associated to the different perspectives, but have very strong common foundations. Perhaps one day a third theory will better grasp this, and that is what theories do, they progressively correct the limits from which we all set out.

Now to the question regarding affect regulation. Well . . . it is a huge question! I agree with Professor Lichtenberg, but this takes us to another great contribution of Lichtenberg's work, that is the relationship between the self and motivational systems, which is the title of his second book. Incidentally, in his book *The Present Moment*, Daniel Stern (2004) suggests that attachment and intersubjectivity are two motivational systems and he tries to examine them using the evolutionary method. I am sorry to say that, from an evolutionary perspective, there are major mistakes in that approach. Intersubjectivity is the self of my Kohutian friends, it is superordinate, it subsumes all other systems, as it is stated – if I have understood correctly – in Joseph Lichtenberg's theory. His theory makes much more sense to an evolutionist than does the theory put forward by Stern, who taps into the basic principles of evolutionism to argue that intersubjectivity is another motivational system. I believe that a careful analysis would reveal that the argument does not stand up and the consequences of this are significant. They help us, for instance, to understand the difference between a secondary attachment disorder in an autistic child and a secondary intersubjectivity disorder in a child with disorganized attachment, which are two very different and distant clinical conditions. Both can be extremely serious. Perhaps a child with high-level autism can be a little better than a child adopted from a Romanian orphanage who has intersubjectivity and attachment impairments which probably cannot be remedied in spite of the best possible care. So it is not a matter of severity but of being able to explain the two clinical conditions – both of which are hard to treat – and their differences.

Which priority aspects the therapist should bear in mind when using this theoretical system? According to me – and perhaps there is a difference here – the therapist is trained by the evolutionary view of motivational systems to constantly and actively strive to establish a therapeutic alliance and to repair the therapeutic alliance. Therapeutic alliance becomes another name for cooperative system. I will try to explain myself better, showing how the evolutionist sees the dynamic tensions – here I am using an expression borrowed from Professor Lichtenberg – among these systems. A small enigma, which is also an example: no animal we know of has young that challenge the dominance of an adult. Human infants begin at two years of age. Between two and four years of age – *the terrible twos*. How is this possible? From the evolutionary point of view, the dominance-subjection system, which has much to do with many aspects of Professor Lichtenberg's aversive system, calculates and assesses the different strength of the opponent. When this system registers that the other's strength is overpowering, it induces a response of arrest accompanied by a signal of surrender. *Invariant* in all species is to bow one's head, lowering or exposing the soft parts to the potential attack of the opponent, as dogs do for instance when they lie on the ground exposing their belly and genitals: these are signals of surrender that are invariant in all species, including man, who bows before the queen or raises his arms. This signal is given immediately when one realizes that the other is stronger. So how can a human infant rebel against a parent's order, 'Eat your food, sweetie,' answering 'No!!!' at age two? This probably happens because we have a cooperative system that qualifies us as *homo sapiens*. So what happens when the child challenges the adult is clear, '*You are bigger than me, but you are like me in intentionality*'; and in that case the challenge is possible, there we see who wins on the level of intentionality . . . so then, bearing in mind these observations – which I have tried to render lively in order to have them intuitively clear in our mind – this is what has priority in the model that I propose: it is the tradition of the therapeutic alliance and of the reparation of the therapeutic alliance as a priority objective, it is what we heard in the presentation of the clinical cases. Professor Lichtenberg raised another very important point. In order to be on equal terms, to repair a therapeutic alliance, he had to engage in *self-disclosure*, he had to say, 'You hurt me when you attack me!' He had to treat the patient as an equal, and the patient – Sister Mary – stated this when she put herself on the same level as Joseph (in the sketch she made of the two of them). This standing with the other on equal ground is constantly present: Sister Mary understood this perfectly well and, according to me, for the first time in her life she had the enduring experience of standing next to someone and observing the same things, perhaps abstract art. This also makes it possible to learn from the other who knows more, and maybe teach the other something he or she may ignore. This becomes an absolute priority. From the first session until the last, throughout the treatment period. So I could say that I agree with affect regulation as having to do with the Self, with intersubjectivity and with consciousness at a superordinate level, and then – within the various motivational systems – with something that constantly compels to privilege this dimension, that of egalitarian cooperation, over all others. I hope the answer is sufficient.

Joseph Lichtenberg

I do not want to squelch the audience but I would like to deal with the question of cooperation very briefly. In my idea, a baby gives all those protest signals that Professor Liotti just referred to. If a mother responds to them and recognizes when the baby is hungry and feeds it within a reasonable time, recognizes when a baby is tired and so on, accepts all the signals of aversiveness in a reasonable way, by the end of the first year the child is securely attached. That is just a given. But after the first year, a child securely attached has to do more than give signals of distress, so the aversive system in the first year of life should not be highly organized. If, in fact, aversiveness is a major component of attachment responses, then that child is on its way to D category troubles and other such things. However, at the end of the first year, the beginning of the second year and continuing on, a child must move out of a dependent affectionate mode into an aversive mode of agency battles. It must do that. It must have a way of saying, 'Well, I see what you want, but I do not want it,' and at that point there are going to be inevitable clashes, and out of those inevitable clashes comes one of the most important aspects of life. Two things begin: one is that all of this gets symbolically represented, so you have a cognitive capacity coming into play that is uniquely human – there are pieces and parts of it in bonobo monkeys, but it is uniquely human to carry it forward. And what the child begins to use is the capacity for seeing what the other is up to and seeing what he/she is up to. He/she is then in a position to negotiate. And so I, in my theory, regard the capacity to negotiate as the central feature of the second and third year of life. And out of the capacity to negotiate comes the capacity to cooperate, because when you negotiate and know how to negotiate you can then jump ahead and say, 'OK, we do not have to battle this one out, we will work it out together.' So, cooperation for me is an outgrowth of learning the capacity to negotiate. And now you have a further development, which I will only take a minute to say. When I meet somebody, because I have had a lot of good experience negotiating, with my mother, with my father, with my brother, etc., I have an expectation that when I meet somebody else who does not have the same desire as I do I will be able to figure out how to negotiate, so I have positive expectations. But suppose all my experiences are pretty lousy and I have not had good experiences, then I develop an expectation which is, 'Things are not going to work out for me. I am one of these people who are going to have trouble every time I get into something or other.' Of course our patients bring us those negative expectations with great regularity. But always, a positive expectation knows it is not always going to be positive, so I also have some ability to recognize that life is not always going to be wonderful and I will work that out. On the other hand, a person with only negative expectations is incurable, because there is no hope, and if there is no hope, you are not going to do it. A person with lots of negative experience who can retain hope retains a positive expectation, and the human being is capable of making a positive out of very little. An awful lot of people who had as little as the kids in the holocaust and who somehow survived still grow up and can be people. So you have the capacity to have hope under bad experiences, we can draw conclusions from every experience, and this is where we get to the cognitive side of life; we enter an experience with an expectation, either a negative expectation – 'Same old lousy world' – or a positive expectation – 'Maybe this time it will be different,' says our patient, 'and that is why I am here, maybe this time it will be different.' And then you have an interaction so things happen between the two of you, or maybe the patient just tells you a story or whatever the interaction is, and the patient draws an inference from it and the inference is, 'Yes, this is bad, and the cause of it is you,' or 'Yes, this is bad, and the cause of it is me.' So you cannot predict what inference, what cognitive stance the patient will take, but you have to follow the patient in whatever stance he/she takes. Or another stance is, 'We are a lousy couple,' at which point you really have a lot of work to do to get that treatment under way. What you pick up in order to get that treatment under way is the emotional state that is there, just like with Sister Mary in the second hour I said, 'Boy, you are angry, and I do not understand it yet.' That was our mutual emotional state. And so from that we then start to work to make meaning, to make sense of something. So that is my overview, in a very broad sense, of the way I picture working and how it grows out of even the early negotiations that are part of the second/third year of life and are critical to it.

Chapter 4

Complex trauma theories and psychopathology

The difficult patient

Antonella Ivaldi

Who is the difficult patient?

ANNA (1)

Anna is a highly intelligent and creative 35-year-old woman. She is easily enthused and just as easily disappointed. Because of this, she changes job frequently and moves from one place to another whenever she becomes involved with someone new. Her father passed away several years ago, after a long illness during which he was housebound and was looked after by his wife and daughter, who recalls that time as a nightmare. She has a very conflictual relationship with her mother, whom she has not untied herself from either psychologically or financially: her mother remains her 'insecure base'. For some years now Anna has been suffering from deep depression, engaging in compulsive self-injurious behaviour: she drinks herself into a stupor, cuts herself and burns her skin with cigarettes or with a red-hot blade. She also binges, fasts and takes too many laxatives and diuretics. She spends days locked inside her room, worrying the people who are closest to her: friends, partners (Anna is a lesbian), her mother – briefly, a group of women who come to her rescue chaotically, in response to her constant emergencies. When I first met Anna, she would come to the sessions accompanied by her mother, her cousin, or another one of her 'women'.

*

In daycare clinical practice, more and more often we receive *difficult patients* with a complex symptomatological picture presenting various forms of Axis I or I/II comorbidity or different traits of several personality disorders. The hypothesis that is pursued in this book and will be presented in Chapter 6 is that there is an etiopathogenic continuum characterized by the presence of a history of traumatic development, insecure-disorganized attachment, and traits like affective instability and impulsivity. The *difficult patient* therefore presents different forms of mentalization, affect state regulation, and behavioural deficits.

*

From the outset, Anna's psychotherapy was structured as a complex intervention in which it was necessary, and indeed useful, to actively involve the significant people in her life in an attempt to curb the negative consequences of collusive behaviours and create a support network that would collaborate in pursuing a common goal. During the initial stage of the treatment, the priority objectives were to steer the course of therapy, set the boundaries of the relationships, and define the therapeutic space. At the present moment, during the individual sessions, we can focus on the (highly conflictual) choice of resorting to pharmacological treatment and on trying to understand what happens when she feels extremely upset, that is just before engaging in impulsive behaviours.

T: *Anna, can you tell me what you mean when you say 'I was really upset'?*
A: *I mean that I was really upset! At one point I just lose it. I lock myself inside my room and stay there. On my way home I bought alcohol, chips, and cookies; I knew I shouldn't but I couldn't help myself. I got home and I wolfed it all down. I couldn't even taste the food. When this happens to me, I can't taste what I'm eating. Then I took the bottle and started drinking, hoping I'd fall asleep. I didn't want to feel anything anymore.*
T: *Do you remember how you were feeling before you decided to buy alcohol and chips and cookies?*
A: *No. I was driving, I felt like crap.*
T: *What do you mean when you say that you felt like crap, can you explain it to me?*
A: *I don't know [. . .] Ugly [. . .] Agitated [. . .] I felt something swelling up inside of me, my head was bursting [. . .] I can't say [. . .]*
T: *Are you describing physical sensations? Do you recall any feelings or thoughts that you had at that moment?*
A: *A combination of [. . .] no thoughts, no [. . .] I don't know. I want to destroy myself! Actually, I don't tell myself 'destroy yourself' [. . .] I don't tell myself*

anything. I act suddenly. For instance, I get up and go eat or drink, out of the blue, unexpectedly, interrupting my daily routine, what I'm doing, what I should be doing.

I ask Anna to try to describe this state better and suggest that when another critical moment occurs during the week she focus on what is happening and write it down. At the next session, she brings her notes.

A: The lower my defenses, the more this mechanism is triggered.

I feel agitated, I try to fight it off but then impulse prevails over reason.

I think I told you that in those moments I think I want it but it isn't true, I don't want it at all!

But, the thing is, I stop thinking and things start to happen. I can stay 'absent' from myself, even after these episodes, or I can 'wake up' while they're happening ... and that's when I choose not to stop, because I hate myself, not before.

I don't choose beforehand whether or not to drink, to hurt myself. When I say 'choose' my brain is actually already shut down and I've already done something stupid. If I'm in a situation where I can't drink right there and then, I start paying no attention to what's around me, to reality.

Everything has vanished already and I'm in a hurry to do what I have in mind.

I usually want to go home where I can do as I please. Yes, I've noticed that before a crisis I feel a sense of urgency; if I'm not home I rush back.

The hatred, the pain surface in the process, or afterwards ... the part of me that says 'What are you doing??,' that 'is aware' isn't there at first and can't be there until it's over, or it appears while it's happening, while I'm eating, drinking, burning myself, but at that point the pain is so strong or the horror for what I'm doing so overwhelming, I feel like such a monster, that I want to do myself in. I can say that that's when the will to destroy myself sets in, I hate myself. Just how reasonable I am, in this case, I can't say, but I know for sure I'm not before.

I can't see and I can't hear, I see and I hear, but with detachment, as if nothing were happening. I'm not alarmed, everything's under control. I feel no pleasure or pain. With the burns it's different: sometimes it's putting an end to it, other times it's adding fuel to the flames in order to breathe, because I don't think I'm even breathing in those moments, and when I'm burning myself I experience physical pain inversely proportional to the emotional pain

– I feel air flowing back into my lungs and I can breathe deeply, I feel relief. Temporary, indispensable relief.

*

The experience Anna describes reveals her inability to identify a consistent sequence of emotions. Physical sensations prevail: agitation, haste, 'I don't feel anything, then I feel pain and it makes me breathe,' and so on.

The experience does not seem to take place within a given context. She does not describe an event. There is nobody else in the scene. Anna is alone in a place that appears to be out of time and space, out of an intersubjective dimension. At times she seems to be in a trance; other times she appears to be driven by a basic, elementary but very powerful need to restore a physiological, homeostatic balance.

Everything seems to arise inside of her, in spite of her, and to be accomplished within her. Although the people who are closest to her are constantly alarmed and worried that she may hurt herself, they seem unable to offer any comfort or be of any help to her.

What happens? How does the dimension of lack of contact with another that seems to characterize some critical moments of Anna's distress unfold? What are the needs, the motivations underpinning her behaviours?

What emerges from Anna's description is a deficit in emotional regulation and an intense and pervasive arousal that seems to come from signals which appear to be insignificant and far removed from the contextual reality. Dissociative states like these are very frequent in the population of difficult patients that we are considering; the point is, we need instruments that can help us to understand the phenomenon and help the patient to recover the sense of self and of what is happening to him or her. At this point, we have to turn our attention to the theory and then come back to reflect on Anna's situation.

The neo-dissociationist view

Phenomena of altered consciousness, in various forms and severity, are the common denominator of psychopathology, according to Janet's '*désagrégation*', that is the loss of coherence and integration of mental activities. Jackson (1932) was the first to intuit this in the late nineteenth century. Referring to evolutionism, he was the first to conjecture a hierarchical architecture of mental functioning: our relational mind, which is part of the world, is constituted of different levels that reflect the stages of the species' phylogenetic course. Every anatomical-functional level has integrated the lower ones, reorganizing the system in such a way as to respond to ever more complex adaptive social objectives imposed by evolution on our species. In order to understand how the complex mental system works, it is however indispensable to view things from the perspective of biunivocal correlation between the independence and the structural and functional autonomy of the various parts of this system and their inevitable structural and functional dependence and integration. That was McLean's intent, for instance, when he stated that the brain is *one and triune* (1973). According to Jackson, psychopathology is an expression of the *dissolution* of the integrating capacity of the higher levels, followed by the emergence of the underlying functions, which are no longer coordinated and modulated. Ey (1975) proceeded in the wake of Jackson and Janet, which had long been forgotten, underlining the importance of an *organic-genetic-dynamic theory* of the mind.

This vision superseded the mind-body dichotomy, much before the contemporary debate on the matter was rekindled, and laid the foundations for an etiopathogenic bio-psycho-social view of mental disorders.

Contemporary literature on trauma and dissociation, which cuts across various theoretical and clinical fields (from cognitivism to psychoanalysis) (Van der Kolk, 2005; Herman, 1992b; Van der Hart, Nijhenius and Steele, 2006; Ogden *et al.*, 2006; Liotti and Farina, 2011; Siegel, 1999; Bromberg, 1998, 2006) has considered and expanded the theories of Jackson and Janet, tapping into new and important contributions of neuroscience (Rizzolatti *et al.*, 2001; Gallese *et al.*, 2009; Schore, 1994, 2003a, 2003b; Porges, 2001, 2003) and the developments of infant research and attachment research (Trevarthen, 1974; Meltzoff and Moore, 1977; Beebe and Lachmann, 2002; Lyons-Ruth *et al.*, 2005). The rapidly developing neo-dissociationist theories are based on:

- the adoption of multidimensional theories on mental functioning;
- reference to evolutionism, in its phylogenetic and ontogenetic component, which leads to a hierarchical anatomical-functional architecture of the mind; and
- reference to attachment theory and multi-motivational theories as a point of departure for the study of a healthy or pathological development.

Trauma and dissociation

A brief history

As is common knowledge, the two concepts of trauma and dissociation are interconnected from the start.

During the nineteenth century, attention was focused on sexual abuse and its connection with hysteria. After years of research and clinical work, Freud, Breuer, and Janet independently reached the same conclusion whereby hysteria was a condition caused by psychic trauma.

Both Freud and Janet recognized that the altered states of consciousness induced by psychic trauma and those induced by hypnosis were very similar, and conjectured that the somatic symptoms of hysteria were manifestations of painful and traumatic childhood events (violence, abuse, incest) that the individual was not aware of and did not remember. The idea of curing these disorders was based on the notion of *catharsis*, in other words, the hysterical symptoms could be alleviated if the traumatic memories were retrieved in the therapeutic relationship and expressed verbally. Such a notion was therefore very close to the modern theories on the treatment of trauma and dissociation. Unlike Janet, who was committed to these hypotheses, Freud lost interest in the matter after publishing *Aetiology of Hysteria* in 1896, in which he stated that at the basis of every case of hysteria there were episodes of premature sexual experience dating back to early childhood.

At the time abuse and maltreatment were very common also in the Viennese middle-class milieus in which Freud practiced medicine. This inevitably generated problems. In the famous case of Dora (Freud, 1905), an adolescent who was used by her father as a sex toy, Freud admitted that abuse had indeed taken place, but he delegitimized Dora's feelings of humiliation and outrage and insisted on exploring the patient's sensations of erotic arousal, as if her condition of exploitation served to satisfy her own sexual yearnings (Ellenberger, 1970).

He later came to the conclusion that the stories of sexual abuse endured during childhood narrated by his hysterical patients were untrue. The presumed distortion of reality by women strongly influenced psychology and its twentieth-century culture, pushing the issue of social exploitation into the background and contributing to neglecting much of the suffering associated with trauma.

Interest in psychic trauma was rekindled as a consequence of World War I, when veterans reported similar symptoms to those displayed by hysterical women.

Abram Kardiner (cited in Herman, 1992), a young American psychiatrist, first treated these veterans and developed a theory on *war trauma* (1941), postulating the essential clinical guidelines for *traumatic syndrome* (very similar to the ones still used today in diagnosing post-traumatic stress disorder (PTSD)). His theory was strongly inspired by that of Janet, who had already intuited that neurosis caused by war represented a form of hysteria. Kardiner highlighted that the use of the term hysteria discredited the suffering of those patients. According to the author, in fact, the word 'hysteria' was culturally associated with evil, perversion, and fragility; it had a pejorative meaning and did little to steer professionals devoted to the treatment of traumatic disorders.

With the outbreak of World War II, psychiatrists tried to find a fast and effective treatment for '*combat neurosis*', highlighting that any fighter could collapse on the battlefield and that psychiatric disorders were directly proportional to exposure to combat. Kardiner and Spiegel (1947) worked on short intervention strategies so that soldiers could return to the battlefield as quickly as possible. Thanks to the use of hypnosis, they made it possible for traumatic memories to emerge, but this was not enough to 'heal' the soldiers, whose psychopathological progress remained uncertain. This did not spark the attention of military authorities, who were only interested in seeing to it that soldiers would return to combat.

In the years following the Vietnam War, the board of directors of Vietnam Veterans Against the War financed numerous studies on the impact of war on the life of veterans. These contributions helped to outline the characteristics of *Post Traumatic Stress Syndrome*, whose symptoms were similar to the '*combat neurosis*' described by Kardiner forty years earlier, and which only in 1980 became diagnosable as a disorder and was listed in the DSM-III (APA, 1980). Moreover, in the 1970s, the American Women's Liberation Movement sped up research on rape which, in addition to promoting the creation of shelters outside the national health system, proved that attacks on women and children were pervasive, endemic, and cultural occurrences, unlike what had been stated during the previous century, when Freud had shed doubt on the truthfulness of such experiences, dismissing them as fantasies (Herman, 1992).

What is traumatic?

The definition of Post-Traumatic Stress Disorder (DSM-IV-TR, APA, 2000) refers to patients who have experienced circumscribed traumatic events and may not be capable of grasping the changing symptomatic displays associated with extended and repeated trauma. Moving from these assumptions, Herman (1992a) proposed a new diagnostic category: *complex post-traumatic stress disorder* (C-PTSD).

The symptoms of a *complex trauma disorder* include deformations of personality, identity, as well as relatedness; these elements are not present in the DSM-IV nosographic category.

Unlike circumscribed traumatic events, complex relational traumas refer to prolonged and repeated traumas in which the victim (child or adult) cannot escape and is under the control of a persecutor (concentration camps, forced labour, brothels, situations of sexual exploitation, abuse, and maltreatment) (ibid.). Additionally, in childhood, complex relational trauma refers to the witnessing of domestic violence (Cook, Miller and Seager, 2009; Van Der Kolk, 2005). This fact is especially important for us clinicians.

We can therefore distinguish between two types of complex trauma which have as a common element an overwhelming sense of powerlessness determined by the inability to escape:

- *complex traumatic event:* one finds oneself in circumstances, limited in time, in which stressful conditions are beyond one's ability to respond and withstand (captivity, accidents, natural disasters, etc.); and
- *complex traumatic development*: that is the particular family and environmental conditions in which a child is forced to grow up, powerlessly enduring constant or repeated abusive behaviours and maltreatment perpetrated by the caretaker (Liotti and Farina, 2011).

Neglect in some family contexts and the lack of attention for the needs that are fundamental to the development of every child are regarded as highly traumatic factors inasmuch as they jeopardize the possibility of staying alive and of developing the psychophysical abilities required to get one's bearings in the world.

In order to understand what is psychologically traumatic, one therefore needs to know what basic objectives the mind pursues besides safety; an event or a chain of events are traumatic to the extent that they severely and persistently hinder the fundamental needs that ensure ontogenetic survival and development.

Multi-motivational theories inform us about the human being's species-specific objectives. Anything that denies evolutionary values in a lasting and uncontrollable way is traumatic (Liotti, 1989; Liotti, 1994/2005; Liotti and Monticelli, 2008; Lichtenberg, 1989).

Traumatic attachment: an etiopathogenic cognitive-evolutionary theory

What can be more menacing than the impossibility of having an attachment figure, a safe point of reference in the course of one's development?

*

MARCO (1)

M: *'Good morning Doctor. I waited a while before calling, but now I'm sure! I really think I need it.'*

I thus receive this boyish young man on a hot July afternoon. I am immediately struck by how quickly he talks and picks up the points for further reflection that emerge during our dialogue. *'What a lively intelligence!'* I think to myself. At the same time, he comes across to me as somewhat evasive; he is like a skipping elf! I can see in his eyes sequences of frames, thoughts regarding himself, his issues, me, and my skills racing in his mind; they race so fast that they almost seem to overlap. There: speed is what characterizes my very first perception of him.

At the same time, I realize that I feel rather alarmed when Marco lavishes praise on me and flatters me in a seductive, somewhat manipulative manner. His flaunted and precocious confidence in me makes me feel duped.

My colleague had forewarned me. *'He seems a little borderline,'* he had said to me about Marco, referring in particular to his tormented love life. I feel drawn in.

The first thing Marco talks to me about is his relationship with Lucia (his current girlfriend).

M: *'I don't really know what to do. I feel very close to Lucia and I really think she's great but I'm not sure I'm attracted to her. Sometimes I am ... but most of the time, it's as if something were missing.'*

He makes a comparison with his previous relationship, which instead was extremely passionate, engaging, but also complicated. During the first three sessions we focus on his sentimental life and every now and then Marco describes with thick, quick strokes significant relational experiences with his family that reveal his attachment history – dry flashes that plunge me into an abyss of pain and fear, which, however, he does not seem to display. I find this striking.

M: *'Yes . . . well . . . when my mother beat me'* (he stops and remains silent, looking at me with an expression that is hard to define, somewhere between defiance and complacency. I have the feeling that he is waiting for my reaction, like in a duel).

T: *'Did it hurt a lot?'* (I do not know why I ask this question. Is it because I need to understand? Or perhaps to restore emotional harmony to the experience that Marco is describing?).

M: *'Well! I ended up in the hospital several times. Once she broke my nose* (he points to his crooked nose and gives a faint smile; his tone of voice and the expression on his face are still defiant. I feel a sense of unrest and mistrust).

T: *'What had happened to you?'* I stall for time and keep asking questions in order to understand, without making comments or dwelling on what I am hearing and thinking, but holding on to the feelings.

M: *'Nothing in particular . . . nothing happened . . . actually, just about anything could serve as a pretext to take it out on me. She was unpredictable.'* He sneers.

T: *'And what would happen after? Who would take you to the hospital?'*

I continue to envision the scene and probe for details in order to better identify with the experience, searching for signs of distress in him that would reassure me. I wish I were not the one feeling all that pain, I would want to give it back to him, but he seems so distant. I need time, I feel it would be dangerous to dwell on the single experiences – grief, fear, annihilation, anger – while he does not seem to let his guard down. I feel he is especially reactive.

M: *'She did! She was a nurse so she was in her element, right? She knew everyone'* (he smiles sarcastically and I begin to feel deeply sorry for Marco. I sense the powerlessness of a boy in the face of the power wielded by an adult who is supposed to be looking after him. The angrier he becomes, the more I feel the pain, like a blade in my gut. I quickly ask the next question, because I am under the impression that dwelling on this aspect of the experience would upset him).

T: *'What happened between the two of you after the beating?'*

M: 'Nothing . . . she usually told me to keep it to myself, to not tell my dad' (his face is like that of a sphynx and I sense defiance).
T: 'So she asked you to keep a secret?'
M: 'Yes, in a way, but . . . she would grow calm again and at that point she would take care of me.'
T: 'But did you get the feeling that your mom regretted beating you?'
M: 'Yeeeess . . . well, I don't know . . . but she was upset afterwards. She was sorry . . . or so it seemed' (he makes that smile again, halfway between cynical and complacent).
T: 'So your dad didn't know about this?'
M: 'No, but he wouldn't have done much even if he did, knowing the way he is . . .' (with a look of contempt).

I watch him and say nothing. I am surprised and search for clearer signs that may help me to understand what is happening and what happened. I cannot immerse myself entirely in the story, some inconsistencies and contradictory signs confuse me. I feel a persistent sense of unrest. I do not trust him. What is going on? Marco's implicit signals (his gaze, the expression on his face, the tone of his voice) disorient me. That sarcastic sneer, the somewhat aggressive attitude that transpires from his gestures and face, the absence of pain as he talks about the – even serious – traumas of his childhood, and many other minor signals strike me more than his words. Suspicion, hostility, and fear characterize the relational climate I feel between us.

While he talks to me about his relational troubles, he immediately brings to me unsettling and incisive elements regarding his suffering (his traumas); he brings them to me in the way he has probably done for years: he does not ask for help explicitly, but rather implicitly, while at the same time he challenges me. Presumably, he would challenge anyone who came close to his vulnerability (can you blame him?). I feel that I have to try to tune in to different emotional states and make an effort not to adhere completely to any one of them, holding them together inside of me. Holding together the pieces of the experience that Marco describes to me and of the one we are sharing together, avoiding hasty conclusions and judgements, continuing to explore – I feel that this is the most useful contribution I can offer at this stage, as we get to know each other.

Our journey has begun, our communication is already proceeding at the explicit and implicit levels and is bringing to the fore how Marco and I function.

*

The child needs a long period of close care for its survival and psychophysical development. Through the relationship with its caregiver, the child learns to know itself and the world in a learning process that requires exploratory spirit and sense of safety in order to proceed by trial and error. The attachment relationship is not linear, rather it is characterized by micro ruptures and repairs that mark the pace of attunement with the other (Sander, 1962; Meltzoff and Moore, 1977; Tronick, 1989). A fundamental condition for good attachment is the mother's ability to accept and stay connected with the child, following with flexibility the fluctuations of the relationship. A steady relationship with the caregiver makes it possible for memories to form in the mind of the child and for the child to develop ways of feeling, of being with the other, of understanding who the other is, what the world is like, which Bowlby defined as *internal working models* (IWM).

When the conditions in which attachment occurs are wanting or particularly difficult the child's development may be impaired, with pathological consequences of varying severity. Among the attachment styles studied so far, the disorganized attachment style seems to best represent traumatic development. When the attachment figure is *frightened-frightening* or *hostile-helpless* (Lyons-Ruth e Jacobvitz, 1999; Lyons-Ruth et al., 2005), severely neglectful or abusive, the child is in a paradoxical intersubjective field that is defined as *fright without solution* (Main and Hesse, 1990). It is an irresolvable vicious cycle of growing fear and incoherent and paradoxical interactions of approach and avoidance, triggered by a parent who turns from being a source of protection into a source of danger. This disrupts the normal functioning of the child who is no longer able to organize experiences and reactions coherently, displaying evident disorganized/disoriented behaviours. The '*fright without solution*' therefore leads the child to adopt a *disorganized attachment behaviour* and have dissociative reactions (Liotti, 1989; Liotti and Farina, 2011).

The signs of a disorganized attachment IWM are identifiable already at age one. They are contradictory and scarcely integrated behaviours that indicate the child's inability to organize a consistent strategy to elicit comfort on the part of the caregiver and are associated with an increase in the release of stress hormones (Spangler and Grossmann, 1999; Hertsgaard et al., 1995). The attachment system (protection against danger through closeness with another) and the defence system (protection against danger through fight or flight) usually work in synergy. In disorganized attachment the two systems clash, creating a situation of *fright without solution*.

Repeatedly failing to access the attachment resources, the motivational system becomes deactivated and non-modulated, and unregulated reactions of the reptilian defence system prevail (Liotti and Monticelli, 2008; Liotti and Farina, 2011). According to the hierarchical functioning of the mind model, when the higher levels (which are phylogenetically more complex and more recent) are deactivated, the lower levels and the entire functioning system that interconnects and harmonizes the various levels are disrupted as well.

Now we can go back to some passages in the dialogue with Anna, which could represent this condition in which the non-modulated and non-regulated reptilian defence system prevails.

*

FROM ANNA'S VIGNETTE

T: *Anna, can you tell me what you mean when you say 'I was really upset'?*

A: *I mean that I was really upset! At one point I just lose it. I lock myself inside my room and stay there. On my way home I had bought alcohol, chips, and cookies; I knew I shouldn't have but I couldn't help myself. I got home and I wolfed it all down. I don't even know what the food tasted like. When this happens to me, I can't tell the taste of what I'm eating. Then I took the bottle and started drinking hoping to fall asleep. I didn't want to feel anything anymore.*

T: *Do you remember how you were feeling before you decided to buy alcohol and chips and cookies?*

A: *No. I was driving, I felt like crap.*

T: *What do you mean when you say that you felt like crap, can you explain it to me?*

A: *I don't know . . . Ugly . . . Agitated . . . I felt something swelling up inside of me, my head was bursting . . . I can't say . . .*

T: *Are you describing physical sensations? Do you recall any feelings, thoughts you had at that moment?*

A: *A combination of . . . no thoughts, no . . . I don't know. I want to destroy myself! Actually, I don't tell myself 'destroy yourself' . . . I don't tell myself anything. I act suddenly. For instance, I get up and go eat or drink, out of the blue, unexpectedly, disrupting my daily routine, what I'm doing, what I should be doing.*

*

Attachment research has shown that from three to six years of age, with the cognitive developments of the pre-school and school period, the behaviour of many children who in infancy were classified as disorganized are replaced by controlling interpersonal strategies aimed to secure the caregiver's attention and engagement. Main and Cassidy (1988) distinguish two types of controlling strategies:

1 The *controlling-punitive strategy,* when children display provocative, coercive, humiliating, and hostile attitudes towards the caregiver, who accepts this type of relationship. For instance, *'Cut it out mom! Quit being an idiot! Can't you see what a mess you're making?'* It seems that the ranking and the caregiving systems are activated together, rather than the attachment system.
2 The *controlling-caregiving strategy,* when children entertain the parent or provide help and comfort through explicit caregiving behaviours. In these cases, a role reversal occurs in the attachment relationship (*reversed attachment*), insofar as these children appear to act more like a parent than as a son/daughter. For example: *My father was violent . . . I had to protect my mother. My father often got angry and beat my mother for trivial things, like not keeping the house in order. I did it for her, I tried to make sure that everything was nice and tidy, in order to prevent my father from abusing my mother.*

Controlling strategies are regarded as adaptations consequent to the malfunctioning of the attachment system (Lyons-Ruth and Jacobvitz, 1999; Lyons-Ruth *et al.,* 2005). Generally speaking, children presenting disorganized attachment in childhood and controlling strategies in pre-school age are at risk for a series of *negative results* including: high secretion of cortisol in response to stressful factors, which are mild during infancy, inhibited or chaotic play in preschool age, high internalization behaviours, aggressive conduct with peers in kindergarten and elementary school, and high rates of controlling attachment strategies with the parents at age six.

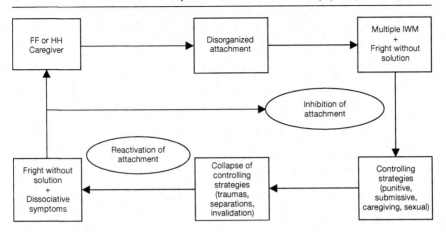

Figure 4.1 Model of traumatic development
Source: Translated from G. Liotti and B. Farina (2011) *Sviluppi traumatici: Eziopatogenesi, clinica e terapia della dimensione dissociativa,* p. 102

Intense and lasting activations of the attachment IMS can cause the collapse of the controlling strategies as well as the re-emergence of the disorganized IWM and of the dissociated and uncontrolled mental states associated to it. This is the basic idea underpinning the conceptual model of Liotti and Farina (2011), which explains the dissociative response to trauma. According to this model, there is no linear correlation of cause and effect between trauma and dissociation; rather, the relationship between the two should be regarded from a multifactorial and multidimensional perspective.

A frightened–frightening (FF) or hostile–helpless (HH) caregiver creates the conditions for disorganized attachment, which causes the child to adopt controlling strategies in response to the caregiver's behaviour that are more adaptive for the little one (activation of the ranking, caregiving and sexual systems). However, when such strategies fail, that is, when triggers reactivate the traumatic experience and the disorganized attachment, IWM *dissociation* can set in.

*

MARCO (2)

The issue Marco seems to be grappling with is deep indecision over his choice of girlfriend, but I have a sense that he has great trouble understanding and handling his sensations, his emotional responses and his feelings. His ambivalence towards an important bond is in the forefront. Desire is accompanied by a strong agonistic activation.

'Lucia really turned me on! We were on a par, it was quite a struggle! She was a bitch almost as much as I was bastard!' When the attachment is active, he feels the need to distance himself from the other, on account of strong sensations of physical discomfort.

'Fiorella . . . I feel like crying when I think of her; she was so sweet and loved me so much. I feel infinite tenderness for her, now that we're not together anymore. But I remember that when we were together she really got on my nerves, I couldn't be near her, I couldn't stand her. Her sweetness, her kindness irritated me so much. Sometimes I treated her badly: "Don't make that silly voice!" I would say to her angrily. Now that we're not together whenever I think of her I'm moved to tears and feel something strong that I haven't felt for anyone else. I would cut my arm off for her. But why couldn't I be with her?'

*

The dissociative symptomatology in response to trauma is to be regarded in the light of mental processes associated with the activation of the attachment IWM regulated by a disorganized IWM (if it were not so, the dissociative symptoms would be less significant and the alterations of the integrating function of consciousness would only be transitory). The activation of the competitive, caregiving, or sexual IWMs for defensive purposes inhibit the activation of the attachment IWM, shielding the individual from the experience of dissociation, even for a long time, sometimes years. So before a new trauma, or a trigger that reactivates the experience, lead to the collapse of the controlling strategies, the *traumatic development disorder* may be expressed through other developmental disorders, such as behavioural, attention, and separation anxiety disorders (Liotti and Farina, 2011).

Traumatic attachment: the perspective of relational psychoanalysis

Clinical research on trauma in contemporary psychoanalysis combines elements of infant research and attachment theory with the principles of relational psychoanalysis (Albasi, 2006).

Various contributions of infant research (Sander, 1962; Stern, 1971; Trevarthen, 1974; Meltzoff and Moore, 1977; Tronick, 1989; Beebe and Lachmann, 2002) have shown that what is crucial for normal personality development is not child–caregiver attunement but, on the contrary, the possibility of repairing interaction errors. The infant acquires an effective/agent, consistent/confident sense of self and a representation of the caregiver as a reliable person through attachment relationships that are open and flexible enough to allow it to experience ruptures and their subsequent reparations as a natural process in which affective ties and the personality are formed.

In *traumatic attachment* the more an infant feels unprotected (activation of the attachment system), the more it has to deactivate the system itself, for the caregivers who should protect and make it feel safe correspond to the source of fear. Under these conditions, dysfunctional interactive models are structured which are based on the paradox according to which intimate relationships become extraneous to the individual (Bowlby, 1969).

Bowlby (1988) speculated that a multiplicity of IWMs exist next to dysfunctional internal working models (DIWMs), which block the development of the ability to regulate one's affective states and to attribute meanings to one's experiences.

The self is an agent system and its integrity is determined by its constant access to a 'storage' of personal memory. This storage is divided into sectors which may be prevented from communicating (*defensive exclusion*). Bowlby refers to research on memory systems: basically, knowledge is organized *semantically* (memories and recollections, according to their general meaning) and *episodically* (memorization of events as specific scenes of the autobiographical past). *Defensive exclusion* is a process that uses memory systems while keeping them separate, as is evident, for instance, in Marco's narrative, in which there is a strong discrepancy between the narrative of the event (episodic memory) and the incongruous subjective experience, which he expresses in the session, relative to the meaning that he attributes to that event (semantic memory).

*

FROM MARCO'S VIGNETTE

M: *Yes . . . well . . . when my mother beat me* (he stops and remains silent, looking at me with an expression that is hard to define, somewhere between defiance and smugness. I have the feeling that he's waiting for my reaction, like in a duel).

T: *Did it hurt a lot?* (I do not know why I ask this question. Is it because I need to understand? Or perhaps to restore emotional harmony to the experience Marco is describing?).
M: *Well! I ended up in the hospital several times. Once she broke my nose* (he points to his crooked nose and gives a faint smile; his tone of voice and the expression on his face are still defiant. I feel a sense of unrest and mistrust).

*

The interpersonal reactions consequent to the activation of the DIWM therefore appear as facts whose principles and rules are only partly comprehensible to the person who enacts them. There is no doubt, no awareness of the incongruity which instead is typical of a conflictual state. The thoughts, feelings, and behaviours may not appear to be connected to each other and to the person's interactive circumstances. The sense of *agency* that lends personal meaning to experience is lost (Albasi, 2012).

*

FROM ANNA'S VIGNETTE

The lower my defences, the more this mechanism is triggered. I feel agitated, I try to fight it off but then impulse prevails over reason.

I think I told you that in those moments I think I want it but it isn't true, I absolutely don't want it!

But the thing is that I stop thinking and things start to happen. I can stay 'absent' from myself, even after these things have happened, or I can 'wake up' while they're happening . . . and that's when I choose not to stop, because I hate myself, not before.

I don't choose beforehand whether or not to drink, to hurt myself. When I say 'choose' actually my brain is already shut down and I have already done something stupid. If I'm in a situation in which I can't drink right there and then, I start paying no attention to what's around me, to reality.

*

The DIWMs appear to be buried deep inside the psyche and revealed only in interpersonal relations, especially at the implicit level of interactions, as my dialogue with Marco shows.

*

FROM MARCO'S VIGNETTE

T: *What happened between the two of you after the beating?*
M: *Nothing . . . she usually told me to keep it to myself, to not tell my dad* (his face is like that of a sphynx and I sense defiance).
T: *So she asked you to keep a secret?*
M: *Yes, in a way, but . . . she would grow calm again and at that point she would take care of me.*
T: *But did you get the feeling that your mom regretted beating you?*
M: *Yeeeess . . . well, I don't know . . . but she was upset afterwards. She was sorry . . . or so it seemed* (he produces that smile again, halfway between cynical and complacent).
T: *So your dad didn't know about this?*
M: *No, but he wouldn't have done much even if he did, the way he is . . .* (with a look of contempt).

I watch him and say nothing. I am surprised and search for clearer signs that may help me to understand what is happening and what happened. I cannot immerse myself entirely in the story, some inconsistencies and contradictory signs confuse me. I feel a persistent sense of unrest. I do not trust him. What is going on? Marco's implicit signals (his gaze, the expression on his face, the tone of his voice) disorient me. That sarcastic sneer, the somewhat aggressive attitude that transpires from his gestures and face, the absence of pain as he talks about the – even serious – traumas of his childhood and many other minor signals strike me more than his words. Suspicion, hostility and fear characterize the relational climate I feel between us.

*

According to post-classical psychoanalytic literature, the mind has two ways of processing information: the *sub-symbolic* and the *symbolic* (Bucci, 1997). *Sub-symbolic* processing occurs at the level of bodily experience in emotional patterns that are expressed by *ways of being*. Symbolic processing occurs at the level of cognitive awareness and is communicated through verbal language.

Traumatic emotional experiences remain non-symbolized at the cognitive level. DIWMs are not simply states, they cannot be evoked like memories; they emerge in a significant interaction, mostly at the implicit level. All patients bring their IWMs into the consultation room, as well as the Self states that have been kept segregated through the dissociative process. Most of the psychotherapeutic work involves recognizing how one functions. From the perspective of relational psychoanalysis, the therapeutic process makes sense if it is regarded as mutual; in other words, what matters is what occurs in the *intersubjective field* in which the analyst's and patient's subjectivities are equally essential.

The ability of clinicians depends mainly on their subjective responses; they thus replace their neutrality with their moods, feelings, fantasies, and thoughts (self-disclosure), which, overall, are regarded as a fundamental technical approach for the identification and comprehension of a patient's problems.

In helping patients to come into contact with their child parts that have not been recognized, that have been segregated through dissociation – which, in jest, Bromberg (2006) refers to as their *gorilla* – analysts must bring their own *gorilla* into play as well.

In psychoanalysis, *enactment* is a dyadic dissociative process by which the patient's emotional patterns deriving from trauma become known and are potentially available to consciousness.

The patient uses the analyst's mind as an instrument to expand the patient's mind, to come into contact with any Self state that was disconfirmed, invalidated or threatened traumatically because it 'created problems' in the eyes of a significant other with whom the patient had established a primary attachment bond that contributed to defining the nuclear sense of continuity.

*

MARCO (3)

After two exploratory interviews in which we focus primarily on his troubled sentimental relationships without referring to childhood experiences, we reach a crucial point. During a session Marco reveals something about himself that puts our relationship seriously to the test.

M: *I don't know where to begin, how to say this . . . well, let's say that sometimes I go on the web and check out, well . . . porn websites, in search of strong emotions . . . websites showing pictures of children, adolescents . . .*

I remain silent, I feel my muscles tensing, I am nervous and do not know what to say or do. I try to reassure myself. 'Stay calm,' I tell myself, 'Try to understand and wait, stall for time, there's no rush to answer.'

Actually, I am aware that I have already partly responded. 'Has he noticed, perceived my response?' I wonder. I continue to look at him straight in the eye while my heart pounds with fear and dread for the images that immediately appear in my mind; I think of my son. I cannot help thinking about my own son. In these fractions of a second, I lose touch with Marco. I am no longer his therapist; my ability to listen and to be open have vanished. I want to leave, walk away. Instead, I sit still and my state of alert is interrupted by Marco, who goes on to say:

M: *I want you to know that I only look at the pictures; never in my life have I done anything that comes close to a real experience. I'm not interested! Actually, I'm only interested in chasing strong emotions.*

There, he has caught on and is going out of his way to reassure me. I do not know whether or not what he is telling me is true and I am not interested in probing any further. I am paralyzed and cannot seem to find anything to say. I try to achieve inner calm and avoid doing too much damage. But I cannot curb my thoughts and emotions. I am reminded of Ed Tronick's still face experiment. Could I make that face in order to prevent Marco from seeing me? Would I do less damage that way?

Our time is running out and, going over the 'handbook of the good therapist' in my mind, I automatically say:

T: *Marco you did well to tell me this; it's very important and we'll take it up again next time we meet* (I cannot wait for him to leave).
M: *Yes, I really want you to know that I've never once considered actually doing anything, it's just a compulsion that compels me to go on these websites* (he continues to justify himself and to reassure me).
T: *Yes of course, I heard what you said, I'm comforted that you don't actually do anything, but going on those websites isn't harmless. There's a business that revolves around this 'abusive market', anyone who goes on the websites takes part in the abuse. We mustn't think it isn't serious.*

My God, I said it! I wonder what effect it will have. We part with the understanding that we will discuss the matter in greater depth during our next session.

It is finally over! I had never felt this way. I wanted to send him away.

I have never agreed with colleagues who believe that a therapist is not necessarily effective with all patients and should indeed choose who to work with, based on his/her own self-knowledge.

I have always thought that a therapist, working with his/her emotions and using him/herself as an instrument, can work with everyone, precisely because the focus of the work is the relationship that is created, especially the difficulties that arise, which become precious material to dwell on.

What was different this time? I felt that I could not do it, I was repelled by Marco, I wanted to send him away, to get rid of him. I thought I could maybe refer him to another colleague, but at the same time I considered how that would make him feel. I had to find a way out of this impasse.

The point was that we could not ignore the implicit level. He had sensed my difficulty and I had to be authentic, but at the same time I had to bear in mind my role and commitment towards Marco. What did all of this mean in the relationship with him and what did it tell me about him? What was the connection between what he was saying to me and the sentimental problems he had talked to me about during the first two meetings? Did the sense of unease that I had always felt with him have anything to do with what was happening to us now? Too many questions; there would be time to figure it out together, but what was being questioned now was the very space where to do this work. How could I refocus and be open to him while reckoning with my own limitations? The key was there but I could not see it. I realized that I had not other choice than to share my difficulties with Marco, after which I could begin to search for a solution.

*

The centrality of collisions and negotiations that define the non-linear process of therapeutic alliance, that is the process which allows our patients to grow, heal, mature, change, has always been a prerogative of the various models of relational psychoanalysis and of its precursors (Sullivan, 1953; Greenberg and Mitchell, 1983; Lichtenberg, 1983; Stern, 1985).

Among contemporary psychoanalysts, Philip Bromberg is the one who most explored and connected trauma and dissociation, developing a model of multiple and dissociated self states and underscoring the *dissociated structure of the human mind*. The ability to dissociate is simply part of the human being and, in this respect, patients and analysts are no different.

Dissociation serves an important function, which is to favour flexible communication among the multiple self states, keeping them dialectically separate and united, guaranteeing a sense of *illusory personal integrity*.

His original contribution to the consolidated attitude of relational psychoanalysis of working on the therapeutic alliance process consists in strongly emphasizing the *dissociative structure of the therapist's mind*.

The process of building a shared awareness requires exploring the mutual dissociative blindnesses. In this sense it is essential that the analyst be willing to accept his/her difficulties and to get to the heart of the dissociative experiences in the consultation room through *enactment*.

The analyst often concentrates his/her efforts, in order to preserve the therapeutic frame, without colliding with complicated elements of the relationship, paying attention mostly to the context. In this case, the patient may respond with an ever greater need to break the therapeutic frame in order to violently offset the analyst's tendency to use words, ideas and concepts rather than being with him/her.

*

MARCO (4)

The following session

M: *I thought about what you said last time. I hadn't reflected on how serious my behaviour is. Actually it's true, I was really struck by your observation, but I want to beat this, Antonella, it's one of the reasons why I'm here.*

T: *I reflected a great deal about it too after our session, Marco. It wasn't easy for me to come to terms with my thoughts and feelings on this matter. Let me get straight to the point. I think it's essential to be authentic at all times during this process, that's why I have to tell you how I feel and what my limits are. When, during our last session, you told me about this habit you have, I was extremely upset; the mere thought of it made me feel so uncomfortable that I had to struggle to stay here with you and to focus the way I usually do.*

M: *Yes, I know, I could tell* (he seems pleased with his intuition; he leans towards me and I sense he is in a state of alert).

T: *I imagined you'd picked up on this, that's why I'm saying that it's important to be authentic at all times and to talk about it. I think you have the right to address the problem, but this requires an adequate space in which you and*

I both feel safe enough. In this case, the point is my limits. What happened to me last time could happen again; I might not be able to tolerate the experiences you describe. I've thought about this very much and the best solution I could come up with was to discuss it with you and to look for a way to deal with it together.

M: *I understand what you're saying and I'm sorry I gave you this impression; actually, I repeat, I never considered doing anything, I like women and I've had experiences only with women* (he seems anxious).

T: *You've told me this already and it reassures me, but you see Marco, it isn't helpful in therapy if I have to worry about myself and you don't feel free to talk about your difficulties. That's why I preferred to come out in the open, so as to avoid you having to deal with my discomfort without having discussed it with me. We're talking about it now and will continue to do so until we find the best solution for the both us.*

M: *AHH! I've had to deal with my parents my whole life, I'm used to it!* (again with an arrogant, defiant attitude; he appears to be pleased with himself).

T: *I have no doubt. That's precisely why I believe it's best that you don't repeat that experience here with me. And that's why I'm saying that we should address these difficulties.*

M: *But . . . do you want to drop me?* (dry).

T: *No. I can't deny that I really wanted to run away, but I didn't. I would like for us to try and find a way to deal with your difficulties, a way that protects us both. That is my intent, but I wouldn't be honest if I were to tell you that I'm sure we'll succeed. We could come to an agreement . . .*

M: *What kind of agreement?*

T: *We could establish that if you were to tell me something that transcends my safety bounds I could point it out to you and we could stop, how does that sound to you? We could proceed one step at a time, take stock of what's happening to us and decide, by and by, whether to carry on and how, what do you think?*

M: *Nothing like this has ever happened to me before! The fact that you're being straight with me about how you feel is shocking to me, in a good way I mean! I like your honesty and I accept the risk.*

T: *Good! As far as risk goes . . .* (I smile) *I'm accepting it too.*

M: *Yes, of course* (we both smile; this time Marco's smile is not sarcastic).

For the first time I feel that there is complicity between us; in spite of the doubts and fears, we are hearing each other, we are both there, connected.

During our dialogue Marco has realized that he had always taken responsibility for his parents, mainly by resorting to a 'controlling-punitive strategy'. This time, with me it is possible for him to face the difficulty with a caregiver who is aware of her limits, who takes her share of responsibility for the problem and encourages Marco to do the same in an active and constructive way.

Such a transaction truly grasps the complexity of all human experiences, especially the ones lived by those who activate a traumatized IWM. A single experience of this sort will not be enough to produce significant change but will probably be the first of many others that will proceed in the same direction and will become consolidated in a new memory.

Later Marco is able to tell me what he is looking for and what he finds on the websites he usually checks out and I am ready to listen to him: he is turned on by the face, the gaze of those young boys who in the videos appear to be enjoying what Marco defines the 'sexual game'.

Whenever he refers to this aspect, I feel a piercing pain at the thought of his body being violated by his mother's beatings and I realize how much he dissociates that pain.

*

According to Bromberg, the willingness of analysts to share their dissociative experiences with patients is indeed the therapeutic element. Self-disclosure is therefore not merely an autobiographical communication but rather an attempt to share an emotional state at critical moments in the relationship – moments of rupture when nothing is sure any longer and one does not know what to do. Since a person cannot transcend dissociation without the presence of another person who is capable of recognizing his or her own dissociation, if analysts are willing to share what they are feeling with patients, experiences of reparation can get under way.

*

I have reflected at length on what transpired between Marco and me and the experience appears to be full of meanings.

I was guided by the wish to preserve authenticity and affective honesty. Consequently, I decided to talk to him frankly about how I was feeling (the various emotional nuances of what I was experiencing), without volunteering ready-made solutions but with the intent of revealing myself.

Perhaps in our experience I was unable to convey to him that it is possible to humbly approach aspects of ourselves and of the other that we do not like, that frighten us, share them and remain together. I believe that by telling him I wanted to expel him, without actually doing it, allowed us to experience the possibility of repairing our self-with-other experiences, which are explored in infant research (Tronick and Weinberg, 1997).

*

When both patient and analyst can have access to and openly share the dissociated experience that was not previously worked through at the cognitive level, insofar as it was too dangerous for the relationship, the process by which this happens renders possible a dialogue that gradually leads to more integrated and complex contents, which are symbolized at the linguistic level and are therefore available for self-reflection and conflict resolution.

Self-disclosure is part of the developmental process which Fonagy calls mentalization (Fonagy and Target, 1996; Fonagy *et al.*, 2002), whereby it is possible for subsymbolic experience to become part of the relational self, rather than be acted out endlessly.

Psychophysiology of trauma

Some research studies (Ito, Teicher, Gold and Ackerman, 1998; Perry, 2001; Lanius *et al.*, 2005; Teicher *et al.*, 2006; Nijenhuis, 2008) have documented the connection between abuse, neglect, and brain anomalies. Reference is made especially to alterations in the development of the right brain, which is specialized in the processing of socio-emotional information and bodily states (the ability to assess facial expressions, gestures and prosody), which is crucial for attachment functions (Henry, 1993; Schore, 1994; Siegal, 1999). Regular development determines interhemispheric organization whereby facial expressions, somatic states, and affective information, processed implicitly by the right brain, should be transmitted effectively to the left brain for semantic processing. Instead, the condition of being in a constant and sub-chronic state of fear, as in the case of severe and early traumatization, abuse, and neglect, over time causes the dissociation of areas of the brain that are normally connected and the non-regulated activation of subcortical structures involved in impulsive, automatic, and aggressive behaviours in response to perceived threats.

As the sequences of the *strange situation* (Ainsworth *et al.*, 1978) clearly show, an infant with disorganized attachment appears to be uncoordinated in his movements, paralyzed, or busy trying to reconcile opposite and coexisting stimuli into a possible, or, rather, impossible synthesis.

In these infants, the psychobiological system of stress regulation appears to have gone haywire, activating abnormal responses. The traumatic attachment pattern remains impressed at the sub-symbolic level of the mind, taking the form of images, dysperceptions of the bodily state, sounds, or smells, and is stored in the limbic circuits as a flashbulb memory, in implicit and autobiographical memory, belonging to the right visuospatial hemisphere (Fink *et al.*, 1996).

For this reason, even the slightest interpersonal stress triggers, if non-modulated, can reactivate painful states that belong to the body memory of the early relational history and are impressed in the amygdalo-hypothalamic circuits of a person's autonomous limbic system (Schore, 1994, 2003a, 2003b).

In our clinical work, this hypothesis can help us to better understand the intense experiences and impulsive behaviours – which may appear to be far removed from contextual reality – of borderline personalities.

*

RITA

Rita arrives in my office with burns on her arm.

R: *I did it again.*
T: *What happened?*

After a few minutes of heavy silence, during which the expression on Rita's face transforms from painful to angry, impatient, sad, and desperate, she says, avoiding eye contact:

R: *Luca and I had just made love. When it was over he got up and went to the bathroom because he had to go to work. Without saying a word, I got dressed quickly and left before he came out of the bathroom. He caught up with me in the street as I was about to take off on my scooter. He asked me what* was the matter and I answered, annoyed, 'Don't you have to go to work? Go on or you'll be late.' He said, 'OK, but tonight we need to talk.' He was upset.

I got home, lit a cigarette and burned my wrists. I had to do something, immediately. I was too upset! I was about to have a fit and wanted to calm myself down.

T: *I'm missing something: what happened when he went to the bathroom? How did you feel? Did something escape me?*
R: No, I don't know . . .
T: *Did something trouble you, or bother you?*
R: (Silence) **I started feeling upset, I felt agitated and had to leave!**
T: *You told me you had just made love, did you enjoy it?*
R: The usual. I've told you already that I can't relax during sex, so at a certain point I can't wait for it to be over. He was sweet and kept telling me I'm beautiful.
T: *Did you like that?*
R: Well, no.
T: *You didn't believe him?*
R: I don't want him to be with me just because I'm beautiful, I mean . . . I don't know, it bothers me.
T: *This isn't very clear to me.*
R: It isn't clear to me either. You see, it's as if he were with me for his own pleasure.
T: *In a way that's true, and I imagine it's the same for you, wouldn't you say? What's wrong with enjoying being together, making love?*
R: I don't know, it's too easy! You're beautiful! You're beautiful! Who cares? I don't know, it just really bothers me!
T: *Can you tell me a little bit more about what it is that bothers you?*
R: I feel tense, I have to move, I feel like I'm going to explode and I have to do something. If I burn myself afterwards I feel better. I focus on the pain and I feel better. There!

The dialogue with Rita is very difficult; she often stares at the wall silently for several minutes. I feel that I am missing significant pieces of the story which could make sense of the experience Rita is describing.

Some time after that session, while on a completely different subject, Rita told me about an episode that had occurred in her family some years ago.

She was taking a shower and had not locked the bathroom door; her father inadvertently walked in, gazed at her for a few seconds, and then left, closing the door behind him. Shortly afterwards, Rita's mother revealed to her a comment that her father had made about her: 'The guy who fucks her is a lucky bastard!' As she repeated the words I was immediately reminded of the episode involving Luca that she had told me about a few months before. I had found a missing piece of the puzzle. Maybe that was why she had such strong reactions when Luca would tell her she was beautiful.

When Rita told me this story she was surprised by the expression she saw on my face (I remember feeling upset by those words, I must have had an expression of pain and indignation). Smiling, Rita said to me that those words were meant as a compliment and started justifying her father as well as her mother who had told her, probably so that I would not judge them badly.

R: *'I know, my dad's nuts, I told you already, he's unbearable! But it was his way of expressing appreciation. Why did my mom tell me, you might ask, and that's fair enough.'*

That episode offered a glimpse of the abusive atmosphere in which Rita had lived; I am not talking about physical abuse, but of behaviours that were psychologically violent, that completely disregarded her needs, her reactions, and the family roles.

*

Childhood *handling* experiences and affective malattunements can be reproduced as physiological responses, emotions, and dissociated actings-out (Valent, 1998). Thus, a traumatic memory remains dissociated in implicit procedural memory without having the possibility of being processed in a space-time context.

This would explain the impulsive and contradictory reactions of many *difficult patients* like Anna (attacks on oneself and/or others, guilt feelings, flight, withdrawal, depression), and their inability to master events adaptively.

The inability to regulate and modulate one's emotions, the lack of integration of one's mental states and the enactment of pathogenic relational patterns make it very hard for patients to identify a need they may have, connect it to emotions, define the context within which all of this emerges and, consequently, behave in a consistent and harmonious manner.

Instead, the tendency to act impulsively and quickly is developed, triggering an emergency spiral, even in the therapeutic relationship, in which a sense of powerlessness can become the prevailing experience.

The anatomo-functional substrates of arousal regulation: the polyvagal theory

Stephen Porges (2001) has helped to shed light on arousal regulation mechanisms by proposing a theory that highlights the link between phylogenetic changes in the autonomic nervous system and social behaviour in humans, focusing on the evolutions of the vagus and on the neural regulation of the visceral state.

Porges refers to MacLean's structural organization of the human's central nervous system (*tripartite brain*) (1973), underscoring the importance of evolution as an organizing principle that has shaped both the structure of the nervous system and social adaptation behaviour, upholding the validity of biological aspects in the study of emotions, and acknowledging the importance of the vagus' bottom-up pathways in the regulation of the upper-level brain structures.

Using anatomical, phylogenetic, and neurophysiological arguments, he proposes a *tripartite model* of the vagus, instead of the *classic binary model*, highlighting the circular biological interconnections between the efferent and afferent pathways.

According to the *polyvagal theory*, adaptive behaviours are determined by three neural circuits, which correspond to different phylogenetic stages of the autonomic nervous system of vertebrates. The order in which these neural circuits emerged represents a response hierarchy in mammals, so that the most recent neural circuits respond first.

The first level is the *dorsovagal complex (parasympathetic)*, which comprises the nucleus that receives inputs, the *solitary nucleus*, as well as the nucleus that transmits outputs, the *dorsal motor nucleus*, situated in the medulla oblongata. The fibers are unmyelinated. It is the phylogenetically oldest branch, present in fish and amphibians, which regulates normal visceral processes during rest and recovery, organizing digestive processes (secretions, peristalsis), and slowing down heart rate and breathing. It is the neurobiological defence system which the body activates in the presence of sudden and unavoidable danger. This activation is associated with loss of muscle tone, resulting in paralysis, bradipnea, bradycardia, sense of prostration and dulling, separation from the body (altered body perception, depersonalization), freezing or fainting (vasovagal syncope). All of these phenomena are interesting for clinical work; we observe them in many patients with different diagnoses and often correspond to depression and panic (consequent to phenomena of derealization and depersonalization, hyperarousal, and the activation of the sympathetic system).

The second level is the *sympathetic-adrenal system*, which is also present in fish and reptiles. The fibers of this system are also mostly unmyelinated. The amygdala receives perceptive stimuli, sends messages up, horizontally, and down, influencing the cortical areas of thinking and acting (basal ganglia and paraventricular nucleus of the hypothalamus), respectively. These nuclei send out signals to the spine and to internal visceral organs by means of the parasympathetic system. The activation of the ortosympathetic system determines the onset of a series of physiological processes aimed to actively prepare the individual for fight or flight: muscle tension, tremor, tachycardia and tachypnea, acceleration of mental processes and muscle responses.

This second level therefore determines a visceral response that helps the individual to attack the aggressor with rage or to flee when confronted with stronger opponents, in both cases feeling active and vital in the presence of danger, unlike the *dorsovagal* level. Heart rate is accelerated, breathing quickens, digestion stops, blood is diverted from digestive organs to voluntary muscles, and the delicate muscles that envelop internal organs tense producing the feeling of visceral tension or a 'stabbing pain' in the stomach. The hormone released is vasopressin, which also serves as a neurotransmitter. The clinical consequences of an overactivation of the sympathetic system can be observed prevalently in some types of panic attacks, as well as in agonistic relational patterns.

The third level involves the *ventrovagal complex*, which appeared in mammals for the first time and further evolved in human beings, allowing for faster and more precise changes in the visceral state. Unlike the dorsovagal system, it consists mostly of myelinized fibers, which are functionally more effective. It originates from the nucleus ambiguus and innervates the face, larynx, and heart, thereby ensuring direct social contact with the other. Its fundamental function is to modulate the activation of the nervous sympathetic system and of action systems associated with defence (fight or flight) by regulating affective states and social behaviour. The hormone involved in this process is oxytocin. Porges defines the various parts of the autonomic nervous system as *phylogenetic substrates of a social nervous system* (Porges, 2001), and, in particular, he defines the ventrovagal innervation as a *social engagement system* (Porges, 2003).

The system governs the cortical components that regulate brainstem nuclei to control eyelid opening (looking), facial muscles (emotional expression), middle ear muscles (extracting human voice from background noise), muscle of mastication (ingestion), laryngeal and pharyngeal muscles (vocalization and language), and head-turning muscles (social gesture and orientation): all of these muscles mediate interaction with the social environment.

The social engagement system is completely formed by the thirty-second week of gestation and is fundamental in regulating dyadic interaction between caregiver and newborn, mediating most attachment modes. Since the ventrovagal system requires maturation (myelinization), that is a favourable environment, the quality of the early care provided by the caregiver may influence the quality of the individual's future functioning, also on the level of autonomic nervous system regulation. In children who have been abused or neglected at an early age, it is possible to observe, even after years, at times serious alterations of visceral functioning (dysregulation of arousal, heart rate, and breathing, as well as an altered perception and processing of stimuli, especially hunger, thirst, pain, proprioception) (Perry, 2005).

A good attachment relationship during infancy and good social interaction favour a sound process of myelinization of the ventrovagal system and of the entire autonomic nervous system. It is evident that the polyvagal theory and infant research studies – especially the ones focused on the first months of life – are in step. *Relationality is a biological imperative* and face-to-face interactions, vocalizations, gestures, prosody in communication, are the first powerful regulators of neurophysiological states that determine mental and physical wellbeing.

This takes us back to the issue of primary and secondary intersubjectivity (Trevarthen, 1979) mentioned previously (see endnote Chapter 2, p. 64). The polyvagal theory seems to confirm the notion of an *early intersubjectivity*. It also appears to be in keeping with Lichtenberg's idea of the *motivational system of regulation of physiological needs*, which combines neurovegetative homeostasis and intersubjectivity.

In this sense, Porges identifies two possible pathways of development. In a favourable and secure relational environment, the ventrovagal system is prevalently activated as opposed to the sympathetic and dorsovagal systems (levels II and I). Social interaction, which is regarded as the fundamental mediator of automatic modulation, reduces both active and passive avoidance responses in the child and facilitates the action systems of attachment, socialization, play, and exploration. Such processes, in turn, allow the nervous system to grow and represent the neuropsychophysiological core of affect/emotional regulation, which is plastically active throughout one's life.

In an insecure relational setting, instead, a perceived danger automatically activates the sympathetic system, facilitating active avoidance responses, that is attacks. The ventrovagal system is inhibited. If the threat persists, the sympathetic system may remain constantly active, causing disadaptive hyperarousal responses (uncontrollable fear, panic, hypertonic block).

When one's life is endangered, when a threat is overwhelming, unavoidable, and it is impossible to escape or attack, in animals and in humans alike the ancient vagal pathway (dorsovagal system) is activated, producing passive avoidance responses (surrender, freezing, numbing, dissociation, tonic immobility, and feigned death). These responses originate from a strong sense of adaptation to ensure species survival, for they induce the predators to abandon the prey. However, they become dysfunctional if the parasympathetic system remains activated also in the absence of danger. We observe this in patients who experience alterations of consciousness (feeling extraneous to one's body and/or the context, body dysperception, numbing, vasovagal syncope).

When science helps us: regulating arousal in the therapeutic relationship

ENRICO

Enrico is a brilliant young professional whose creativity has always helped him to be quite successful, choosing who to work with and how, without having to accept difficult compromises, which instead is very common in his line of work. He seeks my help for what he refers to as 'panic attacks'. Initially he talks to me about his anxiety and symptoms like profuse sweating, tachycardia, and a sense of disorientation. He has experienced these symptoms ever since he was a child and cures himself with benzodiazepines, which his father (a doctor) has taught him to use with some command. Enrico has always known that his father had the same problem, because he told him as much, describing their symptoms as 'anxiety', a disorder that one can live with and that can be cured with the right medicines when necessary. In a way, this has reassured Enrico; he was able to name what was happening to him, knowing that he was not alone in this and that it was not serious, that *it would not kill him*. On the other hand, this awareness has crystallized his experience, discouraging him from exploring what was happening to him and why. Ever since he was little, Enrico thought that he had to live with his problem, finding relief in medication and in the awareness that the crisis would *come and go*, as his dad would tell him. Over time, however, his ailments grew. He turned to me for help when, during his obsessive ruminations, he began to have intrusive thoughts about the possibility of going crazy and hurting his children.

At our first meeting I realized at once that he possessed remarkable personal resources: he was extremely bright and full of energy. Enrico began to explain his discomfort, not always finding the words to describe what happened to him and scrutinizing me from time to time, as if to gather from my reactions whether or not he could trust me. I immediately felt tenderness and, at the same time, esteem and respect for him, perhaps for the dignity he always displayed, even when he was clearly struggling and vulnerable. The boundary between a feeling of mistrust and the vital drive to want to be there and to negotiate what is happening, even in a help relationship, is usually very subtle and hard to identify. But I regarded Enrico's wariness positively, for it seemed to express his wish to remain an active party in the relationship with me. I think that I implicitly communicated reinforcement and liking, which was corresponded immediately.

He talked at once about his anxiety, an easier topic to broach, I suppose, also because the word anxiety has become part of our culture and often seems to give patients a reassuring sense of belonging and normality.

E: *At times I feel very agitated, my hands sweat, I have trouble breathing. I'm overtaken by an uncontrollable fear that I'm afraid of passing on to my kids; I wouldn't want to infect them, like my dad infected me.*

T: *I understand, you become highly alert and your reactions are typical of an activation of the sympathetic-adrenergic vagal system* (I explain what I mean, sharing with him some notions of basic physiology).

E: *That's right, how interesting!* (referring to the information on neurovegetative functioning).

*

The choice to talk about physiology seemed in keeping with my perception of Enrico's need to be actively involved in the treatment process. I do this often, generally for the purpose of sharing some information on how our nervous system works and helping the people who describe to me their symptoms to realize that it is a universal experience. By sharing information I reassure the patient that we are understanding each other and that together we can explore what is happening, thereby coming to a fuller understanding, using together the instruments that scientific literature offers. In my clinical experience, the fact of being informed implicitly restores in patients a sense of control which their symptoms have heavily undermined. Equally important is the relational meaning of this intervention; the *mirroring* and *secure contact in the absence of fear* that develop in the therapeutic relationship are directly proportional to both the analyst's and the patient's ability to make use of their skills. The therapist's choice to share knowledge can stimulate a more equal relationship in which such knowledge is not used as an instrument of power to be wielded.

Proceeding in the therapeutic process, Enrico was able to better grasp his body signals, learning to be more indulgent with himself and to allow himself to feel uncomfortable. Exploring together the meaning of his experiences, in an open and inquiring atmosphere, reassured him and helped him to tolerate.

*

E: *Every now and then I feel agitated, but I'm no longer hard on myself. I feel like smiling and think, 'Here we go again.' When I feel the tension rising, I take something, but it happens less and less frequently.*

T: *Before, you probably not only felt bad but also had an adverse reaction to your symptoms, as if you had to fight them, and this fuelled your agitation and made things worse. Now you are more willing to accept them and this probably makes them last less.*

As his trust in me grew, the experiences that were harder to describe and could not simply be dismissed as 'anxiety' began to emerge. In fact, his states of alert were not what scared him most. Enrico had learned to regulate the hyperactivation through sports. He exercised every day; he had always been very fit, ever since he was a boy. It was essential to him, he could not do without it. He would make sacrifices just to get his daily workout.

E: *It helps me unwind and makes me feel better; I worry when I feel my energy's running low.*
T: *What do you mean you worry? One can sometimes feel tired or under the weather, don't you think?*
E: *No, it upsets me. I don't accept it, I worry, I feel as if I'm sick.*
T: *Yes, you seem to be more comfortable when you feel alert and active than when you're a little out of sorts, wouldn't you say?*
E: *Yes, I need to feel active, I'm less scared that way.*
T: *In the face of danger, we all feel better if we can prepare ourselves to fight or flee. We feel like there's a way out, it's normal. You train your muscles and body to be fit and that makes you feel more reactive. Of course, when the state of alert rises above the danger level, you run the risk of unpleasant effects, which is what happens to you when you get panic attacks, right?*
E: *Yes, that's true.*
T: *Your arousal self-regulation system doesn't work well* (we smile, thinking back to what we shared on the vagal system). *Enrico, can you describe to me how you feel when you're down?*

I had intuited that Enrico was referring to other states of distress that he had not talked to me about before and I could tell he was very scared. I relied on our conversations on physiology to recreate a reassuring contact and only after did I try to probe.

E: *Well, yes, when that happens I feel much worse, in the sense that I experience strange sensations that frighten me* (he pauses and stares into space, he seems reluctant to speak). *Sometimes I feel strange, feeble . . . but it doesn't feel like a healthy exhaustion, like after a workout, for example. I feel disconnected . . . as if I no longer knew were I was . . .* (he pauses again. I realize how hard it must be for him to communicate to me those states that frighten him so).
T: *It's as if you were disoriented?* (I ask, encouraging him to continue).
E: *That's right, as if I weren't myself anymore. My mind is numb, my body slumps . . .*
T: *You feel faint?*
E: *I've never fainted, at worst I feel like I need to sleep, but it isn't a normal sleep, I'm feeble. These are the states that scare me the most. I'm afraid of losing*

my mind, of going insane. That's when I sometimes think that I could go crazy and hurt myself, or even worse, my kids.

He was frightened as he said this, I thought it might be the first time he described what he experienced in such detail. I had the feeling that, as he spoke about it, he was afraid of entering into that state. His stiff posture and fixed gaze gave me the impression that he had plunged into a state of fear with no way out, which triggers dissociative phenomena. I felt that it was a crucial moment for us. Once again, I spontaneously tried to reassure him by referring back to something that we had already explored together, engaging with him at a cognitive level, without going into what I was perceiving with him emotionally, for I sensed that it was too early for that.

T: *We talked about your fear of harming your children already during one of our first sessions. You might recall that we associated it with other thoughts, all catastrophic. We talked about that obsessive brooding, which represents your hypertrophic sense of responsibility, your need to prevent, to make sure that everything is ok, that there are no surprises in store for you and your loved ones, remember?*
E: *Yes, I do, and what you said to me was very helpful because it really made sense to me, and things have gotten much better since we talked about it* (he smiles at me. He seems much calmer now, so I decide to go back to the symptoms he was describing).
T: *Now we can try to understand the feelings that trigger bad thoughts which you were trying to describe to me, what do you say?*
E: *All right.*
T: *They could be known sensations that go by the name of depersonalization, or derealization, which are phenomena of alteration of consciousness; under certain circumstances, all of us can experience them. If they're unfamiliar, they can be very scary, because, as you were saying, you feel like you're losing lucidity, control over yourself.*
E: *That's right, I feel like I'm losing my mind* (he seems frightened but also trusting).
T: *Yes, I understand that. This happens when the dorsovagal system is activated instead of the sympathetic adrenergic system. Remember the polyvagal system we talked about?*

Enrico and I continued to discuss physiology in order to understand and name his symptoms. His panic attacks had a twofold origin: they could be triggered by a state of exasperated hypervigilance or by a state of helpless immobility, like in the face of an overwhelming danger.

In this case too, my choice was determined by the wish to loosen the tension I could sense in Enrico, as he spoke about these states that frightened him so much. His reaction was reassuring; he was curious and wanted to learn more, read up on the topic. The idea of gathering information that would help him to understand what was happening to him had a very calming effect.

Enrico found it very hard to curb his fear during our sessions and when I noticed this I imagined him as a child in his room gazing into space, perfectly still, overtaken by a fear that he could not explain or contain. *Why did he not open that door? Why did he not go to his mother or father to be comforted?* His difficult childhood, his parents' inability to be attentive to his needs slowly emerged. The traumas of his father and mother, which had never been worked through, had made them vulnerable, unaware and, therefore, traumatic for their son.

I could glimpse in his stories a very fragile mother who was *'shut off from the world',* as he would say. She spent a great deal of time at home and was devoted to a husband who, instead, was unfaithful to her with other women; he had many affairs – some occasional, others more significant. Enrico and his brother knew about their father's affairs, as did their paternal grandmother, who would talk openly about them with her grandsons, as if they were something to be proud of. Enrico's mother knew but did nothing about it. Not even when Enrico grew older and started taking various heavy substances. Nobody noticed. Enrico had always managed on his own, he got in and out of trouble without turning to anyone. He would swing between the wish to defy danger and the need to exert control over himself and events, experiencing periods of exaltation and of withdrawal and annihilation. After his children were born the wheels started to creak and his neurovegetative symptoms grew stronger. Whenever Enrico talked about his parents I could sense his anger and the distance he had taken from them.

During our sessions, I was very sensitive to the changes in Enrico's state of alarm, which was prevalently manifested with a tensing of the body: he sat still in the armchair, his jaws locked and hands spread on his thighs. I could sense his fear and withdrawal, and felt very sorry for his suffering, especially for the solitude he had been left to as a child, which was at the root of all this. Talking about physiology caught his attention, stimulated his bright mind, and allowed us to distance ourselves from the paralyzing pain that overtook Enrico, thus re-establishing the contact between us. This represented a short pause, during which Enrico and I were engaged on a more equal motivational level; we spoke as colleagues, friends. We used the theories to try to formulate a hypothesis together and gradually build the puzzle, while implicitly we stayed together, modulating the timing and modes of contact. This had a very powerful rehabilitative value.

While Enrico and I talked explicitly about the ventrovagal system and its arousal-regulating function, we implicitly experienced this. Enrico could see the beneficial effects of our relationship, without comprehending its meaning for a long time. Understanding what had happened inevitably implied touching his traumas, in a circular process: the safer Enrico felt in the relationship with me, the more he could come into contact with his traumatic childhood, but at the same time, coming into contact with his traumas and being able to talk about them together was the rehabilitating experience.

*

Chapter 5

Personality disorders: diagnosis and treatment

How new theories on trauma and dissociation influence the diagnosis and treatment of personality disorders

Mariangela Lanfredi and Antonella Ivaldi

The assessment of trauma-related disorders is becoming increasingly important in clinical work and in scientific research. It is a complex issue, given that trauma-related disorders are often very heterogeneous and display various levels of severity. Epidemiological studies have shown a high prevalence of traumatic events in different cultures: in the U.S., at least 15 per cent of the population reports having been molested, physically attacked, raped or involved in an accident. Moreover, around 90 per cent of people with PTSD experience at least once in their lifetime a comorbid mental disorder (Kessler *et al.*, 1995), the most common being major depression, alcohol and substance abuse, and other anxiety disorders (Brady *et al.*, 2000). Epidemiological studies point to the high frequency of manifest single traumas as well as of cumulative and multiple traumas (Karam *et al.*, 2014). For these reasons, the World Health Organization, in its 2013–2020 action plan, has placed trauma at the centre of its healthcare development plan for mental health, considering it as a proven risk factor. This has been a controversial issue, ever since the PTSD diagnosis was introduced in the third edition of the DSM (APA, 1980). DSM-IV-TR (APA, 2000), which includes this diagnosis in the section on 'Anxiety Disorders' and its definition refers to three clusters of symptoms: persistent re-experiencing of the traumatic event, avoidance/numbing and increased arousal. In this case, the 'traumatic event' is understood as a serious, isolated event that cannot be avoided and that overwhelms the individual's capacity for resistance. In DSM-V (APA, 2013) instead, PTSD is moved to a new chapter entitled 'Trauma and Stress-Related Disorders' where no reference is made to personal response to the traumatic event, which is described as an exposure to 'death, threatened death, actual or threatened serious injury, or actual or threatened sexual violence' (p. 217). Unlike in the previous version of the DSM, the avoidance/numbing criterion is subdivided into two distinct clusters: avoidance and negative alterations in cognitions and mood associated with the traumatic event. The increased arousal cluster covers a broader range of symptoms, which include irritable or aggressive behaviour, and self-destructive or reckless behaviour. Finally, development is considered as well; diagnostic thresholds are set for children over six and adolescents, and for children under six.

Although from a clinical standpoint in trauma survivors dissociative phenomena like compartmentalization of affect, disrupted memory encoding, time distortion, and psychogenic fugue have been observed ever since Janet's studies (see Chapter 3), DSM-IV's definition of PTSD includes only two dissociative symptoms: flashbacks and psychogenic amnesia, while in the ICD-10 and DSM-V diagnostic system trauma-associated disorders are still scarcely represented. DSM-V has introduced the 'with dissociative symptoms' subtype for patients who meet the criteria for PTSD and experience persistent or recurring depersonalization and/or derealization symptoms. In recent decades, different nosographic descriptions have been suggested to characterize the different symptoms associated with trauma, like complex post-traumatic stress disorder (cPTSD – Herman, 1992a), otherwise known as disorders of extreme stress not otherwise specified (DESNOS – Luxenberg *et al.*, 2001), which describes a clinical syndrome that includes pathological dissociation, somatizations, dysregulation of emotions, altered central self and relational schemas, following an experience of interpersonal traumatic victimization. To date, the WHO Working Group on the Classification of Stress-Related Disorders, following a logic of clinical usefulness, has suggested including cPTSD in the next ICD-11 as a separate diagnostic category describing the complex symptomatology that is associated with early and multiple interpersonal traumas (Maercker *et al.*, 2013). The definition of cPTSD therefore refers to the experiencing of severe and/or prolonged traumatic situations, and does not merely identify the effects of devastating traumatic events (like violence or chronic maltreatment), which fall under the category of PTSD or acute stress disorder. Indeed, exposure to particular types of traumatic experiences may result in far more insidious and crippling psychopathogenic disorders than PTSD, compromising the sound development of the attachment behaviour system and of the ability to modulate emotions (D'Andrea *et al.*, 2012). Studies have shown that the BPD diagnosis is associated with child abuse and neglect more so than any other personality disorder (Battle *et al.*, 2004; Yen *et al.*, 2002); research is currently trying to determine whether cPTSD and BPD diagnosis comorbid with PTSD are distinct or should both be regarded as trauma-related disorders (Cloitre *et al.*, 2014).

Several studies have clarified the role of dissociation in the aftermath of early childhood interpersonal traumas. A cross-national study conducted on a large population sample within the framework of the WHO World Mental Health Surveys (Stein *et al.*, 2013) has shown that in individuals with PTSD, pathological dissociation symptoms are strongly associated with an early onset of PTSD, a higher incidence of traumatic events, and childhood adversities. A recent study conducted by Van Dijke and colleagues (2015) using a path analysis has identified pathological dissociation as a mediator of the correlation between childhood complex trauma and cPTSD in adults. Moreover, the longitudinal empirical studies of Lyons Ruth and colleagues have shown the role of long-term predictors of the quality of the parent–child dialogue in the genesis of dissociative tendencies (Lyons Ruth *et al.*, 2006) and borderline symptoms and behaviour in young adults (Lyons Ruth, 2008).

From a theoretical standpoint, according to Liotti and Farina (2011), the difficulty in classifying cPTSD is due to the 'dissociative nature of pathogenic processes underpinning traumatic development' (p. 23); it would therefore be useful to reason in terms of a post-traumatic spectrum comprising different disorders, which can all be traced to traumatic developments and fall within the category of dissociation. Dissociative symptoms are present in BPD and in different mental disorders: somatic symptoms and related disorders (somatic symptom disorder and conversion disorder in particular), in times of crisis in other personality disorders (narcissistic, schizophrenic, dependent), eating disorders, anxiety disorders (panic disorder, generalized anxiety disorder), obsessive-compulsive and related disorders (obsessive-compulsive disorder and body dysmorphic disorder), subcategories of depressive disorders (dysthymia and major depressive disorder in particular), and bipolar disorders.

Dissociation is a multidimensional concept. According to the categorization of Holmes and colleagues (2005), dissociative symptoms are expressed essentially in two ways: *detachment* and *compartmentalization*. Detachment refers to the experience of alienation from one's emotions, identity, or familiarity with the surrounding reality and involves such symptoms as *depersonalization, derealization,* and altered states of consciousness. Compartmentalization refers to dissociative processes triggered by traumas that hinder 'the synthesis, integration, and regulation of ego states which normally produce a unitary and cohesive sense of self' (Liotti and Farina, 2011: 50). Extreme prototypical examples of compartmentalization are *dissociative identity disorder* and *unspecified dissociative disorder.*

A vast literature has considered dissociation as a defence against acute states of physical and emotional pain, which plays an adaptive role in the immediacy of trauma. However, over time, such a defence mechanism causes alterations in the mental processes that generate maladaptive defence mechanisms, which may jeopardize the sense of continuity of one's identity (Lingiardi and Gazzillo, 2014). According to Bromberg (1998) instead, dissociation has an organizing function, which allows for an adaptive illusory integrity and continuity of the self (see Chapter 3). Van der Hart, Nijenhuis and Steele (2006) put forward a theory of structural personality dissociation on three levels: primary dissociation, present in PTSD or in the simple forms of dissociative disorder or acute stress disorder, in which a separation occurs between an apparently normal part of the personality (ANP) and an emotional part of the personality (EP); secondary dissociation, which characterizes cPTSD, other specified dissociative disorders and trauma-related DBP, in which a separation takes place between an ANP and more than one EP; tertiary dissociation, which is present in dissociative identity disorder, in which separation occurs between more than one ANP and one EP that are more complex and autonomous, to the point of having different names and physical characteristics.

Russell Meares (2012) points out that comorbidity between DBP and Axis I and Axis II disorders is the rule rather than the exception; he theorizes that traumatic development is at the root of this simultaneous presence of different symptoms, or clusters of symptoms. Neurosciences are helping significantly to comprehend the impact of early traumatic events and dissociative phenomena in personality development (for a review see Meares, 2012; Sar, 2014). In the light of recent evidence produced by neurobiological and neurophysiological studies, the model proposed by Frewen and Lanius (2014) for disorders of the spectrum relating to trauma that include dissociation has significant transdiagnostic implications. The so-called 4-D model categorizes post-traumatic stress symptoms, from those occurring during the normal stream of consciousness in wakefulness to those that are dissociative and associated with trauma-related altered states of consciousness (TRASC), spanning four dimensions: time (i.e., forms of intrusive recall of traumatic events that fail to provoke a marked sense of reliving versus flashbacks-reliving), thought (i.e., having distressing thoughts in first-person perspective versus voice-hearing in second person perspective), body (i.e., physiological hyperarousal versus depersonalization) and emotions (i.e., feeling numb versus general negative emotions like fear, anxiety, sadness, shame).

It is clear that in clinical work we often come across complex situations that reveal the limits of fixed and rigid representations of diagnostic categories and the need to implement psychotherapeutic interventions that take into account the presence of a wide range of symptomatological profiles in different clinical populations.

Empirically supported psychological approaches to the treatment of personality disorders

Personality disorders (PDs) are pervasive and chronic disorders. Prevalence rates of PDs in North America and Western Europe was estimated between four per cent and 15 per cent (Tyrer *et al.*, 2015). These disorders are associated with premature mortality and suicide and have significant direct costs, in terms of national mental health services (e.g. hospitalizations), as well as indirect costs (e.g., absenteeism from work). Comorbid PDs are associated with poor treatment prognosis of Axis I mental disorders (Reich, 2003). Psychosocial interventions are recommended as the treatment option for BPD and other PDs (Gabbard *et al.*, 2012) and have been applied in a variety of formats, settings, modalities, and dosages. Randomized controlled trials (RCTs) have been used to compare the effectiveness of various therapies based on different theoretical models in the treatment of PDs; most of these studies (19 out of 33 in the review by Dixon-Gordon *et al.*, 2011), however, focused on treatment of BPD. There are few studies on the effectiveness of psychotherapy in the treatment of other PDs: no RCTs have been conducted to evaluate the efficacy of treatments in people with Cluster A disorders (schizoid, paranoid, and schizotypal PD); studies on Cluster C disorders – including avoidant, dependent, and obsessive-compulsive PDs – have gathered little evidence on efficacy. A meta-analytic review (Simon, 2009) showed that cognitive behavioural therapy (CBT), psychodynamic therapy, and social skills training produced clinical gains that were maintained throughout follow-up periods ranging from three months to three years. CBT was found to be effective in reducing symptom severity relating to obsessive-compulsive PD, depression, and anxiety in the wake of treatment (Diedrich and Voderholzer, 2015), but further research is needed to identify the long-term effects.

Cochrane reports (Stoffers *et al.*, 2012) have described such empirically-supported treatments of PDs as CBT, Dialectical Behaviour Therapy (DBT), Interpersonal Psychotherapy for BPD (IPT-BPD), Mentalization-Based Therapy (MBT), Transference-Focused Psychotherapy (TFP), Dynamic Deconstructive Psychotherapy (DDP), Schema-Focused Therapy (SFT), Cognitive Analytic Therapy (CAT), and Systems Training for Emotional Predictability and Problem Solving (STEPPS).

Cognitive-Behaviour Therapy is an overarching term used for treatments that combine cognitive and behavioural techniques (i.e., thoughts monitoring, Socratic dialogue, disputation of irrational beliefs, behavioural experiments) aimed to modify maladaptive schemata and dysfunctional beliefs about self and others in PDs (Beck *et al.*, 2004). RCTs investigating the efficacy of CBT in patients with BPD (Davidson *et al.*, 2006; Tyrer *et al.*, 2003; Cottraux *et al.*, 2009) have shown that it is more effective in reducing self-harming behaviours as compared to treatment as usual (TAU). Emmelkamp and colleagues (2006) compared CBT to brief dynamic therapy in avoidant PD patients: while both treatments produced improvements, CBT proved more effective after 20 sessions of treatment and at six-month follow-up. In an open trial of cognitive therapy, BPD patients displayed significant improvements at 12-month and 18-month follow-ups (Brown *et al.*, 2004). Moreover, a brief CBT package (MACT – Manual-Assisted Cognitive Therapy) was found to be useful in BPD adults deliberately engaging in self-harm when combined with TAU (Weinberg *et al.*, 2006).

Dialectical Behaviour Therapy (Linehan, 1993) is a multi-module psychological intervention which is based on an adaptation of the main principles of CBT combined with mindfulness-based techniques. DBT was originally intended as an outpatient treatment aimed to reduce mood instability and interpersonal problems. DBT emphasizes the principles of providing validation of emotions and acceptance. The program is highly structured and consists of individual therapy, group social skill training, telephone access in times of crisis, and a therapist consultation team. Clinical trials conducted by different research groups (Lineahn *et al.*, 1991, 2006; Verheul *et al.*, 2003; Bohus *et al.*, 2004; McMain *et al.*, 2009; Soler *et al.*, 2009; Priebe *et al.*, 2012) compared DBT with TAU, comprehensive validation therapy, and general psychiatric management (GPM) delivered by expert clinicians, and found that DBT was effective in reducing self-harm and suicidal behaviours in inpatients and outpatients with a diagnosis of BPD. A controlled study by Clarkin and colleagues (2007) comparing DBT with two active treatments (supportive therapy and TFP) observed similar reliable outcomes in various domains for all three treatments. In particular, DBT and TFP helped to bring down the number of attempted suicides and improved depression as well as anxiety and global functioning, while only TFP was associated with reduced anger, impulsivity, irritability, and assault.

Interpersonal Psychotherapy for BPD is a brief manual-based psychotherapy originally developed for the treatment of depression and adapted to the treatment of patients with BPD (Markowitz, 2005). Here BPD is regarded as an attachment disorder characterized by impulsivity, rapid mood swings, and cognitive distortions, with high comorbidity with depression. IPT-BPD emphasizes the assumption that interpersonal functioning and affect states play an important part in the onset and endurance of psychological problems (Bateman, 2012). According to a recent trial (Bellino *et al.*, 2010) conducted on BPD patients, only therapy combined with IPT-BPD proved more effective than fluoxetine for the core symptoms of PD, anxiety, and quality of life.

Mentalization-Based Therapy is a manualized evidence-based psychotherapy originally developed for BPD and subsequently used for other PDs and Axis I mental disorders (depression, eating disorders, substance abuse). MBT draws on concepts from attachment theory and cognitive psychology. Treatment is focused on mentalization, which is considered to be 'the most fundamental common factor' among a variety of psychotherapeutic treatments (Allen *et al.*, 2008). Mentalization refers to the capacity to envision mental states in oneself and in others and is related to reflective functioning and affect regulation. Mentalization is a developmental achievement facilitated by a secure attachment system: genetically predisposed individuals who experienced early neglect are more likely to display impaired mentalization when emotionally challenged. Deficits in the capacity for mentalization leads to the re-emergence of prementalistic ways of perceiving the word – namely psychic equivalence, pretend mode, and teleological thinking (ibid.). Treatment focuses on the patient's current state of mind and interpretation of transference in order to encourage alternative perspectives (similar to the concept of decentering). A recent review (Dixon-Gordon *et al.*, 2011) featured two RCTs conducted by Bateman and Fonagy, which reported a beneficial impact of day-hospital treatment over standard psychiatric treatment at 18-month follow-up, with lower distress symptoms and self-harming behaviours. Five years after discharge, MBT continued to be more effective than TAU in terms of suicide rate, service use, compliance with medication, and symptom measures. The outpatient MBT program is an intensive treatment (18–24 weeks) that involves one weekly session of individual therapy and one weekly session of group therapy, conducted by different therapists. The outpatient variant of MBT was found to be associated with a greater decline in the relative risk of suicide attempts, self-harm, and hospitalization compared to a control group (Bateman and Fonagy, 2009).

Transference-Focused Psychotherapy is a manualized psychodynamic intervention that has been shown to be effective for BPD in different RCTs. TFP is based on concepts and techniques aimed at correcting distortions in the individual's representations of self and others. TFP considers BPD symptoms as originating from a lack of identity integration (Yeomans *et al.*, 2013) – referred to as 'identity diffusion' – which is associated with the use of primitive defensive strategies like splitting that cause affect-regulation difficulties and generate patterns of unstable interpersonal relationships. According to this approach, which integrates elements of object relations theory and attachment theory, 'personality organization' results from early interactions with caregivers and their internalizations. A one-year RCT compared TFP with a treatment conducted by experienced community psychotherapists: TFP proved to be significantly more effective with BPD patients in reducing suicide rates and attempts (Doering *et al.*, 2010) and improving reflective function (Fischer-Kern *et al.*, 2015). Clarkin and colleagues (2007) compared TFP with DBT and supportive psychotherapy (SPT): DBT and TFP were found to be equally effective in relation to suicidality. Levy and colleagues (2006) observed that only TFP (compared to SPT and DBT) yielded positive changes in attachment organization and in reflective functioning after one year of intensive TFP.

Dynamic Deconstructive Psychotherapy is a manual-driven psychodynamic treatment for adults with co-occurring BPD and alcohol use disorder or drug dependence, self-harm, eating disorders, and recurrent suicide attempts (Gregory *et al.*, 2010). This treatment is time-limited (from 12 to 18 months) and combines elements of translational neuroscience, object relations theory, and deconstruction philosophy. DDP is based on the hypothesis that neurocognitive deficits in emotional experience processing account for much of BPD psychopathology. The treatment is geared towards enhancing neurocognitive self-capacities through the development of a therapeutic alliance, identification and integration of distorted attributions, acceptance of limitations of self and others, and differentiation from the therapist. DDP includes some educative elements and explicitly avoids advice, validation, and encouragement, using less of a directive approach. Gregory and colleagues found that patients with co-occurring BPD and alcohol use disorders who received DDP rather than TAU reported significantly better outcomes at 12 months in terms of parasuicidal episodes, BPD symptoms, alcohol abuse, need for institutional care, and medication. Treatment gains were maintained also at 30 months follow-up (Gregory *et al.*, 2010).

Schema-Focused Therapy (Young *et al.*, 2003) is an integrative therapy that combines techniques from cognitive-behavioural and psychodynamic treatment, object relations theory, Gestalt psychotherapy, and transactional analysis therapy. SFT is focused on early maladaptive schemas that become overgeneralized and rigid in the course of an individual's life and are associated to maladaptive coping styles. Schemas are self-defeating core themes developed during childhood and regarding one's view of self, others, and the world. Schemas are activated by environmental circumstances relevant to the specific schema and generate high levels of affect. Schema-coping styles are assumed to be responses developed by the individual to survive the early environment. SFT compared to TFP resulted in lower dropout rates (25 per cent vs 50 per cent) and achieved the most favourable gains in BPD symptoms and quality of life measures after three years of treatment (Giesen-Bloo *et al.*, 2006). SFT, as cited in Rafaeli's publication (2009), has been adapted for different populations: homeless substance abusers, individuals with BPD or anti-social PD in forensic settings, and inpatients with a Cluster C diagnosis. Moreover, SFT for group therapy combined with individual sessions was found to produce significantly greater improvements in BPD symptoms and global functioning than TAU (Farrel *et al.*, 2009). Another RCT involving patients with Cluster B and C personality disorders (Zorn *et al.*, 2008) showed better outcomes in interpersonal behaviour and lower emotional and symptomatic complaints compared to patients exposed to social skills training.

Cognitive Analytic Therapy (CAT) is an integrative intervention that includes elements of psychoanalytic object relations theory, cognitive-behaviour therapy, and Vygotsky's work. CAT is a time-limited integrative psychotherapy (ranging from 16 to 24 weeks) focused on intrapsychic and interpersonal problems common to a variety of PDs (Ryle and Kerr, 2002). Personality disorder is considered as a manifest feature of dysfunctional relationship patterns that are linked to developmental trauma or deficiencies. Narrative and diagrammatic reformulations of emerging difficulties are used to promote new, more functional and flexible mutual roles. Evidence of efficacy is still limited and mainly targeted to the treatment of BPD. One RCT study found that CAT produced a greater improvement in symptoms as compared to TAU (Clarke *et al.*, 2013) in a sample of patients with Cluster A, B, and C personality disorders (68 per cent of participants had a diagnosis of BPD).

Systems Training for Emotional Predictability and Problem Solving (STEPPS) is a manualized, cognitive-behavioural, skills-based group treatment program for outpatients with a diagnosis of BPD, designed to supplement ongoing individual treatment (drug therapy, psychotherapy, or case management). The 20-week program combines cognitive-behavioural elements and skills training with a systems component that involves caregivers or other people with whom the patient interacts regularly. The goal is to teach more useful strategies for the management of emotional intensity and behavioural problems. Two RCTs have shown the efficacy of this training: Blum and colleagues (2008) compared STEPPS plus TAU against TAU alone, and Bos *et al.* (2010) compared STEPPS plus an additional individual treatment against TAU.

Why do different treatment models prove to be equally effective? A hypothesis based on motivational theories

Recent RCTs compared the effectiveness of a specific treatment for PDs – particularly BPD – with other validated treatments or active treatment conditions. Although DBT appears to be more effective in reducing the frequency of suicidal and self-harming behaviours than other interventions, these findings showed that different treatments, when highly structured and administered by clinicians with extensive training, yielded similar outcomes (Leichsenring and Leibing, 2003; McMain et al., 2009; Clarkin et al., 2007).

Manualized treatments of PDs often include a variety of techniques from different theoretical orientations. The efficacy of treatment does not appear to be determined by the consistent application of a coherent and comprehensible theoretical framework, which leads to the conclusion that there is no one theoretical approach that is more effective than others (Bateman and Fonagy, 2000). The Dodo bird verdict ('Everybody has won and all must have prizes,' said the Dodo in *Alice in Wonderland* when asked who had won the race) is the most popular metaphor used to express the notion that a theoretical framework is not crucial in determining the efficacy of different types of treatments.

As regards the treatment of BPD, there are two possible views (Gabbard, 2007). According to one hypothesis, different treatments have common elements that account for their equivalent effects, and most therapies work through non-specific effects. The other hypothesis is that different treatment approaches work with patients who present different clusters of clinical symptoms.

Some authors explored the common elements shared by empirically supported psychotherapies (i.e., DBT, MBT, TFP, SFT, CBT, STEPPS and General Psychiatric Management – GPM) for BPD (Wienberg et al., 2011; Beatson and Rao, 2014). One common element is the use of *a clear, structured treatment frame-work*: appointment times, cancellation or termination policy, agreement regarding telephone calls, confidentiality. This includes a clear rationale for the treatment, which is negotiated with patients prior to the beginning of therapy, and the need to involve and communicate with other staff members. A clear treatment framework can address impulsivity in BPD patients. Contracting can help to identify and preempt problems that are likely to interfere with and jeopardize therapy. Another common factor is that these treatments *focus on the relationship with the therapist*. This involves devoting careful attention to the relationship with a genuinely empathic attitude, and agreeing collaboratively on the goals to be pursued in treatment. Attention to the therapist's countertransference and reparation of ruptures in the course of therapy are necessary. The therapist must take an *active role in the treatment process*. He or she must resort to different techniques – such as self-disclosures, confrontations, problem solving, etc. – in order to stay mentally and emotionally engaged with the patient. Similarities include a *collaborative, cooperative relationship with the therapist* and *attention to affect,* which involves recognizing and identifying emotional states, and using validation and encouragement to tolerate painful emotional experiences. The therapist should also seek *support/supervision,* since countertransference can be an intense experience and may jeopardize the therapeutic alliance. Moreover, these are *exploratory and change-oriented interventions:* behaviour analysis, clarification, confrontation, and other techniques are aimed at improving insight into maladaptive behavioural or thinking patterns. Change is encouraged in different ways by each manual. Development of mentalizing is the core goal of MBT aimed to promote psychological and behavioural changes. Other interventions include challenging self-defeating thoughts (DBT, SFT, TFP), limit setting (DBT, SFT, TFP, GPM), skill training (DBT, SFT), and homework (DBT, SFT).

Beatson and Rao (2014) suggest – though using different terminology – that the factors that validated BPD psychotherapies have in common are the ones that promote the ability to mentalize, which in itself depends on a secure attachment context. Weinberg and colleagues (2011) highlighted that commonalities in manualized treatments are well-suited for the main cluster symptoms of BPD. Attention to affect is consistent with emotion dysregulation in these patients, change-oriented interventions can be effective for behavioural dysregulation, attention for the relationship is consistent with insecure attachment in these patients and with difficulty in preserving the alliance.

Recent evidence recommends an integrated approach to address different areas of psychopathology across multiple functioning domains in patients with PDs (Clarkin, 2012).

Recent literature highlights the need to integrate specific interventions for the treatment of traumatic development with other forms of psychotherapy. Techniques like mindfulness, Eye Movement Desensitization and Reprocessing (EMDR), sensorimotor therapy, or exposure and cognitive restructuring therapies are used to stabilize symptoms and refocus attention. Referring to the relational paradigm that we are adopting (see Chapter 1), we can easily understand that in using different techniques and therapeutic strategies we have to take into account the patients' mentalization and psycho-physiological self-regulation deficits; the severity of these deficits is an indicator of how impaired higher mental functioning is.

In the treatment of serious patients concrete actions are sometimes the only possible language, at least at the outset. The detailed and rich organization of some residential treatment models responds to the need to structure and hold the relationship, and to protect and define the therapeutic space. Intense weekly programs that include several spaces for therapeutic encounter, activities, individual and group sessions, are very helpful in regulating arousal thanks to clear boundaries and structured activities. The distribution of dysregulated affectivity among several workers reduces the stress factors, and this has repercussions also on the therapeutic relationship. Deploying various forces and creating an environment in which to collaborate and to combine resources helps to overcome the isolation that characterizes the individual setting. This enables us to work in safer conditions. In terms of IWMs, we are referring to attachment, affiliation, cooperation, and ranking; we are also referring to a non-regulated activation of the fight-flight system. We know that in difficult patients the attachment IWM is impaired. Traumatic development (see Chapter 3) damages the ability to seek help, thus making it difficult for the therapeutic relationship to grow. Protecting the inception and development of the therapeutic relationship is the central element that all validated treatments have in common. The way in which the relationship can be used varies depending on the model, but every model surely uses techniques and theories that belong to other approaches.

So it is easier to understand why different approaches achieve similar outcomes, thus confirming that for clinicians strict school divisions only stand in the way of the complex work they are called to do.

Once again, the motivation to grow comes from our patients; the different and bizarre clusters of symptoms that some of them display are an interesting incitement for us therapists to train ourselves to deal with the complexity of human nature and to accept our limits. This is where our theories can really help us to venture with a certain margin of safety and much curiosity into what we do not know and will never know completely: the relationship with the other, which is unique and unrepeatable.

Chapter 6

The relational/multi-motivational therapeutic approach (REMOTA)

Antonella Ivaldi

FIRST PART

As I mentioned in the introduction, my training involved an ongoing search for tools and skills, at times in very different areas. While divisions between schools of thought are often determined by academic and power-related reasons, in clinical work we are confronted with other needs, which are closer to those of our patients and have more to do with what we can do to help them and how. Guided by this need, I approached different theories and methods, which could not always be reconciled; however, when this was indeed possible (Wachtel, 1997), it greatly enriched my work in the session room. I have always tried to combine ethics, efficacy, and creativity in my work, often finding myself in the uncomfortable position of having to risk with my patients as I attempted something new, without the reassurance that comes from adhering to familiar protocols.

In describing my approach, I must necessarily point out that it is merely a lead, an experience, a base for further exploration.

That is what it is all about. I will try to tell the story of this model: when, how, and where it came into being.

I will also try to describe the foundations of a way of working, enriching the narrative with clinical examples, in the hope that the reader may gather what is at the basis of a certain type of clinical work, grasp its essence.

The original contribution of this work may consist precisely in showing that it is indeed possible to use different approaches harmoniously, in the light of a meta-theoretical frame of reference on mental functioning; the multi-motivational theory and the relational paradigm (see Chapter 2), in the attempt to stay focused on an etiopathogenic treatment model.

The working context

I have always worked prevalently in a private outpatient treatment setting, following at times complicated patients who are not taken on by the public health service. It can be very hard, risky, and frustrating to assume such a commitment without the backing of a structure that holds and protects the clinical work. We know from the various validated models and from international guidelines that the more severe the disorder, the greater the need to structure the treatment context and methods in order to ensure the safety of patients and workers, as well as the efficacy of treatment (see Chapter 5). This was a challenge for me and for those who, like me, have worked in the private sector. This challenge has compelled me to reflect and to try out methods compatible with the context and the available resources, which offered the greatest possible efficiency. I have tried to expand my skills to benefit from more professional tools; I have learned to use all settings – individual, family, and group – collaborating with psychiatrist colleagues for drug therapy, seeking out collaboration in organizing complex treatment plans to address complex needs.

However, the most interesting aspect of my exploration has been the attempt to use the resources available in the patients' family and social environment. Unlike residential therapeutic protocols, in which patients leave their home in order to benefit from services delivered in a residential facility, outpatients stay closely in contact with their family and social fabric. This, on the one hand, may complicate things in the beginning, but, on the other hand, curbs and reduces problems that inevitably arise when, after a period of residential treatment, patients go back home. Needless to say, this is not a general rule, but it applies when it is sustainable[1] for patients to stay in their own environment during the treatment period. So, considering and – when necessary and possible – involving the patients' significant persons is an additional task and at the same time an additional resource in therapy. This attention for the social context is in keeping with the relational paradigm that we have adopted (see Chapter 2) and distinguishes significantly this type of psychological treatment from the classical approach. Psychotherapy becomes flexible and pliable, as the most suitable settings and tools are chosen on a case-by-case basis. Every intervention is based on the understanding that patients, their problems and treatment are not isolated elements but part of a system and must be addressed accordingly.

From this perspective, individuals are never isolated but part of a social and cultural context to which they belong, which influence and are influenced by the disorder in a circular fashion (Morin, 1990; Vygotsky, 1934). How and when the context should become actively involved in the therapeutic process varies depending on the circumstances and on the therapist's sensitivity and ability to work with individual, family, and group relational dynamics.

The original work hypothesis

I had to reflect more systematically on the procedures I was using when I began sharing my working model and collaborating with colleagues. In particular, in 1998, some colleagues from the Associazione di Psicoterapia Cognitiva and I established a working group for the purpose of combining individual and group models in outpatient clinical practice and of conducting a naturalistic research study to investigate treatment outcome (Fassone, Ivaldi and Rocchi, 2003; Ivaldi *et al.*, 2007).

The patient population we worked with presented various forms of Axis I or Axis I/II comorbid disorders. Some of these are common (eating disorders associated with panic disturbances, and/or dissociative disorders, and/or mood disorders) (Rosenvinge *et al.*, 2000; Zanarini *et al.*, 1998; Oldham *et al.*, 1995; Fassone, Ivaldi and Rocchi, 2003) and, like borderline personality disorder, are associated with a persistent impairment of adaptation and psychosocial functioning. Such forms of comorbidity, which are very similar to the borderline 'dimension' or 'functioning' even though they do not fully meet the DSM-IV category diagnostic criteria for BPD, raise the same problems in relation to the possibility of accessing effective treatment, maintaining it over time, and drawing significant benefits from it in psychopathological and social adaptation terms.

We felt it would be legitimate to assume that a large portion of these patients, together with BPDs and patients with dissociative disorders, represented a relatively homogenous clinical population which followed an etiopathogenic *continuum* characterized by a high exposure to intrafamily traumatic experiences (in the patient and/or *caregiver*), insecure attachment (especially 'disorganized') (Main and Hesse 1990; Lyons-Ruth and Jacobvitz, 1999), as well as temperamental factors like affective instability and the tendency for impulsiveness (Liotti *et al.*, 2000; Pasquini *et al.*, 2002; Battle *et al.*, 2004; Agrawal *et al.*, 2004; Paris, 1994).

From this perspective, it was useful to hypothesize that at least some forms of clinical 'disorganization' (or comorbidities) could represent an epiphenomenon of attachment disorganization (Liotti et al., 2000). On the basis of these theoretical-clinical assumptions, I created a treatment model: the relational/multi-motivational therapeutic approach (REMOTA) for the treatment of patients belonging to this dimensional, etiopathogenic, and psychopathological *continuum* (Ivaldi, 1998; Ivaldi, et al., 2000; Fassone, Ivaldi and Rocchi, 2003).

The original work hypothesis was that patients with BPD or certain morbidity clusters present a disorganized attachment system (Liotti, 1994/2005, 1999; Solomon and George, 1999) that interferes with the establishment and maintenance of a therapeutic relationship, because the attachment system is activated in psychotherapy. Disorganized attachment may give rise to a chaotic relationship, resulting in treatment failure: treatment interruptions, depletion of the sources of treatment. It appeared necessary to protect the therapeutic setting more so than with other patients. One way of protecting the patient and therapist against the destructive effects of such phenomena is to work in a combined setting with an integrated team of experts in order to manage the effects of the dysfunctional activation of the attachment system, as can be inferred from the studies published in literature (see Chapter 5).

The individual and group psychotherapy model that I have created over the past eight years seems to make it possible to curb the relational difficulties described above, judging from clinical experience and from some encouraging results – such as the decline in these patients' drop-out rate – that were published in an uncontrolled naturalistic study (Fassone, Ivaldi and Rocchi, 2003; Ivaldi *et al.*, 2007). In particular, the combination of individual and group therapy delivered by the same therapist seems to allow for a more effective use of the therapeutic relationship (Ivaldi, 1998; Intreccialagli and Ivaldi, 2003; Ivaldi, 2009), promoting better affect regulation (Linehan, 1993) and an improvement in the skills that underpin the mentalization process (Bateman, Fonagy, 2004). Over the years, the treatment model was perfected not only in terms of its structure but also of the possible developments of the therapeutic relationship, becoming progressively enriched by new contributions coming from theory, research, and clinical experience with patients. It was always clear to me that, while it was necessary to protect the therapeutic setting, it was likewise necessary to explore new forms of treatment in order to better respond to the needs expressed by the population of 'difficult' patients. In this sense, although organizing team work and co-therapy proved indispensable, it did not replace the effort required to rethink the therapeutic relationship so that it would be more complex and more in keeping with the needs and difficulties displayed by patients with a traumatic attachment history. From the very outset, this work model has devoted utmost attention to the therapeutic alliance process. From 1998 up until today, the new thrust given by theories on trauma and dissociation have greatly reassured me in terms of the assumptions I had set out from, and further enriched my reflections and way of working.

The structure of the dual setting REMOTA: a simple structure for a complex process

Combined individual and group psychotherapy is organized and presented to patients as one treatment: an individual session and a group session once a week.

Treatment begins with individual therapy; the patient is followed by the therapist for about one year, or for the time needed for the therapeutic couple to build an alliance strong enough to endure difficult moments in the relationship. During this initial phase, the therapist focuses on evaluating the problem presented, identifying the patient's personal resources, and understanding the patient's affective context (contacts with the family and/or school setting, social workers, or others), which will become part of the therapeutic network. From the outset, psychopharmacological treatment is integrated into the therapeutic program. The team psychiatrist is also a psychotherapist and is responsible for dealing with emotional regulation, not only through the use of drugs.

A moderate use of the telephone is allowed, or rather negotiated.

After the initial phase, which lasts from a few months up to one year, the therapist and patient decide to begin the group, alternating group and individual sessions. The criteria for determining when the patient is ready to join a group will be discussed hereinafter. The group session lasts two hours and is conducted by two co-therapists, the same who follow the patients in individual therapy. The groups are 'open' (there is a turnover in patients) and composed of six–eight patients.

All group sessions are tape recorded and filmed, filed, and made available to both patients and therapists. These recordings serve as a therapeutic tool, which may be used by the patients to focus and reflect on some interactions on their own as well as with the individual therapist, with whom they can discuss what they have observed.

Watching the videos with the patients makes it possible to pick up many aspects of implicit communication that are not accessible during the session. When the relational climate is genuinely collaborative, the complicity and trust that characterize it enable highly effective joint exploration that involves a comprehensive bodily and sensory experience. When we observe ourselves in a video, we often perceive ourselves differently than we did during the experience; our voice, for instance, sounds different when we listen to it on a recording than it does when we are talking. Basically, the impact with kinesthetic, prosodic, and proxemic aspects of communication engages the body intensely in the *here and now* and favours the processing of memories that are not easily accessed through cognitive work. Experiences thus induced correspond to the first levels of construction of the sense of self with other and with the world (primary and secondary intersubjectivity). Many contributions of infant research, particularly those of Beebe (1986, 2000; Beebe *et al.*, 2002), are based on the use of video recordings, implicit communication, and the use of the body in the therapeutic relationship. This is in keeping with the new *bottom up* working strategies afforded by the new psychotherapeutic models relating to trauma and dissociation (Ogden, Minton and Pain, 2006; Siegel, 1999: Shapiro, 1995).

The therapeutic relationship and its complexity

While the double setting structure is simple, the therapeutic relationship that is developed instead is highly complex and requires adequate skills and flexibility.

Before going into the various phases of treatment and its peculiar features, in the following paragraphs I will focus on how the therapeutic relationship is understood in the relational/multi-motivational approach and on the analytic attitude that favours an effective psychotherapeutic relationship.

In the therapeutic process the relationship is always active; it represents the framework within which every transaction and act takes place and acquires meaning, in a process of change that is never standard but always different and unique. This process of change involves both patient and therapist, in different ways and to differing degrees. The therapist enters into the life of the patient and becomes part of the story and a protagonist of that story, while respecting his or her role. The case formulation is therefore a narrative that is permeated by feelings that bear witness to the existence and to the nature of the relationship between therapist and patient.

*

SOFIA (1)

I first met Sofia five years ago. When she came into my office she looked just like a lion: a Junoesque woman of thirty-six, with a mane of thick and unruly red hair, and an open, genuine, and compelling smile. The first words she spoke were an invitation to engage with her in an authentic relationship and an ironic sharing of the experience she was about to relate.

Irony came naturally to her, what with her being a real 'toscanaccia' (genuine Tuscan woman), and she had capitalized on her ease in communicating, turning it into a profession. In the past she had worked as a journalist. Sofia had been living in Rome for many years and had bought a home there, because she intended to stay. Up until four years before, she had managed to secure contracts, with mixed fortunes and ups and downs. But the crisis had come down hard on her industry and with the passing of time her freelance work gradually dried up; in the past year, she had been virtually unemployed. Sofia did not have financial problems, though. Fortunately/unfortunately she was the only child of wealthy parents who were now in retirement, but who, up until two years before, had owned and run a small business in the tourist industry. Their business had always been successful, thanks to their knowhow and hard work, which Sofia appreciated and criticized at the same time.

'They always put work first, customers came before anything else – me and my needs for sure.'

Her parents did well for themselves so that they could now enjoy a comfortable life with no financial worries and allow Sofia to live off of private income.

This made her grateful and resentful at the same time, because it created a bond fraught with contradictions and affective blackmail, which characterized her relationship with her parents.

Just as readily as the glow of her smile and hair filled my office, so did the tears begin to flow. I remember the sense of fragility, the tenderness and liking I felt in the face of such generosity. Sofia dried her tears and continued talking, as if nothing could stop her. Certainly not fear!

'You see doctor, I feel terrible, I can't find peace with men! The reason I'm here is that nobody wants me! Or rather, they leave me.'

She told me a long story of sentimental failures, alternating ironic puns and hearty laughs with tears and dramatic overtones.

She had married a man who now worked in show business and their love story had started like a *'fairytale'* only to end shortly after the *'fairytale wedding'*. Sofia had gone out of her way to salvage the relationship, but her efforts had been to no avail.

'We were on a beautiful beach during our honeymoon, doctor, when I asked him dreamily, "Would you do it all again?" and he answered, "I don't know." It was like a cold shower!'

Hence began the decline, and the months that followed were characterized by the lack of desire on his part and by his absences. Sofia told me that she felt terrible and had started putting on weight, which only made things worse. Her physical condition justified – also according to her parents – the fact that her husband was drifting away.

'My parents always find something wrong with me, especially my mother! She looks like a girl, super skinny, my exact opposite. The best of it is that she would want me to be like her. She doesn't like me the way I am.'

Sofia kept repeating that there was something wrong with her, that she wasn't okay and that, basically, no one cared about her.

She fluctuated between discouragement and sadness – because she thought it was only natural that people should not want her since she was not loveable – and anger – sustained by a weaker sense that others were 'shits', hurt her, and, most of all, did not understand her.

I realized that I too fluctuated: I felt tenderness and concern for her when she felt unworthy and dejected, while I understood her anger when she thought that others did not understand her and hurt her. Something told me that I had to make an effort not to adhere completely to either of the two experiences and stay light, grazing my emotions, like a butterfly fluttering above flowers, trying to stay up in the air, coasting above, in order to see more things at the same time from a bird's eye view.

*

How does a relationship differ from a therapeutic relationship?

If it is true that the therapist enters into the patient's story, what place does the therapeutic relationship have in the life of the two protagonists? This question emerges spontaneously, and, throughout the history of psychoanalysis, it has received different answers, depending on the theoretical and conceptual frame of reference (see Chapter 2).

The relational approach, which underpins the REMOTA model, has introduced a theory of psychopathology and treatment that is based on relationships understood as mutuality and reciprocity (Greenberg and Mitchell, 1983).

In keeping with the intersubjective theory, and in the wake of multi-motivational theories (Lichtenberg, 1983, 1989; Liotti, 1989), the relationship is regarded as a space in which the two interlocutors give rise to the clinical dialogue and which becomes the object of joint exploration. In this case, emotions are read and understood as an expression of each individual's inborn basic motivations.

The relationship between therapist and patient is no doubt dense with emotivity and is invariably characterized by the patient's request for help; such a request may be controversial, even ambivalent, but is always present. The therapist, who has acquired knowledge on how the human mind works and on psychopathologic processes in the course of his or her training, is always vigilant and attentive, in a constant effort to capture the emotional phenomena that fill the therapy room. The therapist is constantly seeking to understand the other, his or her requests, and how he or she functions. Above and beyond all the information, historic data, symptomatic signs, and cognitive processing, what is most interesting and enlightening about what happens to the patient involves what happens to the therapist with the patient. The therapist's main task therefore consists in understanding emotions, and that is what characterizes his or her role in the relationship with the patient. Working through emotions, understanding and modulating them together with the patient in order to enable the patient to feel him/herself, take possession of parts of him/herself that are experienced as alien, be aware and be able to regain a sound sense of self, is at the very heart of the therapeutic relationship.

If psychopathology is understood as the various manifestations of consciousness disorders (Ey, 1975; Edelman, 1992; Damasio, 1994), it is easier to understand that the cure lies in the relationship with the curer, and is proportionate to the degree to which consciousness is activated, developed, reactivated, and dwells in an interpersonal dimension (Liotti, 1994/2005; Lichtenberg, 1983, 1989). The therapeutic quality of the relationship will depend on the degree to which the therapist empathizes and attunes with the patient; this will enable both to build a new affective scenario, within which the patient's problematic past can be explored and understood, actualized in the present relationship with the possibility of living significant alternative experiences (Ivaldi, 2004, 2009).

*

SOFIA (2)

When Sofia came to me for help she was frantically seeking bonds: she chatted on the internet and sometimes got together with the people she met on the web. After a few preliminary meetings, during which she told me a little about herself, our sessions focused primarily on what was happening in her love life.

When she talked about her men, Sofia cried rivers of tears. She talked about them as if she were deeply involved and suffered terribly because her feelings were unrequited. Sofia inevitably thought about having a serious relationship and making life plans with any man she happened to be going out with.

I was particularly struck by the naiveté with which she lived this aspect of her life: she seemed ill-equipped and surprised by the fact that many of the men she chatted with were mostly looking for occasional sex. By and by, as our sessions continued, her depression grew deeper, as did her difficulty in regulating emotions. She cried and asked insistently, *'What am I doing wrong? Am I wrong?'* It was no use trying to reflect together on the various aspects of the problem she raised. Sofia did not seem to be willing to drag things out, she was looking for 'the solution' and, at times, she wanted it right away. She was tired of hurting and was impatient with everyone, including me.

She did not say as much, but I sensed it strongly. I imagined that she harboured such thoughts as, 'Here's another one who makes me talk, I tell her things, but there's nothing she can do. Yes, she's patient, she's far too good with me, but she doesn't understand that I'm a disaster, that she should make me change! Otherwise what will become of me?'

I was obviously aware of the fact that my attempt to linger high up above, not delving into any experience entirely, could be rather frustrating for her, but I felt that it would be more dangerous for our relationship if I did otherwise. While I took the time I needed to understand and reflect, she acted and asked for quick answers; she did not seem to have time to spare!

*

I had the feeling that Sofia was unable to combine several emotional shades regarding one person or relationship; she appeared to focus at different moments on different experiences but was then unable to hold them all together in an organic synthesis that would define the overall experience. This corresponds to the dissociative phenomenon of *compartmentalization* (Holmes *et al.*, 2005).

*

During the sessions in which we were not pressed by the emergency of the day, we managed to talk about what was happening to us and I could explain to her how I was feeling and what my thoughts were in relation to her emergencies; I also talked to her about the therapeutic direction we were moving in, in order to negotiate it with her as much as possible. At times she followed me and seemed to agree but then she would inevitably be overwhelmed by a desperate feeling of alarm, as a result of which she would act impulsively and then blame herself, feeling helpless.

*

What analytic attitude on the part of the psychotherapist can promote the development of significant therapeutic experiences?

Before discussing the individual phases of treatment, I would like to say something in general about the personal and professional characteristics of the therapist that can favour the therapeutic alliance. I am referring to characteristics, not specific interventions – as one would find in a manual – because I believe that the most important thing a therapist can do is prepare him/herself to become a *therapeutic instrument* (Ivaldi, 2004; Ivaldi *et al.*, 2007). I have always been persuaded that the relationship that is established at the implicit level is essential and that mentalization, empathy, and authenticity are not acquired through formulas or technical advice. They should flow naturally from a sound development within an affective family setting that favours it, and from the ability to see with a critical eye how the culture and customs of the 'world system' which we are born into and live in influence us. In order to function at the best of our abilities and to enhance the skills that we are genetically endowed with, us psychotherapists – just like our patients – are called to fill the gaps of our less than ideal development. We must also reckon with the contexts in which we work, in which we live, in which others live; we have to consider the rules and principles which these contexts rest on and how they have influenced us, our development, and that of others. Our reflective capacity allows us to be aware of where we are, with respect to what and whom, where and when. From the perspective of the hierarchical functioning of the mind, it is possible to have different experiences of consciousness which respond to the different levels of sophistication of the *categorization* of information (Edelman, 1989), which, in turn, correspond to the different levels of phylogenetic evolution of the human species: from the most basic episodic mind – *primary consciousness* – to the most complex theoretical mind – *self-consciousness*. This is the level to which corresponds the sense of *cultural affiliation* (Ceccarelli, 2005); we can recognize our world because we know other worlds, so it is possible to distinguish and define, by means of constructive critical thinking, the characteristics of our own cultural context.

This raises interesting questions as to what psychotherapy is about, and what role the cultural, economic, and political system which we and our patients live in can play. Turning our attention to the context to which the patient belongs and to the context in which we meet the patient allows us to better understand the patient's problem and request, and the meaning that we could give to the treatment process we will undertake. In the therapeutic relationship that I propose – starting from motivational theories, which point out the universal transcultural invariants that characterize human relational functioning and serve as a point of departure, a limit in which we recognize each other as similar in order to explore – we turn our attention to the multitude of variables that characterize the experience with each individual person that seeks our help. This enables a process of mutual recognition and makes it possible to distinguish that relationship from all others, making it unique and significant. We will therefore ask ourselves what therapeutic experience we will be able to establish with a given patient, what will we be able to negotiate with that patient and how.

How the therapist trains for the complexity of the relationship

Being in a relationship requires personal training for dealing with complexity. As we learn the theory (of reference), we must train constantly in order to learn to listen, to establish empathic contact, which allows us to slowly and procedurally develop the ability to become a *therapeutic instrument*. Training also involves learning to accept the frustration we may sometimes experience when we are unable to grasp some elements of experience and to accept our limits. For a therapist, coming to terms with one's limits is just as important as empathizing. It is risky to think that we have learned everything there is to know about complex human functioning. I think that no matter how hard we strive to achieve this, we never stop learning.

In order to help someone to make therapeutic strides, we need a reference theory by means of which we can try to understand suffering, and we have to be able to see someone past the theories; but we must also be aware of what those strides are and what they entail. In this sense, personal experience is crucial.

Our work requires a combination of theoretical knowhow, specific technical skills, and human skills in a broader sense.

In conducting therapy, we must be aware that our patients will perceive our values and our way of being, whether we like it or not. We must keep this in mind and consider that our profession and our life must be in harmony, just as for our patients there has be harmony between their life and therapy. Therapists must come to recognize their personal characteristics and develop their empathic and reflective potential.

*

SOFIA (3)

For several months, during our sessions we talked about the sentimental events of the moment and some facts from her past, until one day, when she was chatting on the web, Franco came into her life. She became deeply involved with him and their relationship left even less room for our reflections. I had the feeling that we were gathering speed and that the situation was becoming increasingly dangerous.

We were not equipped to go so fast! It was like racing in the Grand Prix with a Cinquecento.

From Sofia's stories, Franco came across as an ambiguous, elusive man with a shady past and an uncertain present. He told Sofia that he belonged to the army elite corps, which is why every now and then he would disappear and could not be reached for days. He said that he could not talk to her about his job because that would endanger her, but he constantly mentioned, offered snapshots of violent and unsettling experiences, which made Sofia think that 'poor Franco' was traumatized and that she could save him. Sofia was confused but captivated by this man; his mysteries made her anxious and intrigued her at the same time. Sofia tried to tighten the bond and find greater intimacy with him. She wanted to know more and wanted their relationship to be out in the open, but it was an uphill climb. She found out from him that he was separated and had a son, but it was only much later that Sofia discovered that he was not legally separated. A great deal more time passed before she tried to make their relationship official. The more Sofia discovered about him, the less likely it seemed that Franco worked for the elite corps, while what gradually emerged was his financial instability and outstanding debts, which Sofia, with her natural generosity and impulsiveness, made the mistake of helping him out with. She lent Franco a substantial sum, which he promised to pay back as soon as he would cash in some payments and, needless to say, never did. Sofia was often angry with her parents because they were somewhat perplexed by this relationship, without even knowing the details. Sofia was used to arguing with her parents and was convinced that they would stand in her way no matter what, *'as they had always done in the past'*.

Sofia wanted to stay with Franco at all costs, build a family, have a child with him. She fought with her parents to get them to accept this relationship, without considering for a moment that their doubts might be reasonable. For some time Sofia took medication, which was prescribed by a psychiatrist I had referred her to: she took antidepressants and mood stabilizers, benzodiazepines when necessary. Understandably, she had mixed feelings about the pharmacological treatment and the person who prescribed it, which is why she switched psychiatrist several times in the course of her therapy. I always tried to collaborate with the colleagues I knew, but I have to admit that more than one responded emotionally to Sofia with impatience.

How could they not? It was hard to keep up with her swings and her frustration at not getting better; I too was frustrated by the fact that I could not get her to slow down. I tried to explain that at that speed we did not have time to go deeper and improve the way she functioned.

This made Sofia feel that she could not be helped. I thought I could read her mind: 'It's useless. I'm a disaster, no-one can help me, there's no way out.'

*

The X factor

The leading clinicians of different schools and with different theoretical backgrounds achieve good results: why? Perhaps the answer lies in the so-called *x factor*, that is, a variable that is mostly unknown and hard to investigate, something like a natural talent that enables one to do this work well. I would like to dwell on this topic, because it is not at all secondary for the good progress of therapy. Researchers speak of it as a variable that is hard to use in research on psychotherapy, because it is elusive and too subjective. But, as we all know, it is the most important variable.

What are the qualities that constitute the x factor? Surely good intuition, the ability to be empathic, *knowing how to be* in the sense of staying connected in the present moment with the person who is with us, attuning ourselves and following our commitment to monitor and reflect on what we are experiencing, by ourselves and with the patient (Stern, 1985; Siegel, 1999; Lichtenberg, 2005).

Referring to a familiar concept, we could speak of mentalization: the ability to be in touch with our emotions and with those of the other, knowing how to decipher them, making sense of what is being experienced (Bateman and Fonagy, 2000; Di Maggio and Semerari, 2003).

It may sound easy, but in actual fact therapists should not only be naturally inclined to do this but, as multi-motivational theories inform us, they should cultivate this natural gift and sustain it through training.

Training is the most complex aspect of the theory because, as I see it, it requires knowledge of relational functioning and its phylogenetic and ontogenetic value, which helps us to understand what needs to be trained and how. It also requires a process of personal development in order that we may become more aware of who we are, of our story, and of our vulnerabilities. By process of personal development I do not just mean analysis, but all the life experiences and the abilities to reflect on these experiences which favour an ongoing learning process and the disposition for exploration.

All good clinicians are naturally inclined to explore, venture, protecting themselves as much as possible, though not completely. This delicate balance between security and risk comes into play in the salient moments of a therapeutic relationship.

*

SOFIA (4)

Our relationship was languishing; I could feel it. I tried to talk about other aspects of her life and herself that were not closely related to her sentimental sphere, but she reverted obsessively to the relationship with Franco.

One afternoon I was working in my office when I received a text message from her:

'Dr. Ivaldi, I don't think our sessions are helping me much, so I've decided to take a break. Regards, Sofia.'

I remember how quickly anger built up inside of me. She was abandoning me! It really felt like I was being abandoned, without having the opportunity to respond. Seconds later, though, I became alarmed. *'Has something happened? Is this a desperate cry for help?'* I wondered. I decided not to wait and called her. She did not answer. I sent her a text message: *'Dear Sofia, I'm very surprised by your message, has something happened? Whatever the problem may be, I'd like to discuss it with you. I don't think our relationship deserves to be dismissed with a message.'*

She called back and the conversation became heated.

P: *Doctor, it's Sofia.*
T: *Sofia what's the matter? I'm surprised . . .*
P: *(interrupting me) . . . Nothing's the matter, doctor, I just don't see any change and have decided to quit* (she sounded upset).
T: *But . . . I'm surprised by your decision, especially by how you're communicating it to me. I don't understand, why tell me with a text message? Just like that, with no explanation and without having had a chance to talk . . . I don't . . .*
P: *(she interrupted me again, sounding even more upset) . . . But doctor! What do you want me to say? I find your reaction strange, it's as if we were lovers! You're acting like a spurned lover! . . .* (she laughed nervously).
T: *It's odd that you don't understand my reaction, considering that you have often felt abandoned yourself and know how it feels. Don't you think it's strange*

that this is happening between us? I don't question your decision, but how you're communicating it. I think we've always been able to talk, why not do it this time?
P: I don't believe this! Two lovers, that's what we're like . . . there's nothing to talk about, I've made my decision.
T: Not just lovers feel bound. We've known each other for almost a year, Sofia, I can't be indifferent to what's happening. I called you because I didn't want to remain suspended, wondering what went wrong, and because I was worried about you. You've made a rash decision, I'm telling you I'm sorry we didn't have a chance to discuss this.
P: All right, I may not have communicated it to you in the best way, but this is my decision.

Our telephone conversation haunted me all night. I kept wondering what had happened. Had I perhaps come too close for her disorganized IWM? Had I made a mistake in calling her? Had I acted impulsively? After all, she had sent me a text message to keep her distance. I was having one of those moments when I question my behaviour, wondering whether it was appropriate or whether I had perhaps overstepped the bounds. Did I break the rules that govern a psychotherapeutic, psychoanalytic or other setting, and venture into unchartered territory?

I was sure that I would never hear from her again, and this made me very angry and upset. Instead, four months later, she called back.

P: *Doctor, do you remember me?* (with a sweet and subdued tone).
T: *Sofia! Of course I remember you* (I answered impulsively with enthusiasm).
P: *Well, doctor, I'm calling because I need your help. Can you receive me?*
T: *Of course, Sofia. How are you? What happened?*
P: *Lots of stuff, I'll tell you in person. I'm pregnant.*
T: *Oh!* (I was surprised. I could not tell whether this was good or bad news for her, but I did not want to discuss it over the phone). *Are you still with Franco?*
P: *Yes, yes. That's the problem* (in tears), *doctor please help me!*

I was really happy to hear from her again. We scheduled an appointment and when we met I realized that she was glad to see me too, although she felt guilty. I found out that she had interrupted her therapy because she had started seeing another analyst, who had been recommended to her, but she was not happy with him either. She asked me to forgive her and to take her back as a patient.

P: *Doctor, I got pregnant and now it's all a mess!*
T: *How does Franco feel about it?*
P: *I don't know, he doesn't say that I should have an abortion but he doesn't say anything about what we should do. I don't think he intends to make any final decisions. I'm scared, doctor, I don't know what to do. I don't want to raise a child by myself. I couldn't do it!*

I decided not to dwell too much on what had happened between us, on the meaning of her actions and behaviours in relation to her issues; there would be time for that. We were in an emergency situation again, this time we were grappling with a very difficult decision to make.

*

The therapist's ability to see his or her own vulnerability, which is inherent to human nature, is a crucial element that reverberates implicitly in the relationship with the patient, conveying a sense of familiarity and equality that is essential in order to get close. How analyst and patient will get close will depend on their personality, characteristics, and difficulties, and will be the focus of the therapeutic relational process.

During training, a therapist must therefore familiarize with vulnerability. Accepting our vulnerabilities is what comes hardest for us, and yet, just like relatedness, it is a biological imperative that we cannot escape.

Therapists are also called to reckon with shame. We live in the Western world, in a highly competitive social, political, and cultural environment. Our own judgement and that of others often dominates the relational scene. As long as we are driven by the need to prove ourselves and to be judged positively, we are not free to be and therefore to stay genuinely in touch with someone. Consider how important this is for us therapists. How can we stay in the present moment with another person in the room if we do not feel free to be what we are? Worrying about having to prove ourselves often diverts our energies and attention from what we are experiencing with the other person. The anxiety of having to perform, appear, hide, or protect ourselves captures our senses, ensnares our mind and does not allow conscious experience to flow.

The intuitive and empathic process is blocked if our senses are not open to perceiving, possibly suspending judgement. That is why a personal development process is necessary, during which we learn to *be* and to *be seen by the other*, without letting ourselves be influenced by fear or shame.

The experience of being seen is crucial in our training. In order for a relationship to cure, an alliance has to be created and one of the essential elements for this is authenticity, that is, the ability to be rather than to appear or to show. It is a little like imagining – metaphorically speaking – that you 'stand naked' before the patient, to indicate how important it is for us to free ourselves from the 'garments that cover us' and sometimes prevent us from achieving true intimacy (Ivaldi, 2008). 'Standing naked' does not mean displaying your emotions, showing off and taking centre the stage; on the contrary, it means not worrying about having to hide your limits and weaknesses, being aware of them, though not focusing your attention on them, and allowing your attention (consciousness) to flow in the interaction with the other.

'A sort of inhibition, paradoxically, a withdrawal of the individual that allows reality to manifest itself' (Translated from M. Zambrano, 2008, *Per l'amore e per la Libertà: scritti sulla filosofia e sull'educazione*, p. 52).

If we use our senses and our mind freely, smoothly, we have greater chances of living experience to the full, staying in touch and journeying with the other. Being open to exploration, being flexible, knowing that we are seen and not feeling the need to hide, suspending judgement, being passionate and curious, riding uncertainty and risk with some degree of safety, not fearing mistakes but knowing how to put them to good use, being creative: these are some of the characteristics that are at the basis of a good therapeutic disposition. It is not necessary to be all of these things at once, for that would be very hard indeed, but it is important to tend towards this, knowing what direction to move in and getting our bearings in order to train our own relatedness to become effective.

I believe it is crucial for a therapist to know and to consider powerlessness, pain, the states that we are so afraid of but are an integral part of life. It is important to be able to stand by our patients when they go through these experiences, modulating fear, recognizing the value of *pietas* and comfort; a gentle caress when there is nothing else we can do. It is likewise important to know that these states exist, even when we do not experience them directly, because knowing it influences the sense of daily experience, gives it vitality. This attitude is in contrast with the tendency towards solitude and the denial of vulnerabilities that are typical of the modern technocratic and mechanistic culture, which is alienating for the individual.

Taking care of someone cannot be a technique, or a therapeutic manoeuvre that we find in a manual and repeat mechanically. Taking care of someone can only be the natural consequence of our having attention and regard for the other. That is why it is essential that we consider the relationship with a patient as an affective relationship, which has clear bounds but is significant for us, so that we may develop a natural intention to take care of others, which is not regarded as a professional duty.

'When the other becomes a real opportunity for me, that is when I give care' (Noddings, 1984, p. 14).

We should grasp the vulnerable essence of our nature, learn to embrace it and take care of it in order to do our job. We can care for the other if we care for ourselves and the world. This, as I see it, is the hardest thing we are called to do in our work and our life. But if we are able to live this we can recognize and use our skills to respond and to change things, whenever possible. We have to accept powerlessness dialectically in order to feel assertive and vital.

In recent years, the contribution of *mindfulness* (of Buddhist origin) has become increasingly widespread. I am convinced that mindfulness is just one way to train ourselves to *stay in touch*. But we have to recognize and enhance this inborn relational disposition in the course of our personal and professional development. The aspect of being in touch with our vulnerabilities is present in all dimensions of spirituality and in religions. This leads us to reflect on the functions of meditation and prayer, which is not just about turning to a God – an *extrema ratio* to find comfort – but probably has to do with stopping in our daily race and re-establishing contact with ourselves and the world, being aware of our limits. Going back to the original condition in which we are born and die, as beings that do not fully know their destiny, the time we are given to live, and the sense of life which – in spite of our inevitable personal quest – remains, for the most part, a mystery.

*

FROM SOFIA'S VIGNETTE

One morning like many others, my cell phone rang. It was Sofia's mother. I recognized that tone of voice and shivers ran up my spine.

'Doctor, she's not answering the phone. We're in the car, on our way to Rome, we're worried. Franco is going home to check, he told me they had an argument.'

I immediately felt weak, listless. I sank into my armchair and it took me a while to come round. For years I had been working with people with personality disorders, at risk. In that moment of dejection, I thought about the most qualified treatments for 'difficult patients' that were developed in the oases of model clinics, where patients and therapists are protected by the structure, rules, protocol, and the great deal of attention that is devoted to the quality of work to ensure that it be excellent, in order to evaluate its efficacy. I thought about how different that is from working with outpatients – the responsibilities and risks one is exposed to, the stress. My first thoughts were, 'I got it all wrong! Did I fail to understand her? Maybe I should have treated her differently. Should she have received intensive treatment, been institutionalized? And yet it seemed to be working.' I was overwhelmed by doubts, but then I thought of the many times I had followed patients who had been institutionalized and, once home, back to their everyday life, had lost the benefits gained from intensive treatment; of how often patients in highly controlled wards commit suicide in the most incredible ways. It is hard to accept that we are powerless. Helplessness, anger, fear, weariness: I had experienced all this and more in those days – and in other days – of my professional life.

This time Sofia had swallowed almost an entire bottle of benzodiazepines; the situation was not as serious as the previous time. She stayed in the hospital only 24 hours and, once home, slept for two days straight, with her parents and Franco watching over her. I was constantly in touch with them; I was still their only point of reference, since they had never spoken with the psychiatrist back home, who was rather strict about time and contacts. We met again, feeling dejected, with only one question spinning in our mind: Why?

*

The first phase of treatment: individual therapy

The relationship between patients and their individual therapist is the backbone of the treatment. The support network – co-therapists, psychiatrists – is important for both patients and caretakers, but it does not replace the individual therapist, who is always the main point of reference for patients throughout their journey and accompanies them in the various treatment phases: from the individual setting to the group experience, until the end of therapy.

*

ELSA (1)

What are your eyes telling me?

The referring colleague had said to me: *'She's been removing her eyelashes ever since she was ten.'* It therefore comes as no surprise when, greeting her at our first session, I meet Elsa's intense and vulnerable gaze. An accurate and teasing streak of eyeliner marks her eyes, which, notwithstanding, appear overly exposed, unprotected.

Elsa is a bright 36-year-old woman, who is bilingual and gifted with remarkable artistic skills. She has changed jobs several times in her lifetime and is currently unemployed. She has been separated for approximately one year and now lives with her current partner in the house of her former husband, whom she is no longer in touch with. Elsa's sentimental life has been characterized by great turbulence, ferocious quarrels with outbursts of verbal and physical violence during which, according to Elsa's accounts, she turns into a 'monstrous' person, capable of harming herself and others uncontrollably. In describing herself this way Elsa is warning me that she is dangerous, but she is also communicating her fears, all the while observing me closely to determine whether I am scared or am sending reassuring signs revealing my willingness to accept her as a patient and help her.

This exchange sums up the essence of the therapeutic dialogue. It is on this that the alliance between Elsa and me will be based – and indispensable bridge towards healing. That scrutinizing gaze, at once fearful and threatening, will always expect a response from me, read it in my eyes, past the words that I will speak. Elsa expresses her fear of wrecking the therapy by enacting behaviours of attack and/or escape, as she does compulsively in relationships in general. I tell her that we must address this fear and that in our first sessions we will need to define the space that we will be working in and create all the possible protections for the therapeutic work that awaits us.

*

A relational therapist regards any exchange with the patient – from the initial phone call, to the first session, to the last – as part of psychotherapy. However, for traumatized and complicated patients it is impossible to ask for and to receive help without experiencing difficulties or, in some cases, without feeling endangered. With these patients, the beginning of therapy may be extremely demanding and hard to handle. In such cases, it is extremely important that the beginning of therapy not be taken for granted;

rather, we must engage the patient in a joint evaluation process for the purpose of building together the working space by means of negotiation. Setting the relational boundaries without taking for granted ideas, biases, and personal theories on the therapeutic process in general and on the nascent therapeutic relationship in particular can protect the relationship itself against the activation of dramatic disorganized attachment IWMs.

Setting and relationship: negotiating the therapeutic alliance

In the REMOTA (Ivaldi, 1998, 2009; Ivaldi, Foggetti and Aringolo, 2009), *negotiation* and *alliance* are expressions of the dynamic nature of the relationship between therapist and patient, in which each individual's particular way of functioning (IWM) – which is the main focus of therapeutic work – emerges. In my experience, the alliance cannot disregard the attachment motivation and does not merely involve the activation of the collaborative motivation; rather, it is the result of a harmonious synthesis – made each time by therapist and patient – of the different combinations of motivational systems that are active in the relationship, based on the priorities required by the circumstances, the therapeutic context, the patient's context of life, and the resources at play. Naturally, the therapist will prepare the relational field in such a way as to foster cooperation, but this will require a process: a series of experiences that bridge the distance between patient and therapist, while their influences, fears, and difficulties will come to the fore.

The first important characteristic of the model is the use of the relational therapeutic process to define the *contract* that is negotiated in the course of therapy. Step by step, the therapist strives to identify the relational space with the patient. The boundaries of this space are gradually marked by the therapeutic couple, bearing in mind the necessary safety margins and the increased ability to mentalize (Bateman and Fonagy, 2000). The boundaries of the treatment relationship are established, priorities and objectives are set. The contract represents a sort of *common space* where it becomes possible for patient and therapist to work in a collaborative climate (Ivaldi, 2004, 2006, 2009). Clearly, the cooperative motivational dimension that can be activated at the end of treatment cannot be the same as that which is encouraged in the initial phase.

Working on the contract in the initial phase involves some important therapeutic steps that must be taken together:

- *Evaluation*: analysis of the referral, analysis of the patient's request, identification with the patient of his/her resources, those of his/her life context that may be useful to therapy, and the obstacles that may hinder it instead; analysis of the resources of the context in which therapy takes place.
- *Definition of the therapeutic plan*: analysis of the patient's expectations, explaining the intervention model, the advantages and limits of psychotherapy; identification and fine-tuning of personalized strategies to protect the setting.
- *Joint redefinition of the therapeutic goals.*

Mind functions, complexity and therapeutic attunement

When the capacity for combining and integrating the subjective experience is impaired, this process is especially complicated. People sometimes present us with chaotic multiplicity, which is indicative of an 'unconscious healing plan' (Weiss *et al.*, 1986). They probably want to attain the functioning complexity that we are all geared for, a 'healthy multiplicity' (Mitchell, 1988; Bromberg, 1998), which requires the ability to integrate the various aspects of reality. One of the most common consequences in people who suffer from such functioning deficits is the tendency to act, often impulsively, creating an emergency spiral that necessarily pulls in the therapeutic relationship, even if it has just come into being.

The possibility of establishing a therapeutic alliance is often played out in the very first minutes of therapy. Such is the case with many patients with whom the therapist immediately engages in an intense relationship (Ivaldi and Foggetti, 2012).

*

LUCIA (1)

Is this therapy already?

It is our first meeting: Lucia arrives in a state of great agitation and sits down with all her bags and packages, which she proceeds to set down next to the sofa.

She overwhelms me with a series of requests and considerations about herself, without giving me the opportunity to reply. She is clearly upset, worried, and angry.

P: You have to help me but I don't know whether you can or want to. I don't know if I can be helped. I'm a mess! Even my previous therapist, who eventually got sick of me, said as much. I'm 37 and I still don't have what women my age already have: children, a husband, a home. I'm a failure! What can I do? Am I a lost cause?

T: Lucia, tell me something more about yourself, because we don't know each other and I don't understand what your problem is very well.

P: (interrupting) I told you what my problem is! You have to help me move out on my own and live a normal life . . . What do you want me to tell you? I come from a hopeless family: my parents are divorced, my father left us, my mother complains and is sick all the time. How was I supposed to turn out? Will you tell me how I can forgive and get on with my life?

T: Who says that you have to forgive, and that all it takes is will power?

P: (interrupting) Everyone! My friends, Father X, the entire community!

T: Lucia, I need some information in order to understand your request. I see you're upset, at times desperate . . .

P: . . . that's right! Desperate, that's how I feel, but how would you feel in my place?

T: Let's consider your request and the most suitable possible solutions.

P: A few meetings just to understand? So when will I find a solution? You see, I can't stand this any longer!

It took a few months to do the evaluation work with Lucia. During that time, it was very difficult for me to talk with her and to negotiate our relationship. I felt that with Lucia it was hard for me to exist, to be seen. I had to raise my voice in order for her to listen to me.

*

The arousal level is very high in the room with Lucia, the pace of the conversation is extremely fast, and the atmosphere is charged with agitation, fear, and mistrust. It seems that in the patient's mind at least two opposite mental representations are present at the same time: the wish/need to be helped and the feeling that it is impossible for her to get help. During the first session Lucia immediately activates with her therapist an interpersonal pattern typical of the *drama triangle*.

The concept was introduced by Karpman (1968) for the purpose of describing relational dynamics, within the framework of the *Games People Play* theory (Berne, 1964). According to Berne, transactions are a measurement unit, chosen by convention, which applies to the communication process. The *game* is understood as a series of ulterior complementary transactions that progress towards a foreseeable and clear conclusion, known as the *final payoff*. This foreseeable conclusion consists of feelings – so-called parasites – that range from fear, sadness, powerlessness, and desperation (typical of the victim in fairytales and classical theatre), to anger and evil triumph (typical of the persecutor in fairytales and tragedies), to concern and compassion (typical of the saviour). The 'ulterior' transactions are characterized by the simultaneous presence of two inconsistent messages, an example being the interpersonal pattern that is activated between Lucia and her therapist: the *social message*, '*Help me!*' accompanied by the *psychological message*, '*You cannot help me, because: I am unworthy of help, no one will really want to help me, if I surrender myself I will be in danger, if you help me I will depend on you forever and you will hurt me, you are inept and vulnerable* (Ivaldi, 2004). This example of a transaction corresponds to what we expect to emerge from a disorganized IWM characterized by *fright without solution* (Main and Hesse, 1990) in the relationship with the person who should be offering help, for in such circumstances the parent is both the source of fear and the solution to that fear.

The shift between the different 'dramatic representations' can be very swift and will tend to increase in proportion to the unregulated state of arousal, like in Lucia's case. When it is impossible to regulate one's fear through a safe contact, one's metacognitive capacities decline, preventing the integration and synthesis of one's mental states (see Chapter 4). Consequently, one will tend to act impulsively and quickly, dragging the therapist into an emergency spiral, in which the sense of powerlessness becomes the prevailing mutual conclusive experience.

Evaluation-contract

Setting the boundaries of the therapeutic relationship, and establishing the rules of the setting and the mutual commitments, are initial steps that concretely define the special nature of the relationship. This helps to counter the activation of dramatic relational patterns where the therapist is the saviour/persecutor and the patient is the victim/persecutor or vice versa.

Therapist and patient face each other and negotiate collaboration, set the boundaries of the relationship, distinguishing it from the relationship that is internalized in the IWM. This is all the more necessary with people who do not mentalize easily, who do not have sufficient differentiating capacities to allow them to negotiate an agreement on the meaning of the therapeutic alliance.

In order to address integration and mentalization deficits, we often need to start from simpler mental processes and proceed towards greater complexity, attuning ourselves to the patient's level of functioning – 'proximal development zone' (Vygotskij, 1962) – during the various phases of therapy, using a language that is conducive to collaboration and growth.

*

LUCIA (2)

During the negotiation phase, Lucia experiences distress on account of the disorderly relational life that she has been living for years. She confronts the therapist with new emergencies, demanding a response that the therapist does not consider advisable. This leads to moments of intense conflict in which Lucia decides to interrupt the sessions but continues to send text messages and threatening emails, some filled with insults. When the therapist manages to meet Lucia again, she reminds her of the rules that she has to follow if she wishes to continue therapy.

T: *You've gone too far, Lucia. I didn't reply because you interrupted the therapy and made an arbitrary use of the means of communication that we had agreed on.*

P: *I wasn't well! I'm sorry I insulted you, but do you have any idea of how I was feeling?*

T: *By interrupting therapy and communicating with me the way you did, you didn't give me the chance to discuss what was happening with you. You dumped all your feelings on me without worrying about how, where and when I could reply. I will not be insulted by you whenever you feel like it, without having a say.*

P: (with a disparaging and critical expression) *Is this how a psychotherapist is supposed to behave? You're getting angry at me; what kind of therapist are you?*

T: *In what handbook did you read the instructions for the good therapist? Of course I'm angry. The therapist is a human being and has emotions. I may even decide that it isn't possible for us to work together if you give me no say and force me to accept your abuse.*

*

Patients may attribute to therapy meanings that collude with their pathological beliefs. Explaining what psychotherapy is and how it is used, what the roles are part of the therapeutic process, means working profitably with patients, addressing the magical expectations they may have and the pathological experience of 'impossibility' that underpins them. The fact that the therapist discusses *what can be done* has another meaning as well. For patients with a disorganized attachment style, often characterized by an inverse symbiosis, 'controlling punitive' or 'controlling nurturing' (Lyons-Ruth and Jacobvitz, 1999), a therapist who defines and sets limits for him/herself and the other may be a new experience. Paradoxically, when the contract is being defined, therapy is already underway, but the therapist will communicate to the patient that therapy will begin only if and when they mutually agree that the conditions are in place to start therapy.

The patient must engage in a process that allows him/her to access ever more complex levels of relational experience. He/she must let go of the past and be open to new attachment experiences appropriate to his/her development and to the 'here and now' of the relationship. During the initial phase, when disruption distorts the interpersonal motivational dimension, it becomes necessary to take concrete steps to protect the relationship and start therapy. In order to take less evolved steps in therapy, paradoxically, it is necessary for the therapist to consider the complexity that he/she is experiencing with the patient and the patient's difficulty. Thinking in a complex way and mentalizing on the part of the therapist also lends a broader meaning to simple actions. The aim is to recover the complexity that the patient can cope with.

*

ELSA (2)

The contract: defining the therapeutic plan

Elsa comes to me thinking that the first thing she has to address is her self-harming behaviour in order to put an end to it. Instead, during this initial phase, we decide to set aside this problematic aspect and attempt to conduct an in-depth analysis of her request in order to come up with a therapeutic plan. During our first meetings I explain how we will proceed and inform Elsa about the therapeutic method and its origins. We begin to share a common language and to lay the groundwork for cooperation. Elsa is very glad to know that she can participate actively in the therapeutic plan: she feels that she can make choices and decisions, she feels considered, less 'sick' and powerless. We establish some protection and holding strategies for her at-risk behaviours, which are not limited to the eyelash-plucking ritual but also include self-induced lesions caused by excessive scratching on her scalp and occasionally on her face, drunk driving, and getting into violent arguments. We agree that the first goal will be to *quit alcohol and drugs*. We decide that, before she starts drinking, Elsa must call me and, if my cell phone is switched off, leave a message. This is the most that can be realistically asked of her in relation to this problem: in this way, she will give herself the opportunity to stop and think a little longer before committing a compulsive act, and me the chance to communicate with her when she is in a state. We consider the possibility of resorting to pharmacological treatment, possibly involving a psychiatrist – a colleague of mine – as another therapeutic figure. We further explore the concept of therapeutic network, which is also intended as a protective response to Elsa's behaviours of aggression and escape, by means of which she preventively imagines she can boycott therapy. Another element of the therapeutic network that we discuss is group therapy, which scares Elsa even more than pharmacological treatment. Notwithstanding her fears, Elsa understands that the network would help to protect our relationship and her therapy. We do not set a timeline for the introduction of the different resources into the therapeutic program, but we decide that, by and by, we will evaluate together the plan of action, thereby monitoring the therapeutic relationship.

*

Even when important goals and behaviours are being addressed, the therapist's attention stays focused on the patient's relational style (IWM). Although the therapeutic couple may have managed to agree on a treatment plan, the therapist expects relational difficulties associated with the patient's trauma to arise in the session room very early on and repeatedly. The initial agreement merely lays the groundwork for working together having reached a common understanding, avoiding early and at times irreparable terminations; however, it cannot take the place of the required experience with the salient moments of the relational process.

Even when we have gone through a lengthy preliminary phase during which we have negotiated the working conditions, agreed on how to proceed, and formally expressed the intention to collaborate, we have to factor in the possibility that something disruptive may occur in our relationship with the patient and that this disruption will allow something significant to happen between us. When, as Bromberg would say, *gorillas* come into the session room (see Chapter 3), we are really at the heart of the therapeutic experience.

*

ELSA (3)

When the relationship cures

There is always a crucial moment in a therapeutic process, a moment when everything that up until then has only been said, described, understood, conjectured, and partly even shared, suddenly becomes dramatically real in the therapy room. This happened to me with Elsa the day she walked into my office covered with scratches and bruises, with a bandaged arm and leg, and a menacing look on her face. *'There now, look at what I'm capable of!'* she says angrily. She bursts into tears and continues, almost in a whisper, *'It's useless, it's all useless . . .'* And then, angrily again, *'You do realize that there's no point in my coming here, in my explaining, in our working out a plan together, when in the space of a second I'm capable of this!'* She cries desperately.

I remember that moment as if it were happening now. I am sitting on the sofa and am slowly bracing myself for a full-blown attack; at the same time, I feel angry but am also deeply concerned as I look at the marks on her face and body while she cries desperately.

I cannot imagine what might have happened and after Elsa's initial outburst, I attempt to ask her.

'What do you think happened?' she answers in shock. *'What happens all the time! I manage to ruin everything. I can't control myself: What I'm capable of is*

horrific. I told you that you couldn't help me!' I try to point out that I still do not know what happened and Elsa, who probably perceives my sense of powerlessness, begins to reassure me: *'You have nothing to do with it. No one has anything to do with it. I'm unfit! No one would want to be with me!'* She cries again.

*

From these fragments of our dialogue, it is evident that Elsa has activated the disorganized IWM (Liotti 1989, 1994/2005) and the dramatization of the drama triangle (Ivaldi, 2004). The patient is going through the painful experience of feeling both victim and persecutor and then, driven by the guilt of mistreating me, also saviour, in a swift and confusing sequence. All of these roles are real, but Elsa is unable to reconcile them. The difficulty she finds in integrating them goes far back into Elsa's past. The very intense experience she is going through does not involve just our relationship and the present moment, but is rooted in a repeated traumatic experience with her attachment relationships. As a child, on account of her particular vulnerability, with her parents Elsa did not have the opportunity to develop her meta-cognitive functions, she could not fully understand what was happening in those vitally important relationships, and was therefore incapable of integrating the different and contradictory aspects of the experience.

*

I gather from what Elsa is telling me that the self-inflicted wounds are the result of a violent argument with her partner. She does not remember the entire episode and is terrified by what she was capable of and by the fact that she was in an altered state of consciousness. She is scared of herself. She hates herself.

It is difficult to choose what to say as a therapist at times like this. All of Elsa's pathological beliefs are there with us and pull me in too: *'I can't be helped, I'm worthless.'* Feelings of pain, rage, shame, humiliation, terror, powerlessness follow in a rapid sequence.

I have to choose how to intervene. The situation is very complex. I would make a mistake if I were to address Elsa's dangerousness and guilt, because if I reassured her I would not be credible (in a sense, the facts support her case). On the other hand, if I were to confirm her self-image, I would be wrong too, because I would confirm her fears and endow her with a negative, uncontainable power, which she does not have.

I choose a caring/protective approach, while respecting the bounds of our relationship. In doing this, it is essential that I refer back to the original contract Elsa and I agreed on.

*

The commitment that was initially agreed upon constitutes a sort of *'free zone'* (Ivaldi, 2004; Ivaldi *et al.*, 2007; Ivaldi, 2008) in which, when the IWM of Elsa's disorganized attachment is activated, it is possible to emphasize the collaborative nature of the therapeutic relationship, redefine its bounds, and therefore avoid the *drama triangle*, thereby restoring the conditions in which therapeutic work can proceed. The desperate experience of powerless rage with no way out, which comes from Elsa's attachment experience and is reactivated in the relationship with me, should thus be at least partly overcome.

*

After telling her that I was very struck by what had happened to her and that I was saddened to see her in that state, I reveal to her my difficulty in choosing where to begin. There are many things that I would want to tell her, but one seems to prevail and I decide to start from that.

'*Elsa, remember the commitment you made to stop drinking and engaging in destructive behaviour – apart from your rituals – targeting yourself and others . . .*' I cannot even finish the sentence because, at the sound of these words, Elsa jumps up angrily and replies with a tone that is both irritated and demoralized, '*Of course I do! I may have made all the commitments in the world and I'm sure that when I did I really meant it, but then . . . something happens and . . . you see, I'm beside myself, it's beyond my control . . . can't you see?*'

In all likelihood, Elsa has activated her IWM and what I said probably made her think that I was scolding her or, perhaps, that I was saying to her, '*You really don't want to be helped!*' just as her mother did. This exchange is very delicate. I answer firmly, contrasting her pathological sense of powerlessness: '*Obviously, if you drink yourself into a stupor you no longer have control over your actions, you don't know what you're doing; anyone would lose control and wouldn't remember a thing. But there's a moment just before you start drinking when you can still choose, and you do. We've been over this already, remember?*'

Elsa is still angry. She remembers the conversation we had about pharmacological treatment to help her stop drinking, and she responds with hostility and despondency to the possibility of being helped that way.

I remind her that, in addition to discussing medication, we had agreed that she would call me when she was about to drink or do drugs. I remind her of the meaning and importance of that commitment. At that point, Elsa does not know what to say. She mumbles that she had considered calling me and did not because she did not want to disturb me, but it is clear to me that she is having trouble coming up with a convincing answer. She has underestimated the importance of the commitment she made, forgetting that it could have been the only way to let me help her in her worst moments.

I ask Elsa firmly to reflect on this and, in light of this experience, to decide whether or not she is willing to make that commitment again: *'Think about it, Elsa, do you feel up to using the telephone in this way and to being helped by a competent colleague with pharmacological treatment? In the light of this experience, I think this is an essential step without which I would decide to terminate the therapy . . .'*

Elsa interrupts me again. She is surprised and irritated, *'You . . . would terminate the therapy . . . This is unbelievable! This is good!'*

*

The moment is extremely delicate. My intervention could very easily be experienced by Elsa as an abandonment, a rejection, because she truly is *'difficult and un-helpable'*, as her pathological beliefs suggest. At this moment, words are not enough to reassure, to explain. The intention with which they are said is transmitted through the eyes, facial expression, and tone of voice.

I am feeling different emotions at the same time. I am sorry and moved, but also concerned and determined to protect her (caretaking); I am also aware that I cannot do this unless she collaborates (cooperation); actually, I worry that I will precipitate with her, without even trying to break the vicious cycle (attachment). I feel powerless in the face of the accomplished fact and a sense of failure in the face of her request for help and my attempt to respond to it (defence system, *dorsal vagal complex*). I am hoping that all the motivations active in me at that moment can reach Elsa, all combined in my response, at the implicit as well as explicit level.

*

Elsa stares at me with menacing eyes, ready to be abandoned yet again. Sadly, I explain that I would interrupt our sessions because, without a commitment on her part, it would be difficult to continue our therapeutic work. *'I'm not willing to see you come to my office again hurt this way, without being able to do anything about it. I'm sorry for you but I think this would be too high a price to pay for the both of us, without even having the guarantee of a mutual commitment towards a common goal.'*

Elsa remains silent. She is upset and taken aback by my intervention. She asks me again if I would really terminate her therapy and I reply: *'Yes, sadly, but I would do it, because I know that it couldn't work, and I don't want to have to worry about you without being able to do anything to really help you, and without being sure that you're with me in this, doing everything you can to collaborate.'* I am hoping that Elsa will understand my position. I am perfectly aware that this is a very risky moment but I tell myself once again that this will not take us anywhere and I do not want to expose Elsa to the risk of incurring yet another failure. *'I can't guarantee it!'* Elsa answers, irritated, but still surprised and unsure.

I tell her that she does not have to give me an answer right away, and that, in fact, it is better that she think about it until our next session. When we part at the end of the session there is great tension and I remember thinking that Elsa's therapy will either end here or turn around completely, so that from now on it will all be downhill.

*

The metacontext: therapy in the real context of the patient's life

Special attention will be dedicated to the idea that psychotherapeutic work has to consider the context of therapy as well as that of the patient's life. In the REMOTA the group is not just a therapeutic setting, but rather a crucial relational dimension which is ever present, in different forms, in the various phases of treatment.

The advantage of working with outpatients as opposed to inpatients

Unlike treatment delivered in a residential setting, where patients live in a more sheltered environment and therapy can be organized outside of their

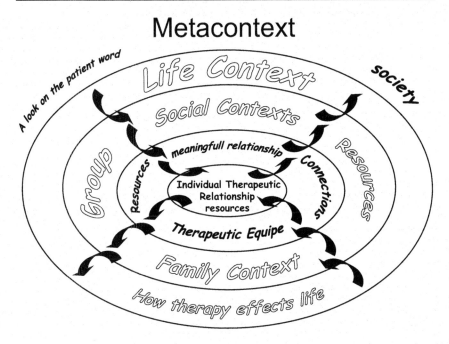

Figure 6.1 Translated from A. Ivaldi (2009) '*Diturbi di personalita e relazione*' Ed Franco Angeli, p. 149
Source: Antonella Ivaldi (2005)

context of life (see Chapter 5), outpatient treatment is more exposed to the risk of interference and dispersion. Most patients, however, prefer outpatient treatment, which is easier to arrange, though harder to keep up. Indeed, drop-out rates in this case are very high. In outpatient treatment, there is a greater need to protect the setting from the tendency to act in a dysregulated way. During the evaluation phase, it is very important to consider the family and the patient's context, or else the therapist runs the risk of being dragged into the pathological dynamics of the context without realizing it when the request for therapy is made. It is useful to try to create a therapeutic network, involving whenever and however possible the significant persons of the patients' social context, in which they continue to spend most of their time. The purpose of this is to curb as far as possible the damage caused by the activation of pathogenic interpersonal patterns leading to impulsive choices and behaviours, as a result of which psychotherapy will tend to focus primarily on emergencies.

Creating the working group considering the patient's context of life

In the model presented, one works with and on the group, focusing on the patient's context of life, sometimes involving relatives and other significant persons. The therapist broadens the scope of observation and work from the outset, gradually establishing the approach and timing. Involving the patient in a joint exploration of the possibility of a therapeutic intervention opens the dual relational context to the *metacontext* in which therapy takes place: the patient's life. The timing of this therapeutic step is determined on a case-by-case basis.

In evaluating and negotiating the alliance, it is very important to consider how and why the patient turns to us. Sometimes the patient is not motivated enough or has not freely chosen to begin therapy. Indeed, in the more difficult cases, the undifferentiated request for help, which is the extreme consequence of a state of exasperation, may come from family members, who are often confused and problematic themselves. They frequently expect us to work miracles and provide emergency solutions.

*

ANNA (2)

My first meeting with Anna was a group meeting. I was not expecting so many people in my office. Anna was accompanied by her mother, a cousin, and other two young women: a friend and another woman who was introduced as her friend/partner. What were all those women doing in my office? I tried to sieve through the myriad feelings I was experiencing. I felt 'crammed', but also activated, slightly alert, and curious at the same time. What did they all want from me? Was I supposed to deal with all of them, or just Anna? I wondered who Anna was. Was she perhaps all of them? Or was she concealed, crushed by those women? They appeared to be perfectly at ease; they proceeded like an army platoon engaged in military exercises, all of them moving together, silently and in perfect harmony in that collective dimension. At times I felt surrounded, other times extremely curious, almost amused by that peculiar relational configuration. Who had taken the initiative of contacting me for psychotherapy was not clear. They all agreed that Anna needed help; they were very involved and concerned by Anna's distress, which at times took dangerous forms. They told me that Anna frequently went through periods of withdrawal, when she would isolate herself, locking herself up in a room and not answering the phone, thus causing great alarm around her. When this happened, Anna had bulimic episodes followed by bouts of vomit and fasting, overuse of diuretics and laxatives; she would cut herself or burn her skin, sometimes quite violently. Anna did not have a submissive attitude, quite the contrary: I was immediately struck by her sharpness and intelligence. She was not sure that psychotherapy would help; she said she had accepted to come not because she wanted to but because the others were worried about her. We went on for months with our evaluation meetings, which involved Anna's women. I had to struggle to get them to understand that they should not take it for granted that psychotherapy would be helpful to Anna. We worked hard on the meaning of their relational clusters, which varied depending on the circumstances and needs, in a dramatic spiral. They shifted quickly from love to hate or vice versa, and everything revolved around Anna's constant emergencies. It took a long time before Anna and I could focus on what happened to her when she withdrew; first we had to work on limiting the damages and emergencies, addressing the dynamics of the existing relational network in order to make it more functional to the therapeutic process.

*

Failing to take into account the patient's context and relational dynamics can be extremely detrimental. Often our patients are financially dependent on someone else, so that a three-party contract becomes necessary. Such is the case with adolescents. It is important to evaluate the extent to which family members may represent a resource or a hindrance to therapy. On the basis of this evaluation it is possible to gradually make decisions regarding the treatment protocol, which will have a significant impact on the therapeutic plan.

Other variables regarding the life of our patients that we evaluate when starting therapy are the patient's social-economic and cultural contexts, significant relationships, and occupation. These can help us to understand the problem and set up a therapeutic strategy that is in keeping with the patient's circumstances.

*

EGIDIO

Egidio is a 35-year-old man who, after being discharged from a residential facility specialized in borderline disorders, is referred to our centre for outpatient treatment. Egidio has been in psychoanalysis for many years and has had a very eventful life: accidents, lay-offs, marriage and separation, violent fights, and abuse of various substances. After the initial meetings, I ask Egidio how he has managed to lead such an extravagant life on the salary of a state employee, which is even lower now that he is on extended leave. *'My mother helps me out,'* Egidio says matter-of-factly. We calculate that he usually spends more than 5000 euros a month, an exorbitant amount, considering that he earns barely over 1000 euros and does not pay rent. Quantifying the cost of his vices immediately brings to the fore an important aspect of his situation: the collusive involvement of the family, which also pays for his therapy. We decide to arrange a family meeting. A joint decision is made to gradually reduce the family's financial support, forcing Egidio to cut back on his expenses and to quit drugs and alcohol.

*

A direct consequence of the functioning deficits of difficult patients can be scarce individuation and differentiation between oneself and others; this coincides with entangled and entangling family relational patterns. The decision to involve the patient's significant persons directly in the therapy is not made only at the outset of treatment but, at times, at crucial moments of the process when the importance of the patient's entire relational system becomes evident.

*

SOFIA (5)

Sofia said that her parents clearly wanted her to have an abortion, which upset her very much. She was almost 40. The first thing I felt like telling her was not to rush things and to reflect on the matter together, although we did not have much time! On Sofia's request, I summoned her parents in an attempt to gauge the resources of her family context. Her father answered the phone and was very harsh with me as well as with his daughter. He thought she should have an abortion because he was convinced that Franco was unreliable and that this child would represent a very complicated bond. He was not willing to talk and was actually rather annoyed by my interference. I thought he was speaking on the basis of preconceived notions, but in a way I could also understand him. I could tell he was worried about his daughter, but the harshness of his tone hurt me, because it made me think about how Sofia must have been feeling in that situation. Franco, who in the meantime had followed Sofia's suggestion and had started seeing a colleague psychiatrist/psychoanalyst, was willing to keep the child, although he did not intend to make too many changes in his life (he was separated from his wife but was still living with her and their daughter). The colleague and I spoke with the consent of our patients and tried to schedule a meeting for the four of us, in order to determine together how to go about the situation.

Unfortunately, the meeting revealed Franco's insubstantiality and the grave superficiality with which he was facing the situation; he was completely oblivious and thought it would not be a problem at all to keep the baby. On the other hand, Sofia got very angry at him and insisted on asking him to take more responsibility, be more consistent, convinced as she was that it was a matter of will. The colleague and I merely underscored their positions and, as is typical in a systemic intervention, what emerged in the four-people context came down on them like an axe.

Sofia seemed to see the distance between her and Franco clearly, although her awareness of this would tend to fade; consequently, she did not behave consistently and effectively.

She was desperate: she realized that she could not trust him, but the idea of having an abortion made her sick. During our following session, we tried to consider the possibility of her keeping the baby. I was pretty sure that at first her parents would react negatively but would then stand by her and help her generously; she knew this was true but did not feel up to it just the same. She was afraid they would resort to emotional blackmail and retaliate. After some tormented days, she terminated her pregnancy.

A period of deep depression followed during which, surprisingly, Sofia continued, amid strong turbulence, to pursue the objective of staying with Franco. Franco acted like the 'missed father', offended by Sofia's decision and by her parents' rejection, and pitted Sofia against them. War broke out. Sofia felt unworthy, fragile, and in her defeat she continued, impulsively, to invest in the failure. She did not trust Franco, nor did she trust her parents, or herself for that matter. She trusted me a little, and clung to that little trust she had in me. I knew it was a fine line, which is why I tried to create a network, and my interventions became direct actions on Sofia's context of life when I would involve her parents and Franco in joint meetings with my colleague.

*

In this case too, the goal of the therapeutic intervention is to help the patient to consider the possibility of engaging the family relational network in a joint process of negotiation on how to address some issues which, in fact, already concern all family members. In the model, the work conducted with the system and the group differs from the classical approach; the setting is neither that of family therapy nor that of group therapy, although the skills required to conduct that type of work are required here as well. One works with relational configurations different from those of the dual setting, and the dynamics that develop in a group entail new psychotherapeutic possibilities. However, one must bear in mind that the families, or the persons whom one decides to involve, are not requesting psychotherapy; what the therapist offers to the persons who are close to the patient is a consultation, for the purpose of further helping the patient.

The therapist asks the persons involved to meet – after agreeing this with the patient – stating the intention to work together with a view to better understanding what is happening, using different vantage points that can be mutually helpful. The therapist acknowledges the importance of the patient's significant persons, underscoring that the reason for meeting is to explore and collaborate, in order to join forces and support each other when facing difficulties.

The patient's mentalization deficits are usually observed also in the family and at times it is possible to make direct therapeutic interventions within the system, always staying focused on the relationship with the patient and the ultimate purpose of the meeting, which is to collaborate on equal terms.

*

SOFIA (6)

Sofia had changed psychiatrist yet again. Needless to say, as soon as she became pregnant, he took her off the mood stabilizer and gradually reduced the dosage of the antidepressant, but after the abortion he reinstated the treatment. The colleague had described her to me as 'manipulative and dramatic'. Whenever psychiatrists talked to me about Sofia, they would say something plausible, but what stayed with me, over and above the diagnostic labels, was the feeling that she was considered untreatable, and a sense of expulsion, rejection. I wondered whether I was the one to be wrong. Why was it that, in spite of the fact that she made me very angry and wore me out, I kept liking her? Why did I feel that I did not want to let go? Was I somehow colluding with her? And yet, after she came back, something had changed between us. We were much closer, we could afford to get angry, without breaking the bond.

It was a morning like many others. Around ten o'clock I received a phone call from Sofia's parents who, with great alarm, asked me whether I had talked to her or had news from her. I realized at once that the situation was serious.

Sofia was not answering her phone and they were on their way to Rome, worried sick. Franco had informed them that he could not get hold of her and she was not opening the door. Hours of anguish and agitation followed. Until Franco decided to break the door down and proceeded to rush her to the emergency room.

Sofia had taken several mood stabilizers and antidepressants. At the hospital, after a stomach pumping, and after we spoke, the doctors decided to keep her for 48 hours instead of transferring her to the psychiatric ward. The colleague who followed her privately for the pharmacological treatment told me that he thought it had been a manipulative gesture on her part, typical of a borderline personality, but that it was to be taken seriously and treated following the standard procedure. I stayed in touch with Sofia's parents, who turned to me, traumatized as they were, seeking help in figuring out 'what to do'.

Meanwhile, Franco was very active in assisting Sofia and never left her for a moment. What had happened became clear later: the two of them had got into a violent argument the morning she attempted suicide, after which he had left and she had locked herself inside her flat. They fought over even trivial matters, but were capable of hurting each other very deeply. Franco was constantly bringing up the abortion, which he held against her, and Sofia was extremely vulnerable on this point. When he did that, she was generally overwhelmed by a sense of self-loathing and, paradoxically, felt Franco closer to her; in her naiveté, she thought this actually strengthened their bond. The gesture of taking the pills appeared to have been an attempt on her part to prove a point and fit well into the escalating conflict of which the aversive element and separation cry seemed to be the main components.

'. . . I thought that, since nobody cares about me, it was best if I just got out of the way. All I do is make trouble! It would've been better for everyone!' (she cried).

After what happened, Franco kept casting discredit on her parents and blaming them. I felt very sorry for them and sensed that Franco was taking advantage of everyone's weakness. Unfortunately Sofia sought him out and was more determined than ever to stay in that relationship. The more she felt unworthy, the more she wanted to be with him.

I shared her parents' concern over the situation. They were devastated by what had happened and let Sofia have her way, fearing that she might do herself harm. The spiral that had set in risked becoming even more pathological.

At that moment, it was crucial to act on the family system in order to restore relational dynamics that were not just post-traumatic responses. After some time, Sofia started to realize what she had done and the consequences of her actions. Some family sessions were particularly difficult and intense. The goal was to break the spiral of fear and this required an effort on everyone's part to speak to each other authentically and to learn to understand the intentions of the other, which was very difficult for that family to do. During the sessions, Sofia's parents were able to talk about their concerns and I openly invited them to be authentic with their daughter, not to fear her reactions. Sofia agreed with some of the things they said about her sentimental relationship and could understand them, to some extent, but declared that she could not give it up at the moment and, after all, she still hoped to be able to change her relationship with Franco. Additionally, she was especially angry with her parents, whom she felt were responsible for pushing her to terminate her pregnancy. In a whirlwind of emotions, fear seemed to prevail in the poor parents, who wanted to be with their daughter at all times. They had to find the courage to let her go and accept the fact that they were powerless, that no matter how close an eye they kept on her, they could never prevent her from making her own decisions. Sofia, on the other hand, had to find the courage to reckon with her feelings and those of the others, and with the conflicts at play, modulating her reactions.

After a series of sessions, I told them that, although I could understand and share their fears, I thought we had to trust Sofia's ability to make her decisions and give her time, and that I would work with her in order to help her overcome the impasse. We decided to touch base every now and then.

*

Working with emotions

SOFIA (7)

During the time that followed, I agreed with Sofia that we would focus our attention on emotional regulation and impulsiveness and that we would be dedicating most of our sessions to discussing her functioning and vulnerabilities. I asked her to make the commitment not to rush, to abstain from making rash decisions and take time to reflect, otherwise we would not go very far. She accepted. Our alliance had definitely grown stronger as a result of the painful experience we had shared. The conflict with the psychiatrists gave us no respite. The latest one thought that medication was not important and that she needed to focus on her psychotherapy, also because he was afraid of prescribing medication after what she had done. Sofia dropped him too and turned this time to a woman doctor, who gave great importance to the abortion and stepped up the treatment with antidepressants and mood stabilizers. A rather long period of time followed without particular emergencies; the love story with Franco continued, with all its problems, but Sofia was able to face the difficulties feeling less exasperated and to fight without causing dramatic ruptures. I reminded her of her commitment to refrain from making rash decisions and to focus on how she was feeling, on her needs, and she was starting to do this. Little by little, she was beginning to see her parents' behaviours from different angles and could feel sympathy for them, above and beyond her anger, for she had seen how devastated they had been by her gesture. At the same time, we could talk about their family dynamics and the triangulation that was always at the basis of their communication. What emerged were the difficulties within the parental couple that Sofia had always unwittingly tried to ease by serving as a 'lightning rod'. As long as the parents were busy taking care of her, the 'difficult daughter', they did not have to come to terms with their own issues. The father was temperamental, like her, and was capable of grand gestures driven by affection and generosity, but he could also be very harsh and aggressive, as I myself had seen at the time of the abortion. The mother, who was hung up on cleanliness and tidiness, was hyper-efficient, extremely focused, 'obstinate and irritating', as Sofia would say; she seemed to be the spark that would start the fire. *'She gets her way quietly, my dad explodes, and so do I.'* Sofia's parents were good people, both with a traumatic family history and the inability for emotional regulation, which they never acknowledged or addressed. The invalidation of the emotional experience and the inability to understand the intentions of the other had been Sofia's daily bread. This had emerged during the family meetings, when in moments of conflicts between them they allowed me to stop the communication in order to analyze it together. It was thus possible for us to explore the different intentions, emotions and motivations, so far unknown to them. Her IWM and the family scenario that we had started to reflect on came to the fore even more clearly during the group experience that we started after her mood stabilized, and she developed a greater capacity for reflection in the wake of the attempted suicide.

*

Emotions are like a compass, enabling us to cross the complex intersubjective world. According to motivational theories, our social behaviour is regulated on the basis of innate predispositions for relational activities (IMS). For each IMS there are different emotions that signal the activation of a given system and its goals.

However, it is unlikely that only one IMS is activated at a time. An emotional state is usually a combination of several emotions and motivations that arise together. In optimum mental functioning conditions, the capacity for synthesis (complex neocortical function) allows us to harmonize different stimuli and different aspects of experience, even seemingly contradictory. Otherwise, in the presence of functioning deficits, the different aspects of experience remain separate and dissociated; consequently, it is not possible to make sense of them and to act coherently.

Psychotherapy is the discovery, with the other, of the IWMs that guide our life and the dysfunctional aspects of the latter that may be the cause of our suffering. All this occurs through the relationship that is established between therapist and patient. Two IWMs meet and the IMSs of each are activated; the therapist works with the complexity of the relationship, which implies his/her own emotions from which to infer those of the other, bearing in mind his/her own internal world, the known and yet-to-be-discovered aspects and the other's internal world, the context in which the relationship develops, his/her personal story, and the patient's story. It is therefore necessary to be empathically attuned with all of the chaotic emotional components of the experience with the patient. The therapist must be inside the relationship and also employ his/her skills to understand the meaning of the experience with the other.

Empathy: a complex process?

Empathy is an important concept that has been extensively debated. Even though it is thanks to Kohut (1977) and to the Psychology of the Self that empathy was emphasized as a value in psychotherapy, the concept has been used in different ways in the various therapeutic and research models. Freud (1974) first mentioned empathy as a process by means of which our emotional experience enables us to approach the emotional experience of another person and understand it deeply. However, psychoanalytic orthodoxy prevented further exploration of the concept, since the emotional involvement of the analyst in the treatment was considered dangerous. From the

1940s onwards, with the advent of the relational movement (see Chapter 2), empathy was recovered not only in the clinical sector but also in research, in scientific psychology, and in neurosciences, thus producing important interdisciplinary considerations that have been brought together with masterly skill in an essay by Williams and Dazzi (2006). The *empathist position,* as the two authors call it, gathers various theoretical and clinical contributions and constitutes the starting point for some particularly significant experiences in the study of processes: the Menninger Psychotherapy Research Project (Wallerstein, 1986), the San Francisco Psychotherapy Research Group (Weiss *et al.*, 1987), Rogers (1957), Frank (1961).

The contribution offered by neurosciences (Edelman, 1992; Baron-Cohen, Tager-Flusberg and Cohen, 1993; Damasio, 1994; Tomasello, 1999; Le Doux, 1996) and by the evolutionary theory (Darwin, 1872; De Waal, 1982; Donald, 1991) show that empathy implies the activation of a network of brain structures that interact with each other and synthesize at different levels of complexity. It is therefore possible to conceptualize a mental activity organized on different stratified levels that reflect more or less evolved functioning capacities in terms of phylogeny and ontogenesis. Of great value was the discovery of 'mirror neurons' (Rizzolatti *et al.*, 2001), according to which empathy may be assumed to be a basic function in cognitive processes, independent of development on the evolutionary scale of the higher mental functions of consciousness. This leads to some interesting observations on the degree and type of empathy that is possible in a therapeutic relationship.

Last but not least is the contribution of developmental psychology in this sense. Authoritative researchers and outstanding clinicians have taken an interest in developmental psychology and infant research, also with the aim of improving our understanding of the nature of psychopathological problems and of the phenomena that are peculiar to the therapeutic relationship. The Boston Psychotherapy Research Group studies mother–child interactions in the first year of life and at the same time seeks significant connections in the clinical field. The repeated absence of emotional understanding and attunement by the parent in relation to a shared experience generate in the child an implicit way of representing self with other and self in relationship with the world that will become the *organizing principle* of the child's relational experience (Stern, 2004). Therapy therefore consists in recovering the spaces of intersubjective sharing that have been denied in infancy and hence provide the opportunity to expand the possible relational experiences and consolidate the sense of self in the world. Beebe and Lachmann (2002) move from the same approach and focus their attention on the processes of affect regulation. Research proceeds in the direction of identifying moments of failure and recovery of the sharing and affect regulation in the mother–child dyad, in order to better modulate communication in the therapeutic relationship. The various authors converge on the age of onset of the infant's ability to understand empathy (see Chapter 2). Since in order to be empathic one must necessarily attribute intentional states to others, some authors, including Tomasello (1999), suggest that this discriminating capacity develops in the infant at 9–10 months of age. Along the same lines, Fonagy (1995; Fonagy *et al.*, 2002) posits that the ability of the mother–child and patient–therapist dyad to communicate their own and mutual affect states is the precondition for effective regulation of emotions.

The variables at play in an empathic process involve several aspects of the therapeutic setting. Feeling one's emotions and understanding them according to the categories of motivational systems in order to understand those of the patient is a complex task. The therapist must be aware of his/her

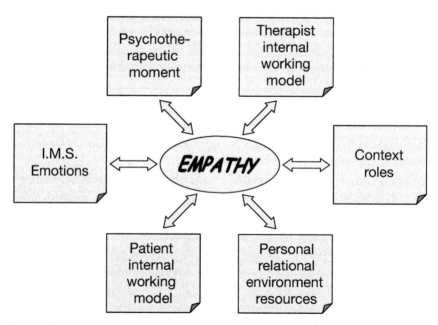

Figure 6.2
Source: Antonella Ivaldi (2005)

IWM in order not to become a victim unwittingly and not to distort the meaning of what comes from the other. He/she must formulate a hypothesis on how the other functions, based on patient history, personal, relational and environmental resources; in a nutshell, he/she must be capable of producing a likely representation of the patient's life, so as to better understand the patient's state in the *here and now* of the relationship and envision the scope for change that is viable and in keeping with the context. Another important aspect to be considered is the step in the therapeutic continuum: how does what the person is telling me relate to our therapeutic story? The patient's anger towards the therapist is not the same if it occurs during the first session as opposed to the twentieth one, for instance; this variable informs us about the different relational meanings of that emotion. Finally, the roles and boundaries in the therapeutic relationship have to be taken into account. The therapist, bearing in mind the mutuality of the relationship (Ferenczi, 1909; Greenberg and Mitchell, 1983; Gill, 1994; Aron, 1996), must consider the different responsibilities and roles in the various stages of the process, and promote differentiation and collaboration, remembering that they will be objectives to be reached rather than points of departure. In the empathic process it is important to ask ourselves from what vantage point are we observing the person and from what vantage point is the person perceiving us; what is his/her idea of the world and of psychotherapy. Furthermore, it is essential to consider the overall context – familial, social and cultural – within which every person's life and the therapeutic process unfold. Being aware of all this and discussing it together is essential for negotiating the alliance and represents a significant developmental stage in the mentalization process. This set of variables, and many others, contribute towards building the empathic process, in accordance with the principles of complexity. The more the therapist is capable of taking all of the variables into account, the closer he/she comes to the complex synthesis of experience – precisely what the patient is unable to do. During therapy partial empathic actions can be carried out that take into account some of the variables but not the whole. This happens frequently and can be very useful for building the therapeutic alliance, but it is important that the therapist be aware of its incompleteness, otherwise he/she will run the risk of blocking exploration and the empathic process itself, colluding with the patients' dissociative mechanisms.

*

FROM SOFIA'S VIGNETTE

When Sofia was called to make the painful decision of having an abortion or keeping the baby, her parents' aversive response hurt and upset her very much and confirmed her conviction that she could not count on anyone. At that moment, she seemed to forget that in the past they had always been there for her – even too much – and that they would do everything they possibly could to help her this time too. This did not allow Sofia to have a complete and clear understanding of their reaction. She failed to see how afraid her parents were of that dangerous man, whom Sofia would be bound to forever if she were to have his child. If, in that circumstance, I had said to Sofia, 'I'm sorry Sofia, I understand that your father's anger and your parents' intransigence causes you pain. They're making you feel alone,' I would have spoken the truth, but I would have empathized with her biased experience of the moment, without creating an opportunity to further explore and better understand the complexity of the emotional exchange between her and her parents. This would not have helped Sofia to exercise the higher mental functions and to synthesize and integrate the different variables of the experience in order to grasp its complexity.

*

In this sense, the therapist's awareness of the partiality of an empathic intervention modifies the meaning of the action which, instead of locking up experience in a limited representation of the other and of his/her problem, becomes a step forward in the shared experience of gaining understanding together and remains open to the construction of new, increasingly complex and hence more exhaustive meanings.

*

T: *Sofia, I understand that your father's anger and your parents' intransigence causes you pain. You must be feeling very alone at this moment. I'm very struck by your father's anger, he seems to be extremely alarmed and worried, don't you think? Of course, it's as if he were trying to protect you by making the decision on your behalf, and quite violently, as if there were no time to negotiate, so great is the danger. It's like what happens when a child crosses the street absent-mindedly while a car is approaching and his mother snatches him away, grabbing him violently by the arm without worrying about how he'll take it, in the presence of such a great danger.*

*

It is more complicated to exercise empathy when there is conflict in the therapeutic relationship and the dramatic experience occurs in the *hic et nunc* of the relationship; such was the case with Elsa in that difficult session (see Elsa: when the relationship cures), when our relationship was overwhelmed by her sense of being beyond help, leaving virtually no room for reflection. When this happens it all comes down to action and in action, even more so, empathy is conveyed for the most part by non-verbal communication.

*

ELSA (4)

During the week that followed that difficult session, I asked myself a thousand questions about what had happened and how I had intervened with Elsa. I was hoping that she had realized that the reason for telling her that I would not have followed her any longer had nothing to do with my wanting to push her away but was motivated by my conviction that only this way could we fight to accomplish something together, that there was hope, and that this was the right way to proceed. I had grown very fond of her, but I did not know whether my words had come across as affective. I was afraid that she might not come back.

But Elsa did come back and she eventually concluded her therapy three and a half years later. Today, her eyelashes have grown back and, after a series of events, she has gotten back together with her husband. She has a job and is doing quite well.

We often discussed that difficult and yet decisive encounter. Elsa admitted that she had considered never coming back. She was very angry at first, but something did not make sense to her. She told me that as the hours went by her recollection of what had happened became clearer and some flash memories emerged, some expressions of my face that revealed my sorrow and also my concern for her, a sense of pity, the tone of my voice, which at times was broken by emotion. Day after day, the feeling that I wanted to abandon her gradually faded. She also remembered the commitment she had made at the outset regarding the telephone calls and medication. She began to realize that she had underestimated it. She did not really know whether she could keep that commitment and how, but she decided to come to the following session, highly doubtful that she could and would be capable of doing it. She came back filled with doubts, also regarding our relationship, harbouring mixed feelings towards me, but determined to clear the air and see what would happen.

I was very glad to see her, I think it was evident. I was ready to clear things up with her, in another climate this time, not in an emergency situation. I was willing to renegotiate our therapeutic commitment, but I knew – actually, we both knew – that something significant had happened.

The communication had been effective; my intentions and my affection had reached her. I had conveyed my wish to stay the course with her, and this had been a powerful message that had destabilized the disorganized IWM, creating new opportunities for further exploration. Her deeply rooted belief that she was beyond help was surely undermined.

All of this happened at the implicit level of communication

*

Explicit and implicit communication

The therapeutic dialogue takes place simultaneously on two levels: explicit and implicit. The two levels are often syntonic, there is consistency between the signs of explicit and implicit language; other times instead there is no consistency or syntony. The most important level of communication is no doubt the implicit level. That is where significant relational experiences occur.

The ability to grasp the other's intentionality is what characterizes our species. It is at the root of intersubjectivity. The other's intentionality is expressed through a language that consists of words and signs (Tomasello, 1999). Facial expressions, tone, intensity, posture, are all signs that engage our perception. The latter is influenced by various factors, so we cannot be sure of our intuition regarding the other until he/she confirms it. Our ability to communicate with the other is directly proportional to our ability to respect the other and regard him/her as a thinking mind (Fonagy, 1995).

*

ELSA (5)

She decides to let herself be helped

I reassured her, telling her that in the course of therapy we would work on her ability to achieve her goals, and I thanked her for expressing the intention to do so.

We spoke at length about her doubts regarding pharmacological treatment, her fears, her prejudices; about how taking medication and calling could collude with her pathological belief that she was *'strange and un-helpable'*.

How could she have called, considering her previous history, especially in a moment of great distress, without expecting rejection or devaluation? We devoted the entire session to going over what had happened the night she fought with her partner; now we could try to understand together where her rage had come from. Elsa seemed to minimize this aspect and insisted on underlining her impulsive and destructive reactions in this as well as in other situations.

Elsa was accustomed to this style. Her reasons, motivations, and needs were in the background in relation to the consequences of her behaviour. In this way, she was invalidated and she continued to self-invalidate her own emotions.

Together we began to explore Elsa's relational experience and tried to distinguish between her needs and the ways in which these needs were expressed, between her emotions and their meaning and the modular expression of those emotions. The nature of her relationship with her new partner, Luca, gradually became clearer. Elsa had clung to him like a sheet-anchor, trying to 'get over' the sudden breakup with her husband, whom she had never seen or heard from since. What emerged from her story was the inability to deal with a marital crisis and the difficulty in choosing to stay in a steady relationship with someone.

Luca, on account of his own difficulties, colluded perfectly with Elsa's weaknesses and reinforced her pathological beliefs; together, they drank and took drugs, which made it even harder for Elsa to regulate her emotions. Luca appeared to be scared when Elsa 'lost it' and things spiraled out of control, making her feel like a monster, but then he would be very caring, for he considered her sick, '. . . *I know you're sick, but I want to be with you anyway*' (Luca had said after their violent fight).

Elsa refused to take medication because her partner had been advising her to do so for a long time. Taking medication would have meant admitting that she was *'very sick'*, as Luca would say, and accepting to finally invalidate her expressions of emotions and her reasons. Notwithstanding, she decided to see a colleague and began drug therapy. The psychiatrist, who was also a psychotherapist, would spend a long time explaining to Elsa how the medication worked and would also go into her emotional functioning. Elsa learned to monitor her mood, her emotions, and became more aware of her needs. She stopped smoking marijuana. She used the telephone to seek help. This marked another important step in the therapeutic relationship. Her calls, which she made in the rare moments of distress and anguish that usually preceded her impulsive behaviours, made it possible for her to experience closeness and caring on my part in keeping with her request, without exposing her to the danger of a negative image of herself as monstrous and un-helpable. The experience of receiving help without feeling devalued for this in the eyes of the other was even more important for Elsa.

*

In this sense, the non-verbal exchange and the therapist's effort to understand and integrate different and at times clashing aspects of the communication (such as for instance the caretaking and the egalitarian motivations) are crucial. Most of the therapeutic work occurs at the implicit level and it is essential that the therapist be aware of what happens at the implicit level and guide the patient in possibly making explicit what is implicit.

*

Elsa had the right to feel acknowledged for her capabilities even at times when she needed help, because for far too long the two things had been dissociated in the relationships that were important to her. If significant people took care of her, they did so as *saviours*, considering her inept and making decisions on her behalf, thus invalidating her and pushing her into a submissive position (Ivaldi, 2004). From the first time we met I sensed how hard it was for Elsa to hold together her vulnerability and her energy, her limits and her creativity. I do not remember ever not seeing these two opposite aspects of her personality. When I was protective of her I was also her friend; talking to her, exchanging views as equals came naturally to me, and I had great respect for her capabilities. We liked each other, we liked being together.

On the basis of this it was possible to build a sound therapeutic alliance. Elsa was able to follow her journey, gradually understanding the various steps with me. Her ability to reflect on herself grew over time and allowed her to overcome every impasse ever more quickly.

At the same time, she started feeling cramped in the relationship with Luca who, in the meantime, found it hard to tolerate the changes in Elsa, which were tipping their balance.

*

The body in therapy: the use of non-verbal communication in the relationship

Non-verbal communication is especially difficult to study and yet it is crucial to the therapeutic relationship. The contributions of infant research have had a significant impact on how care is conceived (see Chapters 2 and 4). Trevarthen, (1980), Lichtenberg (1983), Lichtenberg et al. (1996), Beebe and Lachmann (2002), Stern (2004), Lyons-Ruth and colleagues (2005), rather than focus on the constructs of consciousness and unconsciousness, have given emphasis to the different levels of knowledge and communication, starting from mother–infant observations. The results have confirmed the fundamental role of implicit procedural knowing in a dialogue between two people. In the mother–infant dyad, this form of communication provides important information to the infant about its self and self with other, laying the foundations for the personal sense of identity and for the personal IWM. In a dialogue between two adults, the implicit steers communication in the direction of confirming one's IWM, or not.

So what works in the therapeutic communication?

In classical psychoanalysis, change was determined by the ability to interpret of the analyst, who was expected to know how to choose when to render his/her reading of things, expressing it clearly to the patient. In classical cognitive therapy, techniques were at the heart of therapy; there was no interpretation, but the therapist was still in the position of observing and studying the other in order to offer solutions. The relational paradigm has changed this notion of care; while the therapist observes, he/she tries to understand the patient and communicates at an implicit level much more than he/she realizes. It is therefore essential that the therapist develop the ability to observe him/herself in the interaction, just as much as the ability to observe the other. It is even more important for the therapist to allow him/herself to be observed by the patient. Change happens at the implicit, presymbolic level, and cannot be entirely expressed in a symbolic way.

*

CHIARA

Chiara, a borderline patient who has been in treatment with me for three years, is very upset about a difficult situation she is experiencing with a woman colleague at work whom she is in love with, but who does not feel the same way about her.

She suffers and is afraid she might do something impulsive that she might regret, as has happened other times before.

T: *You're right, it's risky, that's true, it's risky for various reasons: first of all because this person has made it clear that she does not intend to, well, be close to you, or even to communicate with you.*
C: Sure, but that's just the way she is.
T: *Sure, but it doesn't really matter whether or not that's the way she is.*
C: This . . . what . . . I . . . when I used to fantasize about it once . . . well . . . one thing is if I do it with you, because I know that you care about me! That you take care of me. And you know that (she smiles).
T: (She smiles and teases) *And how do you know?*
C: . . . so I don't worry.
T: *And how do you know that I care about you?* (she smiles).
C: You told me (they both laugh).
T: (She continues to tease, smiling) *Oh! I told you? And you believe what I say?*
C: You said it! (smiling).
T: *So if someone tells you they care about you, you believe them?*
C: Oh, come on! (they laugh together).
T: *How can you tell that I care about you?*
C: You told me (she laughs).
T: *Yes, of course I told you, but I didn't communicate it to you in some many words, did I . . . ?*
C: Well, ok! Ok!
T: *I didn't tell you 'Chiara, I care about you' did I? I didn't say that, right?*
C: No, you said . . . I told you, I told you a while back, remember?
T: *Well! I remember many things, because you told me and we told each other many things.*
C: The declaration of love?
T: *A while back?*
C: Last September.
T: (As she recalls the scene) *Hmm.*
C: That story about cleavage?
T: *Yes, I remember.*
C: I said to you, 'But I love you' and you answered, 'Yes, me too.'
T: (She smiles) *Yes, it's true.*
C: And then over the years I've seen that you care about me, although, if I may say so, a little less this year . . . (in a teasingly reproachful tone).

T: *This year I was a bit naughty?* (they laugh together).
C: *Hmm.*
T: *So over the years you've seen that I care about you?*
C: *That you care about me.*
T: *Well, of course, it's true! So you're telling me you can afford these things with me, because I care about you, while you can't afford it with ...*
C: (Interrupting) *With you, yes! Well, because you return my feelings.*
T: *Of course.*
C: *I don't have to worry.*
T: *Hmm.*

*

When I met her, Chiara told me that she was in love with me and for a long time the experiences she talked about were no less problematic and distressing than the ones she talks about today in relation to someone else. It took us a long time to be able to acknowledge the nature of our relationship and to shed light on the feelings, motivations and confusion that governed them. This exchange was especially important for Chiara and I. For the first time she was able to speak explicitly about my affection for her. I was surprised and touched by this. I was especially pleased that she had sensed my interest for her, in spite of her difficulties in distinguishing between affects and their underlying motivations. My provocative questions about how she had understood that I cared about her concealed some embarrassment on my part, but they were also meant to probe how Chiara had come to the conclusion that I cared about her and that she was safe with me. '*By how you've behaved all this time ...*' she says, referring to our history. Time has surely helped us to get to know and to trust each other. Chiara continues, 'You told me, remember? That time about cleavage, I told you "But I love you," and you answered, *"Yes, me too".*' That brief interaction had summed up the mix of feelings that Chiara brought to me. She had understood what 'me too' meant, just as I had understood what she meant by 'I love you.' This exchange summed up the many sessions, at times turbulent and frustrating, during which Chiara thought she was going to have to end yet another therapy, yet another relationship, and I too had doubts about what to do. Now our relationship seems strong; we are free to be ourselves in this relationship and to care for each other. It is hard to describe the intensity of that moment, but I am certain that it is impressed inside us and it becomes evident whenever we feel that we are entering into the deep confidentiality that we have conquered for ourselves. It is at times like this that I sense the importance and value of my work.

Recent developments in theories about trauma and dissociation (see Chapter 4) have underscored the importance of *bottom up* approaches in psychotherapy with difficult patients. Ogden, Minton and Pain (2006) have manualized a treatment model in which the body and body work are the main therapeutic tool for developing empathy and change in the therapeutic relationship in order to address the effects of traumatic development. The sense of this approach, as well as of others like EMDR (Shapiro, 1995), has been extensively described using etiopathogenic theories, which inform us on the damage produced by traumatic development processes.

I believe that different therapeutic practices that actively use the body can reach good results only within the framework of an etiopathogenic model that steers us and allows us to understand the sense of what we are doing.

Trying to consider and recognizing the different levels of mental functioning, and knowing how to attune ourselves to the patient in order to develop an alliance is the focus of a therapeutic process that does not consider mind and body as two separate entities.

The ability to decipher and use the signs of implicit communication belongs to many therapists who consider the body and work with it, although they do not use specific manualized techniques but rather a creative process within the specific therapeutic relationship.

Such an ability is not specific to us clinicians and theorists, but is to be regarded as a human relational phenomenon, which is well represented in the work of universally known musicians, painters, sculptors, poets, and artists who are able to describe in moving ways human vicissitudes that touch everyone's heart. Art can accomplish marvellous syntheses that are universally understood and engage simultaneously in the aaaaesthetic experience the body with all our senses and cognitive skills.

Psychology, psychiatry, and science always lag behind nature and its course.

The real challenge is to be able to integrate knowledge and maintain the freshness and vivacity of a child when facing experiences, the immediacy and creativity of the artist, who follows the flow of his/her mental and physical energy when venturing into experience and being surprised.

SECOND PART

The group: methodological considerations

The group model referred to is inspired by the intersubjective and relational perspective in clinical psychology. The focus is primarily on interpersonal relations. The group is regarded as a source of stimuli, which urge individuals to express their own relational style. Relations among group members therefore carry therapeutic potential (Yalom, 1995).

The therapist is empathically and actively involved in the group, or intervenes where and when appropriate, commenting on what is happening within the therapeutic process. The therapist favours interpersonal interactions and exchanges, directly facilitating an analysis of the communication, with an approach that is inspired primarily by motivational theories. One works simultaneously on each patient's IWM and on the group as a whole, bearing in mind the individual journey of each patient as well as the developmental stage that the group is going through.

In Figure 6.3, one can see the interaction between two levels of communication, the explicit and the implicit. The therapist's interventions emphasize the implicit level of the interaction, 'You seem to be rather irritated Marisa' with questions like 'you assumed it how, from what?' which compel the group members to try to understand the other's intentions.

In Figure 6.4, each one begins to work on his/her ability to understand the other's intentions according to his/her own specific IWM. A group context begins to take shape in which interpersonal learning is possible, which can stimulate decentring and favour mentalization. The group consciousness is expressed in all its complexity.

Every emotional response of the individual members seems to capture a partial aspect of a more complex experience (as shown in Figure 6.5). Marisa later said that she had come to the group carrying all those emotions inside of her.

The setting reproduces a social microcosm, in which the patients feel stimulated to show themselves to others, precisely because the interactions in the here and now bring to the fore important material on personal functioning to be explored together. So the group makeup is heterogeneous: the patients all share the same diagnosis and pursue the same therapeutic

> I can't get men to take me seriously. The other day I asked my husband to give me 100 euros to pay a bill and he said yes, but we have to make love. I said ok, but let's hurry. The door was ajar and our son saw us. When we came out of the bedroom he beat me up and I let him, because he was right.
>
> **Marisa**

But why did you say yes to your husband?

Carla

> I don't know, he insists, he can't accept the separation, he tells the kids that it's my fault we separated, because he thinks I go with other men
>
> **Marisa**

But where are you in all this? It seems like you passively endure everything others do

Sara

> If I didn't have that problem I wouldn't be here, don't you think?
>
> **Marisa**

Marisa, you seem to be rather irritated by what Sara said

Therapist

> She sounded a bit aggressive, it felt like she was attacking, judging, criticizing me, whereas I'm not upset at Carla.
>
> **Marisa**

How did Sara's question "Where are you in all this?" lead you to assume that she was attacking you?

Therapist

> I felt it right away, in my gut. First a sense of irritation, then what seemed like confusion, not understanding what she was saying; then it was how she said it and what she said.
>
> **Marisa**

So you felt by how Sara was communicating that she intended to criticize you. What did the others perceive?

Therapist

Figure 6.3

The relational/multi-motivational approach 173

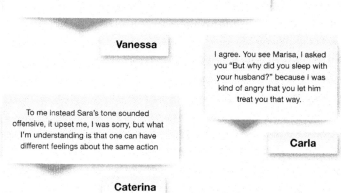

Figure 6.4

Figure 6.5

goals. One tends to de-stigmatize the aspect relating to the disorder in favour of the possibility of experiencing in the group what will and must later be brought outside of the group.

This therapeutic approach integrates different theoretical-clinical contributions and considers the group as a whole (Bion, 1959) as well as the individual group members and their personal therapeutic process.

The ongoing dialectic between the individuals and the whole is one of the distinctive elements of the working model (Ivaldi et al., 2005).

Is affiliation an inborn motivation?

Universality, solidarity, and sharing (Yalom, 1995) are three known group therapeutic factors that make it possible – according to motivational theories – to deactivate the agonistic motivational system, signalling the activation of affiliation and cooperation.

From the beginning of the history of group therapy, various authors have suggested that there may be an inborn tendency towards affiliation. Burrow (1927) spoke of the *primary tendency to aggregate* at a time when the psychoanalytic society was far from making the transition from studying relationships involving two people (the couple) to relationships involving three or more people (small group), which would later represent a revolutionary shift in the history of psychology.

Foulkes (1975) spoke of the *foundation matrix*, Bion (1959) of *values* and *basic assumptions*, with the same intent to describe an inborn tendency to aggregate in humankind.

It was Lichtenberg (1989) who introduced the *affiliative motivational system* (see Chapter 1), which he initially described as an extension of the inborn attachment model, underscoring that the difference between the two universal dimensions lies in the makeup of the unit, not in the affective experience sought. The goal is a sense of shared belonging, which enables and enriches personal growth. The child observes its family not as individuals but as a unit. In the recent revision of the motivational theory, Lichtenberg, Lachmann, and Fosshage (2011) define affiliation as an IMS distinct from the attachment system.

The motivation to form a group is not always affiliative. Groups are often formed for aversive reasons; for instance, one joins forces to fight an external enemy. Freud's view of groups was prevalently negative and, like him, several authors have underscored the worst and potentially dangerous aspects of the combination of affiliation and aversive motivations. It is easy to find such examples in the various types of 'pack-like groups', gangs that pursue extremely destructive goals.

Although there is no denying the destructive potential of a group when it is driven by an agonistic motivation, Lichtenberg insists on the sense of affiliation as being a fundamental and aggregational motivation. Affiliation is a resource by means of which the individual *'calms him/herself down, asserts him/herself, and finds confirmation of his/her value'* (Translated from J.D. Lichtenberg, 1995, *Psicoanalisi e sistemi motivazionali*, p. 151).

From the point of view of evolutionary cognitivism, it has not been possible so far to find the invariant that could define – from an ethological standpoint – affiliation as an inborn motivation like the others. It is equated to egalitarian cooperation, the last IMS to be included among IMSs in the cognitive-evolutionary theory (Liotti and Monticelli, 2008).

The invariant for these motivations emerged from the studies of Tomasello (1999), which emphasized the ability to understand and interpret others as intentional agents, capable that is of elaborating symbols and meanings and communicating by means of a shared language. According to these studies, such an ability belongs exclusively to human beings as compared to non-human primates. Tomasello underscored that the development of this species-specific skill is associated with the *'ultrasociality'* of the human species. It thus becomes possible to learn not only *from* others, but *through* others (Cacioppo and Patrick, 2008).

The 'combined attention scenes', which constitute the invariant in ethological terms, imply a shift from a dyadic to a triadic relationship. We are talking about a small group.

Over time, the relationship with the other, the understanding of intentionality, and the transfer of information among individuals, flow into *cumulative cultural evolution*. In other words, as cultural traditions become more complex *they can deal with a broader range of adaptive functions* (Translated from M. Tomasello, 1999, *The Cultural Origins of Human Cognition*, p. 56).

Whenever a significant evolutionary step is made, things start over from there. According to Tomasello, we are what we are today thanks to this twofold evolution: biological and cultural.

Being in a relationship using two session rooms

The other distinguishing feature of the REMOTA model is the interconnection of group psychotherapy and individual psychotherapy. The individual therapist is present also in the group and this lends continuity to the therapeutic work, favouring timely interventions that have an impact on the relational process under way. The fact that therapist and patient move from one session room to the other is the most significant element.

'I'll see you in the group.' When does the alternation between the two settings start?

We have seen that already during the first phase of treatment the therapist expands the context, preparing as far as possible an intersubjective field by tapping into the resources available in the patient's life, negotiating with him/her the meaning and nature of the therapeutic relationship. When the therapeutic couple has established a common space for collaboration, the therapist 'goes with' the patient into the group. Before this happens, the patient must first address the relational difficulties he/she may have with the therapist–what Kohut (1971) calls self-object transference–as opposed to the repetitive transference (see also Segalla, 1998), in order to create a basis for collaboration (what I refer to as a 'free zone') to set out from and go back to in the stressful moments he/she will face during group therapy.

*

ELSA (6)

The group

Each important step in the therapy was marked by a rather intense activation of Elsa's profoundly negative experience. This also occurred when she started group therapy. It was the group's first encounter, not only Elsa's. A colleague of mine and I grouped together various patients who could benefit from a dual setting – the individual and the group setting.

Elsa arrived late that day. While some of the more outgoing people were keeping the group entertained, I thought about what might be happening to Elsa. Then she arrived, apologized quickly and sat down with the others. She was struggling. She seemed to be projected back into the past: her distressed expression, at times hostile, the evasive eyes and the movement of her hands, nervous and discordant with the rest of the body, which was perfectly still. Two years of therapy suddenly seemed to vanish. At the end of the session, Elsa literally ran away without saying goodbye to anyone. I was worried and, after reflecting on the situation at length and discussing it with my colleague, I decided to call her. It was the first time I did this. I told her that I was worried and that I wanted to know what was going on. Elsa was happy I called, although she felt uncomfortable. Once again, she needed help, but this frightened and upset her. She told me that she was having trouble and that she was angry at herself for how she had dealt with the group. At the following individual session, we further explored what had happened.

My phone call, which came at a particular stage in the therapeutic process, marked an important turning point in our relationship. I was able to have a caretaking attitude at a difficult moment for Elsa because I felt that our alliance was already well-tested; Elsa had made great progress, to the point of establishing a sufficiently trusting relationship with me, understanding that help did not necessarily have dangerous implications and that her vulnerability did not jeopardize her ability to choose how to be in a relationship, how to be helped. I was also aware of how the change in setting was benefitting the therapeutic relationship.

We experienced for the first time the possibility of leaving the individual therapy room together, meeting other people, and then returning to it and commenting on what happened.

*

Such an experience creates interesting opportunities for therapeutic work: a dual setting organized in this way makes new relational scenarios possible. The vantage point changes, it is not always the same; we observe each other as we engage in different interactions. During the individual session we comment on some events that we experienced together: it is not quite the same as working with narrated events.

*

In this case, we discussed Elsa's fear and shame, her dread of being labelled as *'weird'*, a *'serious case'* and *'difficult'*, of being judged negatively by the therapist in comparison with the others and, therefore, of being rejected. In following sessions, Elsa talked about the difficulties she experienced in the group. She started making eye contact and slowly began to explore new ways of expressing herself and of asking in relation to her needs. Elsa revealed herself faster than other group members and her initial impasse was quickly overcome. Much of the work in this sense was done in individual therapy, where our alliance, which was already quite strong, evolved significantly, leading to an ever greater differentiation and individuation on Elsa's part. At the same time, in the group, surrounded by peers, she was be able to thrive from a direct exchange with other participants, which allowed her to explore different interactive styles and problematic aspects of communication directly related to her IWM.

The therapeutic process in the group setting prompted significant great changes in Elsa's life, such as her break-up with Luca. Elsa realized how different they were and how fragile were the foundations upon which they had started building their life together. It gave Elsa the support she needed to be on her own and to endure Luca's insistent attempts to restore the old equilibrium which was based on turbulent fights and various types of 'highs'.

Some time later, Elsa ran into her former husband, Giovanni. Their chance encounter was very emotional. Elsa was happy to see him, the anger seemed to vanish all at once, but she was distraught when she discovered that he had another woman. During therapy, Elsa went over their relationship and saw some events in a different light compared to the past. She came to realize that she was still very attached to Giovanni and that before she had not understood how much he meant to her. After some time, during which they had many intense encounters, Elsa and Giovanni got back together again. His sudden and mysterious disappearance after their separation also started to make sense: their feelings had remained intact, almost frozen for some time. In the light of a new awareness gained during the time they were apart, Giovanni was able to experience those feelings again and face many of the difficulties the two of them had encountered. This reconciliation was extremely important for the final phase of Elsa's therapy, during which we addressed the self-harming ritual of removing her eyelashes.

*

What is the developmental benefit of creating a group?

It is no news that all human beings need each other and that by joining forces it is possible to achieve sometimes unhoped-for results. These two reasons alone would be enough to explain the importance of creating a group. According to my experience, however, there is more to the value of group work.

The first contracting stage of treatment paves the way for more sophisticated levels of clinical dialogue. Entering a group provides more opportunities to reflect on interaction with others and to become aware of qualities and shortcomings. Work with patients takes place in the two session rooms and in their real life, involving many people, but always with the same companion, the therapist, with whom they dialogue constantly. This experience will have an impact, implicitly and explicitly, on their IWM. The presence of the same therapist in both settings makes it possible to observe a wide range of relationships according to different combinations. Such a network enriches therapeutic work exponentially. Sometimes the individual therapy room becomes a place where to discuss what was experienced together. Dysfunctional behaviours, which in the individual setting can be inferred only from the stories told by the patient, are revealed in the 'here and now' of the group setting. This often coincides with a turbulent period during which good use can be made of the two different therapeutic contexts. Relational difficulties with the group members bring to the fore issues discussed in the individual setting or help to identify new ones. It is possible to reflect on significant interactions, on one's way of behaving, and to consider the point of view of others, in an exchange that involves all the persons who have shared an experience. The group therapy context may also represent scenarios in which it is easier for patients to recall 'model scenes' relevant to their own family group and the first social groups they have belonged to.

*

MONICA

Monica, a young patient suffering from borderline personality disorder, after an initial period during which she has accepted the role of the 'fun and resourceful one', starts to develop an interest in Luca, a young group member, and to seek comfort in him outside of the group. The young man picks up on the ambiguous attention, and is annoyed and worried by her insistence. He discusses the matter with his therapist, saying over the phone how he feels, and the two, encouraged by their individual therapists, decide to talk about it in the group. During that difficult session, Monica says she understands Luca's concern, but his reaction makes her feel rejected. Tension rises and Monica becomes more hostile and unwilling to dialogue with the rest of the group. She can only see her own point of view and seems overwhelmed by humiliation and shame. At one point she stands up and heads for the door, crying angrily. Before leaving the room she screams, *'It's always the same old story, I can only make trouble. I'm the disruptive element! I should just leave!'* She bursts out of the room. Everyone is paralyzed for a few seconds, then her individual therapist follows Monica out of the room, leaving the rest of the group with the other therapist. Her therapist persuades Monica not to leave, to manage the crisis differently than she usually would. Her mind filled with persecutory thoughts and a sense of exclusion, the patient comes back into the group room and says she is willing to stay, provided that the episode not be discussed with the group and that she may talk about it with the individual therapist during their next session. The group accepts Monica's request, respecting her moment of crisis.

*

In this episode, the therapist functioned as a 'vicarious mind', leading the patient to explore the possible mental representations and her own as well as the group's emotional states at the heart of experience.

Needless to say, such traumatic experiences had occurred repeatedly in Monica's life and had already been discussed in therapy through Monica's stories. This time, however, it all happened contextually; patient and therapist were part of a 'model scene' and could go over it together. The episode provided valuable material for the therapeutic couple to work with, first in the individual and then in the group setting, highlighting different elements of the relational context. At the same time, it was possible for Monica to experience a relationship of closeness and sharing with her therapist (caregiver), which allowed her to explore new ways of coping with distress with respect to her IWM.

Working in a group with one's individual therapist makes it possible to go over problematic aspects of one's IWM related to the affiliative motivational system. In keeping with Lichtenberg and Segalla, I believe some of the traumas suffered during childhood and in adult life stem from the dysfunctional characteristics of the context one belongs to. In family groups, just like in other groups, the agonistic motivation may prevail over the affiliative motivation and intertwine with it. This may generate a traumatizing context, like a disorganized attachment relationship with a caregiver which, from this point of view, is part of a context. Just as it is possible to use the dyadic therapeutic relationship to overcome the traumas caused by an insecure or disorganized attachment experience, we can use a larger context like the therapy group with the same individual therapist to deal with pain associated with traumatic affiliative experiences.

The therapeutic relationship and the group

I have learned from experience that, even when only the individual setting is used, having some training in group dynamics is an important resource for the therapist. The ability to turn one's attention simultaneously to the many variables of a context becomes an essential skill that can be tapped into under many circumstances.

The group in itself is a complex reality, a 'dynamic whole', quoting Lewin (1948). In order to understand and to leverage its complexity, it is necessary to adopt various vantage points that are constantly communicating. To be a group therapist, one must acquire the ability to broaden the scope of one's observation and perception before what is observable and perceivable. One must also be able to synthesize and make choices after rapidly assessing the many variables at play, according to the priorities. The therapist works on the individuals and on the whole at the same time, exercising his/her empathic skills in a more complex way than in the dual setting.

This reverberates on the patients, whose ability to experience complexity not as a chaotic but as a harmonious multiplicity thus improves. Learning to deal with complexity is therefore one of the most important resources of group work.

In a small group of six or seven people it becomes possible to work interactively, harnessing most of the group's therapeutic potential. Every group has its own intensic qualities resulting from the combination of its members, the context in which it is formed, and the motivations that sustain it. Every group has an identity of its own, which evolves in the various phases of the process.

The group thus becomes an additional therapeutic resource in the sense that it is used not only as a container, but also as a *multiple context of vitality* (Ivaldi, 2009) that sheds light on the internal dynamics which the participants reflect on during the stages of treatment, clearly with the help of the therapist.

Many patients find it harder to expose themselves to a group than to just one individual. The fear of being judged is easily triggered. The group context evokes scenarios from the past – one's family, school context, first peer groups. The group forces everyone to address the problem of 'what others will think of me' and, therefore, the fear of being seen. Using this constructively, one can reveal one's fear of being judged and of making a mistake, of being seen or not being seen. This usually transforms competition into solidarity and sharing. Another interesting aspect is that the therapist will be seen by the group, which reinforces the egalitarian and mutual nature of the relationship with the patients. Furthermore, when a patient joins a group, the relationship with the individual therapist changes because aspects of both, which did not emerge in the individual context, inevitably surface. Each one will have the opportunity to observe him/herself during the interactions with the others, and for each individual living that relationship in a broader context will elicit significant memories of their early family affiliative dimensions.

*

What was surprising about the experience was the new 'angle' from which group work allowed each of us to see ourselves, our strengths as well as our weaknesses. Even more surprising was getting to know the therapist individually and then 'discovering' him in the group.

*

From the I to the we: cohesion, not fusion

The concept of cohesion and the sense of belonging are comparable to the notion of 'therapeutic alliance' which refers more specifically to the individual setting. Cohesion is understood here as the development of a sense of solidarity that holds the group together. More than a therapeutic factor, cohesion is indispensable in order for group therapy and work in a group in general to be successful. When there is a high degree of cohesion, it is easier to express feelings and to analyze them freely in an atmosphere of mutual help and solidarity, in which one feels free to both criticize someone else's work constructively and to commend it. An indication of the degree of cohesion in a group is the participants' ability to manifest their difficulties and to talk about their mistakes.

The level of cohesion is an expression of the group's ability to function, at a meta, superordinate level, in an affiliative and cooperative way.

A cohesive group is formed by individuals who distinguish themselves and recognize each other.

One of the main issues addressed by a group is that of identity/diversity. It is in a group that a dialectic process involving the I and the We becomes possible.

The sociologist Elias (1987), tries to overcome the opposition of the two terms I/We by resorting to the image of the *network* (Foulkes, 1975), suggesting that people change *in* and *through* their mutual relationships. It is fundamental for the individual to distinguish him/herself from the others. This, however, implies recognizing the others.

Differentiation is a process and necessarily involves problems and conflicts.

Facing the conflict in order to cooperate

In order to achieve a sense of cohesion and belonging, it is therefore necessary for a group to be able to face and to manage conflict in its conscious and unconscious components. In this sense, one clearly understands the therapeutic value of the clinical group and the crucial role played by the therapist.

It is not hard to realize that there are few truly cohesive groups.

Many people, on account of their difficult life experiences, beginning from a history of insecure and disorganized attachment, do not experience such a relational condition and consequently do not easily aspire to it. Western society, with the laws of its economic and political system, pushes people in the direction of competition and individualism, certainly not towards cooperation, whose developmental goal has nothing to do with the consumption of material goods and with profit. On the other hand, emotional wellbeing and serenity do not have much to do with consumption and profit, as far as we can see working with discomfort. Consequently, although affiliation and cooperation are a value, a goal to reach and a condition from which to start over in order to live more serenely with others, it is very hard to attain.

To feel a deep sense of cohesion and belonging it is necessary to renounce asserting oneself merely as an individual, which must not be confused with defining oneself and being assertive, which instead are indispensable in order to be with other people, avoiding the risk of fusion.

The group poses the conflictual problem that '*in order to be oneself one must experience the different, or rather the possible "differents"*' (Di Maria and LoVerso, 1995: 21).

It is crucial to distinguish the sense of cohesion of an affiliative nature from the cohesion of a group dictated by purposes which are considered important but primarily of an agonistic nature, of the '*union is strength*' sort. The affiliative motivation pursues a purpose of high existential value. The sense of deep joy one feels when one exchanges a look of complicity with or feels affective closeness to someone else, is in itself a fundamental value for us human beings which reflects our sense of vulnerability as well as our developmental priorities. All this is passed on to the patients if the therapist has learned and experienced it first hand during his/her training.

Achieveing collaborativeness is therefore a goal to be reached, not a given at the outset.

It is possible to overcome conflict only by being in it, provided that one acknowledges how important it is to growth. The group therapist plays an important role in this sense: the developmental advantage of affiliation and cooperation must be clear, and he/she must not be afraid to go through conflictual stages to achieve them. This will help the group to handle the anxiety that is usually present in moments of crisis. The therapist must tolerate difficult moments where aversive motivations prevail over others, and the participants do not have full awareness of what is going on.

In these cases, the leader's ability to understand and tolerate feelings of alarm and anger is very important, even more so than the verbal ability to stimulate reflection on different aspects of each member's personal experience. This ability at an implicit level should influence the group. This task does not differ much from what the therapist does in an individual session, but in the group it acquires a different meaning on account of the context.

The group peers play an important role in managing the conflict, making it possible, through their personal contributions, to shift the focus insofar as they stimulate others to see another point of view, the same reality from a different slant. Moreover, time and space are subdivided differently than in the dyad.

*

SOFIA (8)

The group
The invalidation of the emotional experience and the inability to understand the intentions of the other had been Sofia's daily bread. Her IWM and the family scenario we had started to reflect on came to the fore even more clearly during the group experience we started after her mood became stabilized and she developed a greater capacity for reflection during the period following the attempted suicide.

The group was no news to Sofia, who was already familiar with how I work and had known from the start that, in the course of her therapy, she might have had the opportunity to alternate individual and group sessions. She brought a great deal of life into the group. Her congeniality, hearty laughter and irony captivated all the participants at once. However, not much time passed before her ability to involve and become involved took on more dramatic tones. The first clashes with the other members brought out her vulnerabilities, as quickly as only a group can. Just as she had presented herself as being open to a genuine communication, she proved to be rigid and withdrawn whenever misunderstandings and conflicts arose. Sofia's Model Scene came to the fore early on. On the basis of her very sharp perceptions, Sofia amplified the emotion and sense of alarm, which was triggered by her *automatic* interpretation of the other's intentions – without checking, without reflecting. Her reaction was powerful, like an overflowing river, hyper-emotional. The forcefulness of her reactions inevitably placed her at centre stage; the group focused its attention on her, forgetting how it all started and who it started from. The responsibilities of the others were pushed into the background while she stood out for her behaviours, which irritated and/or scared everyone. She became the problem. She was perceived as being 'the weird one'. The more Sofia felt she was judged by the others, the more she exploded in a blend of desperate rage and fear and, like a lion in a cage, she wore herself out, showing her teeth, reminding everyone that she would fight until the end. The phenomenon had occurred countless times in her life, in her family and now also in the group. The relationship of trust between us seemed strong enough to withstand the conflicts that arose in the group, although it became very tiresome at times. It was very hard to interrupt what was happening and make her stop and reflect because she was unable to mitigate the sense of finding herself in a situation of 'red alert' and consequently she could not give herself time to think and feel. Her fight-flight system was activated and the arousal seemed so high that she could not think straight. There were moments when it was necessary, and indeed useful, for us to watch the tapes of the group sessions. On those occasions, Sofia and I were able to find the tranquility we needed to notice the details of the interaction and reflect together. Like in slow motion, we could discuss the reactions she and the others had had and everything that had escaped her during the experience emerged and surprised Sofia, who felt somewhat disoriented but curious. She began to understand that sometimes her interpretation did not correspond to the actual intentions of the other. She also started to recognize the sense of alarm that became pervasive and made her react violently and so quickly as not to be able to reflect and stay in contact with herself and the others. It was just the embryo of a new awareness, but the two of us took good care of that first form of life.

The group was troubled by the experiences of conflict and by Sofia's reactions. Cohesion was uncertain, some members were particularly judgemental, and in spite of the fact that we had discussed this, the sense of shame prevailed at times in the group, causing some people to withdraw, close up and take a distance. As far as Sofia was concerned, her strong reactions triggered the 'scapegoat' phenomenon, in other words the group would join forces, feeling sound, right, and isolated Sofia as the 'weird one', the 'sick one'. In this way, the group avoided really coming forward and fooled itself that it would be spared judgement.

It was not easy to analyze these dynamics, but it was exactly what we were called to do in therapy and, little by little, the model scenes of each participant became clear. Sofia was surely an explosive force that perturbed the group and did not allow it to work comfortably in an atmosphere of 'polite' sharing. With her you had to get to the bottom of things and, especially, past appearances.

*

The therapist stimulates the group to proceed in the direction of cohesion and affiliation, which make it possible to reveal oneself, establish intimacy and go through conflict; at the same time, in a dialectical sense, going through conflict will promote a greater sense of cohesion and cooperation in the group. The therapist must be capable of following this ongoing dialectical process, intervening when necessary to stimulate the group to proceed towards cooperation, but also making room for the group's therapeutic potential, stepping aside when his/her intervention is not required.

If the therapist's intervention stimulates reflection on the nature of the conflict, within a framework that is as free from prejudice as possible, he/she will help the group to observe the same phenomenon from the same vantage point, trying to understand it together. Within the group context, such a dimension of joint attention is enhanced by the presence of a third person who changes the representation of the relationship. Both patients and therapist avail themselves of this.

Why does the integration of the individual and the group setting improve working conditions? A biopsychosocial hypothesis based on evolution theory

Transitioning from the individual to the group setting facilitates therapeutic work by making it easier to reflect on the relationship together. I would now like to dwell on one of the possible reasons why a setting thus organized should work in terms of effectiveness, reducing drop-out rates and facilitating therapeutic work, thereby improving the living conditions and curbing the dysfunctional behaviours of our patients.

We will refer to the relational paradigm, which allows us to combine the contributions of authors who have tried to integrate neurobiology and psychosocial knowledge (Donald, 1991; Schore, 1994; Siegel, 1999; LeDoux, 1996), authors who have worked on identifying the neurobiological processes of consciousness (Edelman, 1989, 1992; Damasio, 1994), and multi-motivational theories (Gianni Liotti's cognitive-developmental theory and Lichtenberg's Psychoanalytic theory) into one biopsychosocial consciousness model.

According to Edelman, all mental functions are an expression of one skill – categorization – which is structured according to different levels of complexity (perception, simple emotion, complex emotion, language, consciousness). Each level corresponds to a different way of organizing the various types of relationship between the self and the environment (interaction, rapport, relationship in the various expressions of complexity).

'The various functions are built within a developmental process that allows for the progressive quantitative and qualitative enhancement of the ability to categorize; from the initial constraints of concrete and immediate experience to the final freedom afforded by abstract imagination, by the discrimination and generalization of meanings' (Ceccarelli, 2005: 242–3).

Every transition to a higher level makes one aware of the level below. The developmental transition from simple emotion-nuclear consciousness to complex emotion-extended consciousness, for instance, corresponds to re-categorizing from a level of the 'self with the other' to one of the 'self with the group'. Consciousness makes it possible to modulate the behaviour that pertains to the type of relationship characterizing the underlying level, insofar as it broadens the differentiation of the self-representation and of the representation of the type of environment with which the individual interacts at that given level. This would explain the clinical findings on patients treated by integrating the individual and group settings, which point to an increase in meta-cognition and an improvement in therapeutic working conditions. The patient's transition into the group activates a higher functioning – that is difficult to attain in the dual setting alone – which allows one to be aware of oneself with the other, that is, to achieve a greater differentiation of self and other, which is required in order to modulate one's behaviour in the relationship. In order to be aware of oneself in the group it is therefore necessary to activate the higher functions: secondary consciousness and then self-awareness, which entail a more complex categorization of the 'self in society'.

In the working model presented here, the transition from the individual to the group setting facilitates mentalization processes inasmuch as it allows the therapeutic couple to work on itself. This is very difficult – if not impossible – to do with patients presenting serious metacognitive deficits associated with the activation of attachment. Such a transition occurs at an implicit relational level: the mere fact of being in an enlarged context with their therapist allows patients – even in the presence of metacognitive deficits – to distinguish the dual relationship; this makes it to reflect on the latter at an early stage. By shifting to the higher levels of mental functioning the group can reflect on itself. The cooperative and affiliative motivations become more complex with every transition and it is possible to grasp more sophisticated meanings of 'being with'. In order to achieve this, it is sufficient to shift from a dyadic relational dimension to a relational dimension extended to the small group, which should automatically facilitate access to awareness of self-other relationships. The therapist must however bear in mind the difference between the levels of activation of consciousness, hence between the different therapeutic objectives that can be pursued with the patients. The group leader must be aware of the greater value of the group cooperative dimension and of belonging, even when the patients are not. This will greatly impact the way in which group work is conducted.

*

SOFIA (9)

Before turning forty, Sofia was finally able to leave Franco: it was not a painless process, but at least there was no drama involved. As was to be expected, Franco reacted by pressing her and refused to accept her decision. However painful, Sofia knew it was inevitable. The dream had died long ago and she was able to see clearly the situation she was in and the person she was with. She had started to be kinder to herself and to others and was saddened by her decisions, including the abortion, and by the fact that she had failed to fulfil her goals.

There was no trace of depression and the psychiatrist started to reduce her medication. Sofia was glad about this and began to experience the new encounters she had more lightheartedly; she now took time to observe herself and did not need to expose herself immediately in relationships that were just beginning. It was a good phase for her, which was crowned by a gift. While chatting, Sofia met a man. Sofia described Mario as an interesting person, very polite, different from the other men she had met in the past. She thought he was attractive but found some of his attitudes ridiculous. She did not think this story stood a chance; on the contrary, she did not feel anything resembling falling in love. However, she was interested in Mario and, in a way, she did like him . . . Sofia continued to see him and remained suspended; she kept telling me stories in which he always appeared ridiculous to her. She described him as being *a little slow*, not very smart, with many hangups. Basically, with me and in the group Sofia acted like a 'princess' who measured her suitors and enjoyed making fun of them. She was amused by the fact that he talked about love.

'*Doctor, he tells me I'm beautiful, that he's falling in love with me! Can you imagine? . . . In love with who? Can't he see that I don't feel the same? Here's another guy who doesn't get me! And most of all, he doesn't know what he's talking about!*'

Her tone was very sarcastic. In the group, some identified with her critical, at times cynical attitude towards love; others instead took Mario's defences and told her she shouldn't hurt him or lose him. I listened to her and sometimes laughed along, but I volunteered no opinion regarding Mario and what she told me; when she asked me, I merely agreed with her that she could not force herself to fall in love and that she had no responsibility for that. Deep inside though I felt that there was something very good about that story. I felt it had the potential to become a great love. I kept these feelings to myself, waiting for signs confirming this hunch. Sofia kept seeing him and did not let go, because she sensed there was something worthwhile in him and would be sorry to lose him, but she also felt anger and impatience building up inside of her. One of the many times she questioned herself as to why she could not fall in love with Mario I said to her:

'I've thought several times about the fact that you think it's strange that he should be interested and in love with you. Are you sure you're not scared, Sofia? Why all this anger? You could simply be indifferent, don't you think? Instead you get very angry with him. It's as if you were putting him to the test: Regina reginella quanti passi devo fare per arrivare al tuo castello con la fede e con l'anello?' (Children's rhyme that goes something like 'Oh queen, beautiful queen, how many steps must I take to get to your castle with a wedding band?') Sofia laughed. 'We can't challenge the fact that you're not falling in love, but we can explore the fact that you feel so angry, because it's a little strange, don't you think?'

Not only did she agree, but she felt very stimulated. She began to see things from a different angle and started to develop a passionate interest. Something extraordinary had happened to her. Mario had really been a gift, as Sofia would say. This man withstood her anger without giving too much importance to her impatient reactions. He seemed to be humble enough to put himself out there. He endured the trials the princess was putting him through and was passing the test. Sofia, who had developed a greater awareness of her fears, became more and more involved and felt happy, but still very frightened. I was happy for her. In the group Sofia was considered lucky: she was willing to reach out to the others thanks to her spontaneous generosity, but also because at times she felt guilty towards those who were not as lucky and perhaps a little envious. There were conflicts in her relationship with Mario, as with all couples, especially when they moved in together. They were measuring each other and negotiating the relationship. Sofia was still on the lookout, she was not sure yet that she could stay. Sofia's parents had established an excellent relationship with Mario, and this made her even happier. Some time passed and things seemed to proceed well. Sofia was off her medication, she had cautiously started considering the possibility of having a baby, they renovated their home to make room for a nursery. Everything seemed to be going for the best. But Sofia relapsed and acted impulsively once again: she took too many benzodiazepines that she kept at home, thus causing panic and despair among her family, us caretakers, and the group members (see Sofia (6), p. 155).

Sofia and Mario had gotten into an argument and she had had an outburst. Mario was not used to such scenes and left when, in a fit of rage, she told him to get out. He had gone back to his place and had not called her that night or the next day. He wanted 'time to think and let things simmer', he later told her. Sofia had called him a few hours after the fight and when she heard his calm voice, associating it with the fact that he had not tried to contact her, she took it as a sign of lack of interest on his part and concluded that he was going to leave her.

'I couldn't stand it, doctor, I wanted to sleep! I didn't want to feel any more and I looked for the drops: I wanted to calm myself down and downed the whole bottle. It was like going back to the ferocious fights with Franco, I couldn't stand it!'

Sofia looked at me beseechingly:

'Please believe me, I had no intention of killing myself this time! I just wanted to get some sleep! You have to believe me, please!'

She was afraid of the consequences of her gesture, felt guilty and ashamed for having caused so much concern again, was terrified that no one would believe her, that people would stigmatize her and think that her disorder had become chronic. The psychiatrists were adamant: they put her back on medication, prescribing high doses of mood stabilizers and antidepressants. 'It's standard procedure,' they would say. It was a tough blow for Sofia. She was trying to have a baby and knew she would have to delay her plans for who knows how long.

'Please doctor, I don't want to put my life on hold again, I'm 40! I'll never stop this way, I'll be on medication for the rest of my life! And what about Mario? What will he make of all this?'

But the psychiatrists were not willing to negotiate. No one felt like taking responsibility for failing to prescribe treatment. What had happened had generated alarm and dismay around her and, although I believed her and thought it would be possible to try not to follow standard procedure, my opinion was not enough and I did not have the power to make that decision. On the other hand, the fact that she had resorted to such a gesture for the second time had inevitable consequences and I felt that, in a way, it would not be good for her to try to avoid them. So the therapy proceeded, while I tried to help Sofia to cope with the consequences of her actions without losing hope and to work towards change. After the initial alarm and distress, the emotion that prevailed in me, her parents, the group, and the people closest to Sofia was anger. Once again fear risked becoming a pathogenic factor. So, when the time needed to metabolize the fact was over, I felt ready to sustain the people around Sofia – myself included – in voicing their experience authentically. The first to speak up were the group members.

Mara: *'This isn't possible, it just can't be! Do we have to think that whenever you have a problem you attempt suicide?'*
Matteo: *'There are people who experience more serious losses, illness, and they don't react this way, did you ever think about that?'*
Elisa: *'Don't you think that the people around you are suffering? Don't you realize that you hurt them this way?'*
Katia: *'Why didn't you ask for help? Otherwise what's the point of therapy?'*

This obviously introduced new material for our reflection, but we had to distinguish between expressing our emotions authentically and simply passing judgement, conveying the idea that *'There's nothing that can be done! You're hopeless!'* During the last year of therapy, in the group and in our individual work we focused on overcoming fear, accepting the sense of helplessness and remaining open to the possibility of learning also from our worst experiences. Sofia was right, she did not intend to commit suicide, but it was important to lend value to the gesture and its consequences. Taking responsibility, dialoguing, exchanging views, staying open to exploring, not just in the group and with me, but also with her parents and with Mario who, fortunately, after the initial surprise, stood by her side and established an even deeper bond with her: all this was a significant experience for Sofia. They are getting married in July, and the whole group will be with them. The last year has been very intense and Sofia has become 'almost wise'. She has retained her passionate temperament but now she is capable of reflecting, asking for help, understanding what is happening, also in complicated situations. She has grown and become stronger, and this makes her less exposed. She tells me cheerfully about episodes in her life in which she practices reading what happens in the interactions with others and we are both surprised by how well she grasps the undertones of emotional experience. For some months now Sofia's medication has been scaled down. The psychiatrist who followed her recently and was reluctant to reducing the dosages is surprised by how far she has come and admitted to me that the medication does not have much to do with it. I took that as a compliment, but I received the sweetest gift when, during a family gathering, Sofia and her parents said to me, *'Doctor, you're part of the family now!'*

*

Conclusion

In this model, psychotherapy begins with individual treatment and ends with the group. The therapist who in the beginning has 'stood in the front line' in order to respond to the patient's requests, to steer the work and negotiate the therapeutic relationship, can say he/she has succeeded when he/she feels like an active participant in the group. The empathic ability required of the therapist in the initial stages in order to understand which direction to follow while fully engaging in the relationship – being at times very down to earth – will also help him/her to understand when it is time to step back. The therapist will make room for the group and the individual participants to develop significant relationships that will heal the wounds and represent a secure base to go back to, even when therapy is over. Overcoming the natural conflicts that arise when different minds meet, as well as the personal traumas of the participants in a group, makes it possible to reach a state which may not appear to be as useful as the agonistic ones, but is no less important and existentially significant. The feeling of calm and wellbeing one experiences when exchanging a look of complicity with, or feels affective closeness to, someone else, is a fundamental value for us human beings. It is a reflection of our sense of vulnerability and of our strength.

The group can be regarded as the common space in which differences are accepted, people are confronted with others who are different from them, with the purpose of using diversity as a resource that can help to pursue common objectives within an affiliative meta-motivational framework.

Reflecting on groups and on their dynamics, understanding the context of our life and that of patients', allows us to approach our individualistc culture with a critical mind and provides instruments of care that resonate directly with our social and economic context.

*

ELSA (7)

The eyelashes grow back

We are finally there. The moment in the therapeutic process has come when it becomes possible to consider putting an end to the ritual that has been part of

Elsa's daily life for years. The times of impulsive behaviour, of 'getting high', of living like a *'strange, dangerous, rejected animal'* are far behind. Elsa conducts a more balanced life while maintaining her originality. She has managed to work constantly in the past year and now she works in advertising with her husband, using her artistic skills. Our sessions are now mainly characterized by exchanges on her relational life. We talk about emotions in an ever more articulate way. We have gone over her life story, particularly her childhood and adolescence. Elsa has managed to relate her suffering as a child to that of her present life. She has started to accept her story and to see some possibilities for not relapsing into her traumas. We have identified some nubs in Elsa's affective sphere, which, if stroked, sometimes still provoke impulsive reactions or cause pain and deep distress. It is still very hard for her to show her weakness and to seek help and support in difficult moments. She manages to do it with me, with the group, and with her cousin Chiara, with whom she has a very tight relationship. She is starting to do it also with her husband, whom she has allowed herself to get closer to after getting back together with him. Still however, when she feels misunderstood, frustrated because her requests are not met, Elsa responds by reactivating her usual pathological patterns. This happens especially with her husband, whom she is more intimate with. *The final part of Elsa's therapeutic process focuses precisely on this difficulty in asking for help and surrendering herself, which is closely connected with her ritual.*

So far, we have very cautiously approached her deep-set habit of standing for hours in front of the mirror torturing her eyes, realizing that for Elsa this has to do with much more than just self-harm. It appears that the time has come for her to let go of this behaviour, without however neglecting its meaning and, more importantly, the need it expresses. We have discussed all this many times with Elsa. We know that it will not be easy and for this reason we decide to study in depth the most appropriate and protective strategy for her. Therefore, we address at once the profound meanings of the gesture as well as the strictly practical aspects – essentially, how to stop. As a result, we identify various resources that may offer support: Elsa's husband Giovanni becomes involved, saying he is ready to participate; we decide to consult a dermatologist and an ophthalmologist to find out about the difficulties we might encounter in the process of trying to make her eyelashes grow back. In attempting to chart the course and foresee its stumbling blocks, one in particular emerges: the fear of being on her own and not knowing how to cope with possible emotional distress, which, given the importance of the enterprise, she imagines will be very intense. We then consider the possibility of a brief period of residential treatment in a clinic, Villa Margherita, where some of my colleagues work with patients with serious borderline personality disorders and with difficult patients.

I speak with my colleagues, with whom I have been collaborating for a long time and who have a similar theoretical approach to mine. I explain to them my particular request to admit Elsa. They understand and agree to see her. Elsa travels to Vicenza, accompanied by her husband, and speaks with a colleague who explains the treatment protocol and listens to her needs. They make arrangements for her admission after the summer. Elsa comes back feeling highly motivated. She liked the clinic and now has to reflect on how she will go about asking for help during her stay in Vicenza. The meeting at Villa Margherita allows us to further probe Elsa's most delicate issue. Her mother's words, *'you are un-helpable'*, echo in our minds as we reflect on and organize a support network that will be available and ready for Elsa.

Elsa goes on vacation with her husband and comes back in September with a surprise for the group. She has let the lashes of her lower eyelids grow back. She is proud of this result, which was achieved also thanks to Giovanni's supportive presence. Elsa couldn't wait to come back to the group and share the results of her efforts. The group is moved and many feel encouraged by her experience. We all acknowledge the value of the group.

Needless to say, she does not go to Vicenza, but keeps open the possibility of being admitted if the need arises.

In light of these events, all the aids that were set in place turn out to be a response to Elsa's fears rather than an actual necessity.

Elsa is very happy but continues to be rather anxious about her ability to complete the work she has started. She slowly begins to realize how important it is for her to be overly reassured in relation to her efforts, not so much on account of actual dangers, but rather – probably – to validate her experience. I recall Elsa's words, *'My parents did not notice that I would remove my eyelashes . . . they did not realize many things about me.'* This time, what is happening to Elsa cannot not go unnoticed.

This time she is not alone. The group and I follow her and accept her apprehension whenever Elsa expresses it. Even when I have a clear sense that she is not exposed to any real danger, I help her to take precautions because I am aware of the value of that joint effort, which is as a sign of recognition for Elsa that helps to heal old wounds, an intense and reparatory emotional experience.

The most complicated aspect in this final phase of therapy does not involve so much learning to seek help but rather learning to tolerate frustrations in this regard, avoiding relapsing into her negative, desperate and despairing experience in which everything loses meaning and seems pointless. It is this past that triggered Elsa's most destructive behaviours.

So, at the end of the process, the greatest effort consists in helping her to 'actualize' her need for help and closeness. Actualizing a need involves distinguishing between the childhood experience of attachment/affiliation and the current attachment experience with her various caretakers (myself, her husband, her cousin, the group, and so on), differentiating roles and contexts. We reflect together on the different meaning of an attachment relationship with a parent when a child is small and helpless and its very life depends on the care provided by that parent, and an attachment relationship with another person whom one may turn to as an adult. The relationship with a parent and with one's family has no way out, one has no choice, and the conditions of a child are so weak, relative to the different stages of development, as to render parental support indispensable for survival and unique. Different is the condition of an adult who seeks help in moments of need. We discuss these in depth in order for her to accept her past traumatic experience of attachment/affiliation and learn to reactivate her need for attachment by contextualizing it by and by. Such reflections involve all group members, who thus have an opportunity to also consider their own traumas.

This last leg of the journey is not as simple as it may seem. Various difficult moments are experienced in the individual as well as in the group setting. Nevertheless, Elsa manages to complete her therapy. Her eyelashes grow back and she concludes therapy with a particularly moving group session during which, in tears, she talks about her personal experience with every group member. She speaks of her *'travelling companions'*, leaving something to each of them and taking something from each of them with her, saddened by the end of an experience that will never happen again, but full of affection, gratitude, and a deep sense of belonging and affiliation, which is chorally shared by the group.

*

Notes

1 Sustainable means that the life context is not a threat to the patient's physical and psychological wellbeing and a serious obstacle to change.
2 The clinical case of Elsa is from the article published on Psicobiettivo 'What do your eyes say' (Ivaldi, 2006).

Chapter 7

Some methodological considerations on outcome research in psychotherapy and results of a naturalistic study in the treatment of patients with severe axis I/II comorbidity disorders

Giovanni Fassone

Some food for thought

Before discussing the results of a naturalistic study conducted on a sample of difficult patients, it might be of some interest for the reader to consider some aspects regarding the significance of research and its results.

The following reflections are not intended as an attack on research *per se*, nor do they represent an anti-scientific position or a rejection of the current scientific paradigm. They are meant to stimulate a critical reflection on some problematic aspects of medical and scientific research in general. So the question is: *What do we talk about when we talk about outcome studies in psychotherapy?*

It may be useful to begin with two examples that take us straight to the heart of the matter, namely: What do we talk about when we talk about research results, and what do they actually mean for us as researchers, clinicians, and patients?

Some time ago, I was talking with a friend who is a researcher in cancer cell biology. She told me that one of the biggest problems is – believe it or not – the authenticity of data. That is, *literally*, the problem of being sure that the data obtained are real, true, not invented or manipulated. She said that in the last few years the number of scientific retractions of studies and research has increased significantly. In other words, more and more studies that could not be replicated had to be retreated by magazines or researchers, causing serious damage to the scientific community. I remember being very surprised to hear this from one of the most brilliant researchers in her field.

The second example involves a conversation I had with a patient of mine a few years ago. Her partner, a university researcher doctor, was suffering from lung cancer that had metastasized to the bones and brain. He was bedridden, cannulized, fed with a nasogastric tube, unable to provide for his most basic needs, and in a state of floating consciousness. Everyone was very concerned and distressed by this situation. My patient and I grappled with the following conundrum: some colleagues and friends of her partner, as well as his oncologist, had suggested that he enroll in an experimental program involving a recently introduced chemotherapy that had proven effective in extending the life of patients suffering from the same condition by a few weeks. My patient wanted me to help her figure out whether this treatment could actually help her partner and relieve everyone's anxiety. I remember that she brought a copy of the experimental article, which actually highlighted (by means of an RCT study) that patients with a similar clinical condition to that of her partner has survived six weeks longer. After debating the issue and reading the article together, I asked my patient a simple question: *'Is surviving at least six more weeks in these conditions really desirable or not?'* In other words: What do we mean when we talk about the 'survival' of a human being? I remember that it did not take much time for the patient to realize – with tears in her eyes – that her partner, the one she lived with, knew and loved, would never want to survive another six weeks in those conditions.

Now, without venturing into such an impervious field, suffice it to say that the extreme competitiveness in all areas of research, the interests at stake, the need to get and to renew funding, the natural pursuit of career advancement, the incentives expected for results that could bring fame and visibility and, last but not least, the existence of a conflict of interest that involves researchers, are just a few of the problematic aspects that jeopardize the quality of scientific results.

Furthermore, the desirability of an event, or *wishful thinking* – in my patient's case 'survival' intended as a mere lengthening of life – can make us lose sight completely of what can still be considered as 'life'.

With this we do not want to suggest that biomedical research and research in psychotherapy are absolutely unnecessary. They are necessary, and indeed crucial for progress. We only want to draw attention to some *caveats* which, in our opinion, should always be borne in mind when analyzing the results of a research study, for instance on the evaluation of the efficacy of psychotherapeutic treatments.

The gold standard for research on outcomes in medicine and psychotherapy: is all that glitters gold?

The standard for research in psychotherapy, as well as in medicine – the so-called *gold standard* – is represented by randomized clinical trials (RCTs). RCTs are a very powerful tool employed by researchers to establish a linear causality between two events: the administration of a treatment (independent variable) and the outcome of this treatment in patients who received it (dependent variable).

The most important benefit of the experimental design of RCTs is that two compared groups of subjects, if randomly distributed, are theoretically similar to each other in terms of both the known and (especially) unknown variables that could influence the treatment outcomes.

This means that possible changes in the clinical condition can reasonably be ascribed to the only variable that makes the groups different, that is the prescription of either the experimental treatment or the control treatment.

The RCT's experimental design is therefore a highly effective instrument for detecting linear causality between two events. In medicine, for instance, it is useful to evaluate the efficacy of an antibiotic on some kinds of infection. In this sense, this methodological approach is parsimonious as well as simple and efficient. Currently, no treatment – not even in psychotherapy – can be considered effective if its efficacy has not been documented through an RCT. In this respect, we would like to reaffirm that RCTs are still irreplaceable.

However, as far as the efficacy of psychotherapy is concerned, the key question is: *Which treatment, delivered by whom, under what conditions, for what kind of patient, can be considered effective?* The next question is: *Can RCTs provide an answer to this crucial question when it comes to evaluating efficacy in psychotherapy?*

There is evidence that the linear causality model is rather unsatisfactory for outcome studies in psychotherapy. Many variables come into play which determine and influence the efficacy of psychotherapeutic treatment; most of them have nothing to do with the treatment protocol or with the type of treatment provided.

Factors such as the selection process of the clinical sample (both the experimental sample and the control sample), the experience of the therapists involved, their motivation and engagement in research and clinical work, individual features of patients in terms of their previous history as well as of their reactions to events that can occur in their life, factors unrelated to the treatment that could influence a patient's wellbeing or distress, the crucial aspect represented by the resources and resilience of a patient as compared to another, that is a patient's personal ability to benefit from a certain type of treatment at a particular moment of his/her life, are all very important factors which determine the outcome of all psychotherapeutic procedures.

While it is easy to standardize two groups of patients suffering from pneumonia to which two different antibiotics are prescribed, and it is reasonable to assume that the effects obtained are produced by the specific drug that is being administered, in psychotherapy the multitude of factors that we have listed above play a crucial role.

In this respect it might be of some interest to make a simple methodological reflection. A fundamental aspect of the method used to conduct clinical studies in medicine consists of the double-blind approach. In double-blind tests neither the patient nor the doctor who administers treatment are aware of which treatment the patient is actually receiving. This in order to avoid 'biases' that could influence how the physician administers the treatment and the patient's compliance, responsiveness, and tolerance.

For instance, a physician who is going to test a new drug could be enthusiastically and inadvertently inclined to underestimate its side effects and to emphasize its clinical effects. By the same token, a patient who is going to receive a new treatment that has not been tested yet and is essentially unknown could have a propensity for showing or experiencing more side effects, or, on the contrary, could be hopeful and persuaded that the new treatment is more effective than the ones attempted previously.

At this stage one could easily object that simply resorting to unbiased outcome measures could solve the problem. That is true. In fact, most of the standards used in medicine are instrumental, objective, and unbiased. The values for blood pressure, for instance, are measured in a standardized way by staff that is unrelated to the experimental procedure. But how can one adequately control the other factors that could influence blood pressure, even occasionally, such as changes in lifestyle, amount and quality of exercise, salt intake, amount and quality of sleep, diet, stress levels determined by one's occupation and working conditions, family and economic situation? Some factors that can mystify the results, such as weight, tobacco smoke, and glycaemia, can be kept under control, but what about the other factors that we have just mentioned? Researchers have made great efforts to minimize the effect of uncontrolled variables, and in the case of blood pressure treatment reasonably satisfying results have been achieved.

Now, what if we were to we ask the same questions in relation to the evaluation of efficacy for patients with borderline personality disorder? As we have seen in other chapters of this book, several therapeutic interventions have proven effective with patients with a borderline disorder. All the procedures and models considered effective have already conducted one or more RCTs to evaluate efficacy, and, according to the parameters employed, their efficacy has been proven without a doubt.

But a satisfactory answer has not been given to our question: *Which treatment, delivered by whom, under what conditions, for what type of patient and with what disorder can be considered effective?* And: *Are the results obtained actually generalizable and applicable to the entire population affected by that specific disorder?* For instance, a study demonstrates the efficacy of a specific treatment for BPD patients with parasuicidal behaviour who have been hospitalized. Can we say that this type of treatment is equally effective in a population of BPD outpatients with prevailing dissociative symptoms? Some people may think that this is not so easy, I being one of them.

Some problems with RCTs in psychotherapy

The experimental design

As we said before, the first problem with RCTs in psychotherapy is that double-blind tests cannot be used. Indeed, in psychotherapy it is not possible for both the therapist and the patient to be unaware of the specific treatment that is being administered and that differs from the previous treatments. This has some significant implications, which will be discussed later.

A second problem has to do with the fact that the experimental design of RCTs implies the use of numerous samples of patients, substantial financial resources, and a logistical and organizational structure that can guarantee the correct implementation of all experimental procedures. In psychotherapy the sample size may not necessarily be a problem, but the availability of substantial financial resources and of an adequate logistical and organizational structure could be such a limiting factor as to exclude most clinics and researchers involved in evaluating the outcomes of any psychotherapeutic intervention protocol. Furthermore, the applicability of the RCT experimental model, and the randomization of patients in particular, would be virtually impossible in such contexts as private clinical practices, where the random allocation of patients to a given treatment is simply unfeasible.

However, considering that in some countries, like Italy, the vast majority of psychotherapeutic treatments are delivered within the context of private clinical practice, we have to accept the fact that in such contexts reliable data on the efficacy of treatments provided is not available. Indeed, in Italy very few RCTs have evaluated the effectiveness of psychotherapeutic treatments and they are mostly related to relatively simple protocols, applied in the treatment of well-defined disorders like major depression, panic disorder, hypochondria, and so on.

The sample

Paraphrasing Archimedes' 'Give me a place to stand and with a lever I will move the whole world,' the inventor of case/control studies, Jeremy Cornfield, would say: 'Give me a good control group and I will prove anything to you.' In other words, the selection of the control group and of the sample in general is of capital importance in the setting up of a trial. Variables such as type of patient, selection criteria, generalizability of the characteristics of the sample to the entire population of subjects suffering from the disorder, to name but a few, are all crucial when it comes to assessing the criteria of validity of a study and the generalizability of the outcomes.

If randomization solves issues relating to the differences between groups, it does not solve issues relating to the sampling of a group that has not been randomly taken from the general population to which it belongs. In other words, an experimental group of borderline patients can be randomized in a treatment group and a control group, but there is no guarantee that the original group is effectively representative of and comparable to the general population of borderline patients, treated or not, hospitalized or not, on drug medication or not.

As was previously mentioned, the patients of a public mental health centre who suffer from a given disorder (like BPD) are not entirely comparable to patients who are treated in private clinical practice contexts. This has nothing to do with clinical severity or complexity, but with other independent factors, such as social background, family context, economic situation, level of education, personal resources, and resilience. Such factors cannot be reliably controlled in an RCT design when a sampling bias occurs.

The control treatment, or 'do you like to win easily?'

In the early 1990s there was an overwhelming spread of so-called SSRI antidepressants, of which Prozac was the forerunner. Many molecules, currently widely used in the treatment of depression, were tested and marketed using documentation from RCTs.

In that case the problem was that (almost) all studies used amitriptyline as a control drug. Amitriptyline is a tricyclic antidepressant which back then already appeared to be the least effective among TCAs and the one with more side effects than any other of the same category (imipramine and clomipramine). The advantage being? Easy. However badly things went, the new drug would have a much more favourable tolerability profile compared to the control drug, thus resulting better and 'easier to prescribe', thereby skillfully confusing efficacy with tolerability. The same problem arises with psychotherapeutic treatments. Let us take BPDs as an example again: the first studies compared the experimental treatments with the so-called 'TAU' (treatment as usual). Some rightly argued that the TAU was *not* an appropriate control treatment, precisely because the TAU (which usually consisted of generic and non-specific 'clinical management') appeared to be a harsh and obviously inappropriate way of treating patients with BPD.

The effectors of treatment (psychotherapists): which therapists, for what treatment, with what motivation, skills, predisposition, human qualities, and inherent capabilities?

Why is it that if we have to look for a surgeon for a delicate abdominal surgery we look for an endorsed, competent surgeon that we have heard good things about and who has technical and personal skills ('the surgeon's hand') that reassure us? Why should we not do the same when we need to treat a severe borderline personality disorder? Can we really say that these issues are not important in the choice of treatment, in influencing its effects as well as the patient's compliance to the psychotherapy program, the interventions, and the definition of goals?

The human factor – all the more so more in the psychotherapeutic treatment of serious disorders – is, needless to say, a fundamental implicit factor that determines the treatment outcome.

Some might object: *'But we certainly cannot consider all of these imponderable variables when evaluating the effectiveness of a psychological treatment. It is enough to randomize!'* All right. I agree. Why then, I wonder, has nobody ever considered randomizing therapists as well? Simple: because no one randomizes surgeons. Have I made myself clear?

Effectors of change: treatment techniques, life events, external factors unrelated to the therapy

The relevant role of evaluators combined with the absence of the double-blind test poses important limits to the evaluation of the results of a psychotherapeutic treatment tested with the RCT method.

The allegiance effect is a first effect worth mentioning, and it essentially consists of a phenomenon whereby researchers who clinically evaluate the results of a treatment in which they are personally involved, find it rather difficult – as it were – to report the negative results of the treatment in question, while they tend to overestimate – even unwittingly – its positive effects as compared to the control treatment. This is an understandable and, to some extent, accepted phenomenon, but sometimes it can be a more relevant and significant problem in the genesis and interpretation of results.

The fact is that there are very few published RCTs that show a substantial equal efficacy between any experimental treatment and the treatment it is compared against. If this is a general problem for medical-scientific literature (the problem of negative results or negative trials), in our case it seems to have greater importance, on account of the personal involvement of the experimenters (all researchers want their treatment model to be the effective one for the treatment of that disorder).

Good randomization on a sufficiently large sample of subjects, strict control of the quality of data and an equally rigorous analysis of the data by third parties, the use of objective and unbiased outcome variables solve the problem in part but do not eliminate it altogether. If, in addition, we consider that patients may also be influenced, in varying degrees, by the fact of undergoing an experimental treatment different from the treatment received in the past (for instance a more intensive, multimodal treatment which commits them for a longer time and involves more workers and resources), we cannot rule out the possibility that this may have an effect on the outcome of that treatment.

That is one of the reasons why this issue was raised fifteen years ago already: in the case of the treatment of borderline patients, the TAU did not seem to be a reliable basis of comparison, since all TAUs were grossly ineffective, expensive and useless for most outcome variables (number of hospitalizations, self-harm, impulsivity, psychosocial functioning, treatment drop-out, etc.).

Moreover, the role played by factors independent of treatment, such as events of personal or family life, which are often random and uncontrollable (accidents, falling in love and separation, bereavement and illness, economic changes, layoffs and promotions . . .), can have very significant effects on a person's life and, therefore, on a patient's life.

I am reminded of the story of one of my patients, Lucia: with my help, she battled for years against a condition of deep depression, in which the theme of her personal 'inadequacy' in life went hand in hand with that of 'bad luck'.

At the age of 38 Lucia had the misfortune of being diagnosed with breast cancer, which was treated with radical mastectomy and chemotherapy. Eight years later, she was also diagnosed with Hodgkin's lymphoma.

Can we say that these events had no influence on her main issues (inadequacy in life and bad luck) and that they did not influence the treatment and its outcome? So as not to lose the taste for paradox, I will say this: they most certainly did have an influence. Lucia, in fact, is still very much alive, and she battles on with her psychotherapy . . .

Conclusion

The purpose of this discussion on the limits of the RCT experimental design is not to belittle the value of RCTs. Nevertheless, we do believe that this methodology provides an answer to some important questions but not to others, which we believe are equally relevant to the proper evaluation of outcomes in psychotherapy. After all, the ultimate goal of research should be to influence clinical practice and promote a further spread of effective therapeutic practices. If the crucial issue is the spreading of effective therapeutic practices, then we must think that the therapeutic practices we are talking about are adaptable, accessible, and reproducible in the naturalistic context in which the diseases that they intend to treat are cured in most cases. Otherwise, why even talk about them?

A psychotherapeutic treatment model which is exceedingly manualized, complex, expensive, multimodal in the sense that it requires multiple logistics (hospitalization, day hospital, multidisciplinary team, etc.) is a model that can be adopted only in a few facilities and accessible only to a few patients; thus, even fewer patients will actually benefit from it. I personally believe that an intervention model should not only be effective but also feasible and adaptable to the naturalistic environment. Otherwise it is likely to fail in its primary goal, which is to ensure that the greatest number of people can benefit from the treatment that is proven effective by RCTs. Those who work in public health are all too familiar with it, and I also believe that it should be a current topic for clinical practice in mental health, both public and private.

As a starting point for the reader, some complementary approaches to the RCT model could further enrich and complete the overall assessment of a treatment's effectiveness and viability. Here is just a short list that the reader may examine in greater depth, if he/she so wishes (Carey and Stiles, 2015). The benchmarking practice, that is designing clinical studies which, using outcome measures from other published studies, can be used for comparing effectiveness (for example with the instrument of meta-analysis through the effect-size). Comparing the treatment in question in contexts of naturalistic care, as close as possible to clinical and real-life conditions, where the majority of patients will ask for psychotherapeutic help and assistance, in the absence of a conflict of interests. Naturalistic studies have many limits (mainly that of not being RCTs), but they offer some advantages that should not be underestimated, having to do with feasibility, viability, and transferability of results. Another approach is that of clinical case series or studies which include the systematic study of a series of single cases, treated and followed over time with specific customized methodologies that can offer guidance on what a particular type of patient needs, when and how. The data obtained through serial replication can be very useful. The reproducibility of a model (an essential component of the medical-scientific paradigm) in different contexts, with patients in different conditions, with therapists working in different structures (clinics, day hospitals, outpatient facilities, both public and private) lends great value to the results obtained in terms of what we call outcome evaluation and treatment effectiveness, even though the results were not obtained with the RCT model.

So, addressing the original question *'What do we talk about when we talk about outcome studies in psychotherapy?'* requires a remarkable effort in terms of a theoretical and methodological reflection, to which I hope I have given even a small contribution that readers can reflect on as they wish.

Results from a controlled naturalistic study in the treatment of severe comorbid axis I/II patients

Objective and methods

The objective of the present study was to compare cognitive-evolutionary intersubjective therapy in the form of integrated individual-group therapy (IG-CEIT), the *'experimental group',* with the same type of individual therapy (I-CEIT), the *'control group'*. Comparisons between the groups regarded the likelihood of maintaining and completing therapy as well as benefitting from it both clinically and in terms of psychosocial functioning. As was already discussed in Chapter 6 'the original working hypothesis', patients were selected on the clinical criterion of being reliably diagnosed as having a personality disorder, with or without axis I/II comorbidity (such as eating disorders, panic and anxiety disorders, mood disorders and/or dissociative disorders).

Selection of patients

The study population consisted of individuals who, in the period from January 1999 to May 2006, had sought mental health care at selected outpatient mental health care facilities in Rome, and who were diagnosed with one of the following disorders, according to DSM IV criteria: BPD (DSM-IV criteria), in association with other Axis I disorders or not; other B cluster personality disorders in comorbidity with Axis I disorders; transversal comorbidity in Axis I (persons who simultaneously met the DSM-IV criteria for more than one disorder) or longitudinal comorbidity (persons who over time met the DSM-IV criteria for more than Axis I disorder).

All of these patients (n=129) were offered integrated double-setting individual-group co-therapy (hereinafter referred to as 'individual-group cognitive-evolutionary intersubjective therapy', IG-CEIT) or individual therapy (I-CEIT). Allocation to the *IG-CEIT* or *I-CEIT* group was made on the basis of three factors: waiting list (longer for IG-CEIT), logistic variables (i.e. incompatibility of IG-CEIT schedule with work, patient living too far from the healthcare facility where IG-CEIT was delivered), refusal to undergo IG-CEIT. Among these three factors, waiting list and logistic variables were the most frequent.

Patients with schizophrenic disorders, delusional disorders, type-I bipolar disorders, or psychorganic syndrome were excluded from the study. We also excluded patients who during treatment could not have access to IG-CEIT for logistical problems but agreed to undergo other forms of integrated psychotherapy (psychotherapy/drug therapy) (20 out of 129 patients). Drug treatment was provided as needed in both groups.

Evaluation and tools

All participants were evaluated for: a) *motivation to undergo treatment* (on a scale from 0 to 5, where '0' was *unsatisfactory* and '4' was *very good*); b) *drop-out* during treatment (non-consensual interruption); c) *harmful behaviour* towards self or others; and d) *impulsive behaviour* (alcohol/drug abuse, sexual promiscuity or aggressiveness towards others, binge eating). The following tools were used for psychometric evaluation: Global Assessment Functioning (GAF), Behavioural and Symptom Identification Scale-32 (BASIS-32) and Quality of Life Index (QoL-I). Evaluations were performed at baseline (i.e., right before beginning treatment) and at 12, 18, and 24 months into treatment. Diagnoses were based on the DSM-IV criteria; all diagnoses were discussed and systematically reviewed by two of the authors (GF and AI). The diagnostic concordance (K) among evaluators ranged from 0.77 to 0.83.

Treatment

IG-CEIT, which was presented to the patients as a single regimen, consisted of two two-hour group sessions and two one-hour individual sessions per month (the sessions took place every other week). Group therapy was conducted by two co-therapists, one of whom was the same therapist who conducted individual therapy. The group, which was 'open', consisted of six to eight patients. Peer-to-peer clinical discussions of cases were held monthly among all therapists. All group sessions were audio recorded or videotaped; the recordings were available to both patients and therapists. I-CEIT consisted of one one-hour individual session per week; drug-therapy sessions were also provided upon request (generally one session every two weeks as required). Both regimens lasted 24 months, unless otherwise indicated.

Procedures

Methods and procedures have been extensively described in other sections of this book. In this section we will go over only the essential elements, for the sake of clarity.

Startup with evaluation, individual therapy, and contract

Therapy begins in an individual setting, where the therapist and patient draw up what can be referred to as a 'contract', agreeing on the objectives of therapy and defining the setting, stressing that both patient and therapist must make the necessary commitment towards achieving results. The contract also establishes the boundaries of therapy and of the patient-therapist relationship, in addition to priorities and objectives, especially in terms of feasibility. The contract thus represents a sort of 'free zone', a shared space where patient and therapist can go back to when the therapy becomes conflictual. The concept of 'contract' thus has a direct impact on the relational process, clearly steering it towards the development of the best possible collaborative relationship as early as the initial sessions.

Telephone use

The contract also envisages a set of rules regarding the use of the telephone. As in other treatments (i.e., DBT), the patient is encouraged to use the telephone to call the therapist when at risk of impulsive or self-harming behaviour. In fact, patients are clearly requested to use the telephone to seek help *before* engaging in any potentially harming behaviour. On the other hand, the therapist has the right to call the patient if some difficulties arise with the therapy (i.e., drop-out from single or group sessions, stress-related events in patient's life, etc.).

Beginning the group (IG-CEIT)

The patient is gradually *introduced* to group treatment by the therapist who performs the individual therapy and who, with a co-therapist, follows the patient throughout the treatment. The relationship between the patient and the individual therapist is the backbone of both individual and group therapy. The existence of a referral network involving a co-therapist represents a key resource for both patient and healthcare workers and for the success of the treatment. The group co-therapist is introduced to the patient at the very beginning of the treatment (within the first three sessions), to stress the concept of team-working and treatment scheduling.

Theoretical and therapeutic tools

The use of certain descriptive and therapeutic tools, such as the theory of interpersonal motivational systems (IMS) (Liotti, 1994/2005; Liotti and Monticelli, 2008; Fassone *et al.*, 2012; Fassone *et al.*, 2015) and the dramatic triangle (Karpman, 1968; Ivaldi, 1998, 2004), is greatly facilitated in group therapy, where it is possible to work on interactions in the here and now (Yalom, 1995). The group model belongs to the intersubjective tradition (ibid.). The two therapists are actively involved in the group, experiencing and showing empathy and favouring interactions and interpersonal exchanges in relation to the evolution of the group itself and facilitating the analysis of the interactions, mainly based on the IMS theory.

In the individual-group CEIT, typically cognitive-behavioural techniques and tools are also used. In particular, the patients are assigned tasks, like filling out self-observation forms (regarding what goes on in the group) or doing a written self-monitoring of episodes of lack of impulse control.

Results

The main socio-demographic and clinical variables are shown in Table 7.1.

Table 7.1 Sociodemographic and clinical variables for individuals undergoing IG-CEIT or I-CEIT

	IG-CEIT n=85 (%)		I-CEIT N=24 (%)	
Age (in years)	31.4 +/–		30.4 +/–	
Gender (male; per cent; female; per cent)	29 (34); 56 (66)		9 (62); 15 (38)	
Educational level				
Elementary school	–		–	
Middle school	10	(12)	2	(8)
High school	53	(63)	17	(71)
Graduation/degree	21	(25)	5	(21)
Diagnoses in Axis I				
None	11	(13)	3	(12)
Eating disorders	30	(35)	8	(33)
Anxiety disorders	14	(16.5)	3	(12)
Unipolar depressive disorders	23	(26)	8	(33)
Bipolar II depressive disorders	3	(3.6)	0	(-)
Dissociative disorders	8	(9)	5	(21)
OCD	10	(13)	0	(–)
Somatoform disorders	2	(2.5)	1	(4)
Sexual disorders	6	(7.5)	0	(–)
Substance abuse/addiction	7	(8.2)	6	(24)
Diagnoses in Axis II				
None	18	(21)	2	(8)
BPD	30	(35)°	15	(62)°
Other cluster B personality disorders	12	(13)	2	(8)
Cluster C disorders	13	(15)	2	(8)
Cluster A disorders	3	(4)	1	(4)
NAS	8	(9)	2	(8)
Comorbidity	65	(77)	20	(83)
Previous drug therapy	46	(54)[†]	18	(75)[†]
Drop-out from previous psychotherapy	No			
Yes			25	(37)[†]
			43	(63)
	11	(73)[†]	4	(27)
Previous hospitalization	10	(13)	7	(30)
Previous harmful behaviour (average episodes per month)	2.9	(+/–3.1)	3.6	(+/–3.3)
Previous substance/drug abuse (average episodes per month)	1.4 (+/–2.7)*		3.2 (+/–3.3)*	
Estimate of motivation towards therapy	2.6	(+/–1.1)[†]	1.7	(1.3)[†]

Source: Used by permission of Eastern Group Psychotherapy Society and GROUP Journal
*p<0.01, univariate ANOVA, 95% CI; [†]p<0.01, chi square test, 95% CI

Baseline

When comparing the two groups, there were differences in the initial values for GAF, BASIS-32, and QoL-I, in addition to the history of hospitalization and previous drug therapy, psychotherapy, and drop-out. In Table 7.2, the scores for the clinical and psychopathological variables are presented for the IG-CEIT group (n=85) and the I-CEIT group (n=24).

The two groups also differed in terms of the distribution of BPDs, which was relatively more common in the *control* group. Subjects in this group seemed to have a more severe disorder; they were more prone to drop-out and impulsive behaviour and were less motivated to undergoing treatment. These differences can most likely be explained by the differences in distribution in the diagnosis of BPD. In fact, when repeating the analysis only for persons with BPD (n=30, corresponding to 35 per cent of subjects in the IG-CEIT group and n=15, corresponding to 62 per cent in the I-CEIT group), there were no differences for any of the variables considered, except for BPD patients undergoing IG-CEIT that had a significantly lower previous drop-out rate than the individual CEIT group [7/30 (23 per cent) vs. 9/15 (60 per cent), respectively; p=0.02, chi square test].

Outcome

The drop-out rate during therapy was significantly lower in the IG-CEIT group [16/85 (19 per cent) vs. 16/24 (65 per cent), respectively; p<0.001, chi square test]. The observed difference in drop-outs was attributed to an excess of diagnoses of BPD in the control group. In fact, as expected, persons with BPD showed significant differences as compared to the patients with other diagnoses, for the considered variables (GAF, BASIS-32, substance abuse, self-harming behaviour, estimated motivation, previous drop-out), all of which are potential indicators of a worse outcome. In particular, previous drop-out was in absolute terms more common among patients with BPD as compared to the rest of the study population, independently of the treatment received during the study. We therefore repeated the analysis for BPD patients only, in both groups.

The data provided in Table 7.2 show that the patients in the IG-CEIT group do better than those undergoing I-CEIT. The subgroup of BPD patients undergoing IG-CEIT also showed very significant improvement

Table 7.2 Average values for GAF, BASIS-32, and QoL-I, and the variables "self-harming behaviour" and "substance/drug abuse", at baseline and at 12, 18 and 24 months of therapy, for persons undergoing IG-CEIT or I-CEIT

	IG-CEIT (n=85)		Individual CEIT (n=24)	
GAF				
Baseline	50	(+/–7)	48	(+/–5.3)
12 months	57	(+/–8)	54	(+/–5.3)
18 months	61	(+/–7.4)	58	(+-5.4)
24 months	65	(+/–7.5)*	59	(+/–6.7)†
BASIS-32				
Baseline	66	(+/–15)	74	(+/–13.7)
12 months	54	(+/–16.6)	58	(+/–18.3)
18 months	45	(+/–12.9)	37	(+-4.7)
24 months	36	(+/–13.7)*	48	(+/–18.6)†
QoL-I				
Baseline	5.1	(+/–2)	4	(+/–2.3)
12 months	6.7	(+/–1.7)	5.1	(+/–2)
18 months	8	(+/–1.6)	6.5	(+-2)
24 months	8	(+/–1.5)*	6.6	(+/–2.7)§
Self-harming behaviour (average episodes per month)				
Baseline	2.9	(+/–3.1)	3.6	(+/–3.3)
12 months	1.6	(+/–2)	2	(+/–2.4)
18 months	0.8	(+/–1.5)	1.6	(+-1.9)
24 months	0.7	(+/–1.3)*	2.2	(+/–1.2)§
Substance abuse (average episodes per month)				
Baseline	1.4	(+/–2.7)	3.2	(+/–3.3)
12 months	0.8	(+/– 1.6)	1.8	(+/–1.7)
18 months	0.9	(+/–1.5)	1.1	(+-2)
24 months	0.5	(+/–1.2)*	1.3	(+/–1.9)§

Source: Used by permission of Eastern Group Psychotherapy Society and GROUP Journal
*significant with respect to baseline: p<0.001, t-test for paired data
† significant with respect to baseline: p<0.01, t-test for paired data
§ p>0.05, not significant; t-test for paired data

for GAF, BASIS-32, QoL-I, self-harming behaviour, and substance abuse at the end of treatment (24 months), compared to the beginning of treatment (initial GAF vs. final GAF: 47 vs. 63; initial BASIS-32 vs. final: 75 vs. 42; initial QoL-I vs. final: 4.8 vs. 7.6; initial self-harming behaviour vs. final: 5 vs. 1.2 episodes per month; initial substance abuse vs. final: 3.6 vs. 0.9 (episodes per month); p<0.01; t-test paired data).

Discussion

In interpreting the results of this study, some of its limitations need to be discussed. As far as this is not an RCT, a number of methodological limitations may be raised.

First and foremost, since there is no randomization, some crucial outcome variables are not distributed haphazardly among the two groups. This makes it impossible to definitely state that differences observed in the two groups in terms of effectiveness of treatment depend on treatment itself.

In our study this is confirmed by the observation that the condition of subjects enrolled in the I-CEIT group was more severe than that of subjects in the IG-CEIT group. This could mean that '*more severe*' and less motivated patients have a worse outcome *per se*. Although these differences are substantially related to an excess of BPD patients in the control group – BPD patients in both groups are comparable for most clinical and psychopathological variables – it is nevertheless a methodological limitation that reduces external validity of the study.

Selection of patients based on waiting list or logistical criteria, or based on the refusal of IG-CEIT, also represents a problem: less motivated patients choose less engaging treatments. In fact, only a minor portion of patients actively refused IG-CEIT, while other variables seemed to play a role in auto-selection of patients to one group or the other.

The fact that the therapist who conducted the therapy was also one of the evaluators may be another limitation, potentially affecting the validity of the results. Although the diagnostic concordance among evaluators calculated at the beginning of the study was satisfactory, the evaluators may nonetheless have been influenced by the fact that they also acted as therapists in the study. For this reason, Pearson's correlations were calculated on a random sample of outcome scores for different patients, and coefficients were satisfactory.

Moreover, the reliability of the diagnoses, particularly for the diagnoses related to personality disorders, may have been limited by the lack of homogeneity in the clinical sample diagnoses (diagnostic polymorphism), together with the fact that DSM-IV diagnostic criteria were used, yet structured diagnostic interviews were not. However, the diagnoses of personality disorder and especially BPD were discussed and reviewed by one of the authors (G.F.) together with the colleagues who had made the initial diagnoses. Nevertheless, it is important to underline that the goal of the study was to compare two treatment settings of CEIT in the treatment of patients whose psychiatric diagnoses were polymorphic as defined in methods and related to a history of early trauma experiences. Furthermore, it is worth recalling that even borderline personality disorder is far from being a homogeneous disorder. In fact, BPD diagnoses according to DSM V criteria refer to a polymorphic disorder, where different clinical features may prevail in different subjects with the same diagnoses (affective instability vs. identity dissociation vs. impulsiveness, substance abuse and self-mutilation), thus defining patients with distinctive clinical and treatment implications.

Finally, although a two-year period is considered sufficient for obtaining appreciable results in this type of patient, the fact that treatment can be prolonged according to need introduces an element of uncertainty, in relation not only to duration but also to costs and to the commitment of the patient and the therapists.

Despite the above-mentioned limitations, some interesting conclusions can be drawn. Controlled semi-naturalistic studies provide a 'snapshot' of the operative and clinical reality in which various healthcare workers conduct their activity, located in different areas of a city with a population of approximately 4 million people, with the advantage of providing a control group which used the same recruitment process (preselection, referral to a suitable facility, evaluation, and enrolment in a daycare program) and evaluation, independently of the type of treatment received. The evaluation scales have been validated and are simple to use for the therapist.

The control treatment (cognitive-evolutionary individual therapy) was performed by the same therapists. The treatment model is relatively flexible, simple, and accessible in terms of both time and commitment for nearly all patients. Thus IG-CEIT can be considered 'cost-effective'. As part of the package offered, the patient may undergo one or two additional individual sessions and can consult the group co-therapist if drug therapy is needed (it would be much better if the team consisted of one psychologist and one psychiatrist with a strong background in psychotherapy). The co-presence of therapists facilitates contact and exchange on the evolution of both group and individual therapy, which is considered fundamental for the success of the therapy. Small teams of stable and devoted therapists who share the theoretical-clinical model must be created. If any of these characteristics are missing, it is difficult to continue the therapy without risking negative consequences for the patient and the quality of the work.

Finally, it might be useful to underline some crucial issues with regard to previous considerations about RCTs methodology. If we had been able to conduct an RCT with positive results we certainly would have reached a major and remarkable result in the scientific community. The point was that randomizing those patients was simply impossible as well as somehow careless. Actually, they were all patients requiring our professional skills, and they were all looking for the best possible and feasible treatment option. *Possible* and *feasible* are – in this case – key words. The possibility of carrying out a good treatment is better than the desirability of an unfeasible best treatment. Last but not least, in this case there was clearly no conflict of interests (and no 'allegiance effect'): all patients in both groups were private clients, all of them were able to pay for their treatment and they were all equally important as individuals seeking mental care. So, our conclusions are that whenever possible, BPDs as well as comorbid patients with early interpersonal trauma history should be treated with an IG-CEIT approach for the following reasons: lower dropout rate, greater effectiveness in terms of the improvement of symptoms and psychosocial functioning, lower re-admission rate and self-injury. Last but not least: less burn-out in the individual therapist involved in the treatment of people with overwhelming emotional dysfunction in interpersonal relationships.

Chapter 8

Group psychotherapy
Addressing impediments to engaging the affiliative motivational system

Rosemary Segalla

Using motivational systems theory as a tool for observing group process is uniquely useful for the group therapist. It enhances the therapist's ability to attend to the process of individuals as they engage intersubjectively as well as make observations about the process of the group as a whole. Lichtenberg, Lachmann and Fosshage in their recent book, *Psychoanalysis and Motivational Systems: A New Look* (2011), have incorporated advances in neurosciences, attachment research, and dynamic systems or complexity theory to further explicate motivational systems theory.

The authors originally proposed five motivational systems. These were physiological regulation, attachment/affiliation, exploration/assertion, aversive and sensual/sexual. Recently added were the care giving system and affiliation as a system, separate and distinct from the attachment system. It is clear that the distinctive qualities of these two warrant their addition as separate systems. In the earlier version of the theory, attachment was seen as the primary system with affiliation developing later as an expansion of the capacity for attachment. This subsuming of affiliation as a developmental aspect of attachment did not sufficiently underscore the differences between the two. The authors explain their decision to separate affiliation based on several findings:

> First, research on the family triangle (Fivaz-Depeursinge and Corboz-Warnery, 1999) revealed that children as early as three months work to include a parent who is not in their immediate attachment interaction, indicative of the earliest stages of the family as a group. Second, the early distinction made between the familiar group as safe and the racially or ethnically other as questionable is guided by the parent's

affiliative biases. In addition are evolutionary pressures for intragroup cooperation and non-intragroup competition and territoriality

(p. 19)

While the quote explains the authors' reasons for separating the two systems, there is considerable confirming data from other fields. A brief example: E. O. Wilson, writing in his newest book, *The Social Conquest of Earth* (2012), speaks of the inevitability of group membership in which our affiliative motivations are met. He states:

To form groups, drawing visceral comfort and pride from familiar fellowship, and to defend the group enthusiastically against rival groups- these are among the absolutes universals of human nature and hence of culture (p. 58).

He goes on to address our inevitable intersubjectivity:

The social world of each modern human is not a single tribe, but rather a system of interlocking tribes . . . (ibid).

People savour the company of like-minded friends and they yearn to be one of the best . . . (ibid).

Implicit in these statements is the inevitability of group membership. What happens then, when we come upon patients who are minimally involved in groups of any kind? The concern for us as clinicians is why they avoid group membership as part of their experience in the world. This question is the basis of my exploration of the impediments to the activation of the affiliative motivational system. This avoidance can also occur within the context of the attachment system. Although these two are separate systems, they are inevitably intertwined. We may see someone in treatment who embraces and functions quite well in a dyadic relationship both with those who people their world, as well as with the therapist in individual therapy. The puzzle is why a patient successfully negotiates a dyadic relationship but avoids group contexts. This is stated in black and white terms. It is rarely this stark. In the therapeutic setting, aversion to group engagement usually emerges gradually as the therapeutic work unfolds. It may not become obvious until the therapist suggests group therapy as an addition to the recommended treatment. It can often be disguised because these patients often have to, by necessity, function in some kind of group, be it work, school or other social organizations. The exception is the patient who begins therapy with a complaint or concern about some problem they are having in a group setting. This however, is not the usual avenue that prompts a therapist to suggest group therapy. That is, issues with the affiliative motivational system may be more hidden and subtle in their manifestation. It may take time for these motivational issues to emerge in the treatment.

There are also those who have considerable difficulty attaching even within a dyadic relationship. It becomes obvious that their engagement in group settings is also impaired. This difficulty in both individual and group treatment demonstrates a marked incapacity for trusting engagement at any level. Speaking in attachment terms, this individual may be insecurely attached leading to problems that may impact both individual and group work. It appears that these individuals may be somewhat dissociated and what often emerges in the treatment is a troubling trauma history. There are of course, other possibilities and examples of impediments to affiliation.

What does viewing this population through the lens of motivational systems offer? Lichtenberg, Lachmann and Fosshage suggest the following:

> In our view, motivation involves a complex intersubjective process from which affects, intentions, and goals unfold. Motives are not simply givens; they emerge and are co created and constructed in the developing individual embedded in a web of relationships with other individuals
>
> (p. 13)

Affects, intentions and goals may be viewed as the necessary therapeutic focus to both discern and work within individual psychotherapy or psychoanalysis as well as group treatment. Considering group therapy through the lens of affects, intentions and goals gives some focus to group process, a constantly unfolding, often chaotic process. It can be difficult to consider these within the group setting. We might ask, whose affect, whose intentions, whose goals? This becomes the work of the group therapist as he attends on several levels, the group as a whole, subgroups and individuals as well as on his own experiences.

Functioning in groups

As indicated, once we raise the issue of group therapy, we are immediately thrust into an exceedingly complex world. It demands that the therapist attend to many levels of human engagement. This presents an enormous challenge to the group therapist, encouraging him to create a multidimensional approach to treatment. For example, should attention be focused on the intersubjective field between individuals and therapist, between two or more group members, or on the group as a whole? While all of these levels of engagement are at play in any moment, where the therapist chooses to focus his attention usually depends on his theoretical perspective. This of course means that many levels of group engagement are ignored. When one or more members are unavailable to participate in the group action, remaining passive or withdrawn, the therapist may find himself either ignoring the quiet member or being distracted by their silence. Swept into the confusion of the moment, he may choose to ignore the quiet member and over focus on the very active members. This is one of the reasons that attending to the affiliative motivational system offer a kind of holding structure, allowing the therapist to focus on the group action. By attending to affects, intentions and goals, both in the group as a whole and within any other combination of membership, the therapist may make observations that are meaningful to the entire group, moving the process forward.

Attending to affects, intentions and goals of the group imply that the therapist believes that the group as a whole has a life of its own, quite beyond the input of any individual member, including the therapist. Because the group as a whole comprises a complex system, it can be difficult to make observations or interpretations that feel valid for each individual in this complex system. This can lead to the activation of other motivational systems such as attachment, aversion, exploratory, sensual/ sexual, physiological needs as well as the need for caretaking within individual members. In this therapeutic chaos, it is not difficult to imagine the way a therapist struggles to find, and put language to, that aspect of the process that feels dominant to him. It becomes imperative, not only that he is guided by the outline of a theoretical stance but also, that the action observed must necessarily be guided by a strong internal sense of what happens in groups. This is a developed skill that emerges from many experiences of working with groups. In this chapter, my attempt is to explore the functionality of using a motivational perspective to consider group action, particularly in situations in which dissociated aspects of individuals and the group as a whole creates chaos, leading, hopefully to a tipping point that allows the group to grow in new direction

Affiliation and group membership

For those who do group psychotherapy, there is a keen awareness of the distinct power of affiliation, particularly its usefulness as a vehicle for healing the individual member of the group. My emphasis on the affiliative system serves several functions. It allows consideration of the powerful need for affiliation and it also opens to further dialogue the rather limited use of group psychotherapy, particularly in the United States. I would like to understand this under utilization of a treatment approach that addresses the inevitability of our group membership and the crucial role it plays in the development of the self.

There is considerable research on group behaviour and its role in the development of the self in many fields such as biology, anthropology, social psychology and philosophy. This research is incorporated in the thinking of the group therapist who wishes to understand this research in order to create more effective group treatment. Interestingly, in a conversation with a psychoanalyst, I discovered that it is the opinion of many psychotherapist and analysts that group therapists are interested primarily in the experiential rather than in the theoretical and research perspectives that form the backbone of group treatment. I found this view difficult to understand because it belies the rich theoretical perspectives of many, many group therapists. The majority of those I encounter as I work as a group therapist are deeply interested in understanding the origins and development of group behaviour and how group participation is an inevitable aspect of being human. Its impact is felt at every level of the culture and its failure often results in dire consequences, not only for the individual but also for the entire system in which the individual is embedded. The group can hold and heal in a way that may not be available to an individual, standing outside group contexts. Returning to E. O. Wilson, we see the inevitability of group membership. It is our role as therapists to attempt to understand the impediments to affiliation with others. This understanding comes out of our work as group therapists, working to aid in the establishment or reestablishment of group membership for our patients.

Why many therapists choose not to include group treatment in their practice captures how our own limitations impact how we choose to work. Doing individual treatment, either psychotherapy or psychoanalysis, is an isolated and isolating experience. Many address the loneliness of this profession by engaging in peer supervision of some type, individual to individual or in peer group settings in order to share difficult cases, and also to address the isolation engendered in this profession. Although therapists find these settings immensely useful, few make the obvious connection to doing group treatment.

These choices may reflect our own issues with affiliative motivations. It may be that we are as uncomfortable in groups as some of our patients purport to be. It can also be difficult to find a way to breech the differences between sitting behind the couch or in a chair facing one patient with the more complicated work of a therapy group. It can be that we do not have any training in doing group work or that the theoretical perspective we embrace makes little allowance for working in a group setting. The possibilities are endless. Perhaps what we should be left with is to consider our choices, examining our own affiliative issues that may prevent us from such a consideration. Most important, the decision not to place our patients in a group denies them access to a treatment process that might be especially useful outside the safer space of individual treatment. I have suggested elsewhere, (Segalla, 1998), that we are often surprised to see patient attitudes and behaviours emerge in a therapy group that have never appeared in the individual work. The modality provides a unique window into both attachment and affiliation. What is apparent is that it is impossible to consider an attachment motivation without an understanding of affiliative needs and visa versa. What may be more difficult to discern in individual treatment may become apparent as the work in group therapy reveals other aspects of the patient's difficulties. Thus, placing a patient in group therapy may offer entirely new dimensions to explore in the individual work. What often emerges is a rich interplay between what is observed in the two modalities, offering healing on new levels, moving a patient to a healthier activation of the affiliative motivational system. This interplay emerges as the therapist engages in what is described as a combined treatment model that utilizes both individual and group work. Working with this combined model richly expands the exploration of complex intrapsychic and intersubjective realms of both the patient and the treating professional.

Aspects of affiliation in group therapy

Group action can be explored on many levels based on the therapist's style and codetermined by the inherent patterns of behaviour in a given group. My approach to treatment is based on several basic premises of self psychology, intersubjectivity and complexity theory, all encompassed in motivational systems work. Therefore a basic premise of my work is that therapeutic action is unpredictable, thus we do not know what will perturb the system, activating a tipping point that may illuminate an interaction, for example, or throw the group into chaos. This unpredictability gives the group therapist the creative edge in working with the process. It allows for an unfolding of group interactions that happens when a particular theoretical stance is loosely held. Thus, at one moment, the selfobject experiences of a particular group member may be the focus as members work with that person, clarifying what is needed/desired by them. Or an interaction between two or more members may highlight the group's need for fulfillment of groupobject needs (Segalla, 1998). That is, the group unconsciously attends to keeping the group energized in order to fulfill needs for affiliative experiences. Disruption to selfobject and group-object experiences is an inevitable aspect of group action. It can erupt suddenly as a result of empathic failures among members or be precipitated by a therapist's intervention. For example, a general observation made by the therapist about an absence of affective engagement and its possible meaning was experienced by several members of the group as a strong criticism of them, resulting in anger, tears and rejection of the observation as well as strong feelings by two members of not being 'good enough'. The session ended on a disrupted note, leaving the therapist to explore whether she had been feeling critical. The discussion resumed the next time the group met. The members most impacted immediately began to talk about their reactions, both taking responsibility for their reactions, relating them to their own issues, as well as demanding that the therapist give some explanation for her seemingly critical observations. The therapist, describing her own observations after the disrupted group, admitted to feeling bored in the process, suggesting that she unconsciously enacted the boredom by stirring things up with her statements. As the therapist explored her own affective response, group members began to consider their own desires for more affective engagement and what might be inhibiting them from doing so. What emerged was some fear that they might be criticized, anxiety about being left alone with strong feelings, desires for more attachment that might not be met. The dialogue of the group was lively and affectively open. The group began to consider that the members were generally afraid that affiliative and attachment needs would not be met in the group as was their experience in the world. This was attached to their anxiety about any display of aversiveness because their affiliative and attachment needs had generally been met with rejection when they behaved in any way that could be seen as aversive. These were important realizations for this group in which affect could be very effectively stifled. The therapist came to see that her own affiliative needs prevented her from being more challenging when members operated at a superficial level of engagement. She observed that in this particular intersubjective field, she had unconsciously activated her own fears around affiliation that helped impair the groups' movement into a more lively engagement with each other. The theme of the group focused on the individual members needs for attachment overriding their desire for affiliation, as if one could not have both needs met. It became clear that basic attachment had been disrupted in their lives, preventing them from the exploratory work necessary for the development of affiliation. What should be apparent is that any other motivational system can potentially prevent healthy development of the affiliative system. While all motivational systems are in operation at all times, it may be that a certain groundedness in attachment, exploration, aversive, sensual/sexual and caretaking systems are needed for a therapy group to embrace the need for affiliation before it can become a cohesive operating unit. Often, in practice, it may take a considerable amount of individual work with the therapist before a patient will agree to become a group member. Rarely do I see someone who wishes to quickly add group therapy to his or her individual treatment. This attests to the need to have basic motivational needs addressed before entering group therapy. It is why a combined treatment model can be so important. If a patient has had some success in addressing other motivational needs in the individual treatment, they may be better equipped to deal with the inevitable disruptions of being in a therapy group. This forms a safety net that allows the individual work to sustain them as they are learning to experience the group as a useful tool for growth, experiencing group cohesion as satisfying rather than terrifying. Despite the fact that we are inevitably embedded in systems from the beginning of life, starting with the family system, the development of the affiliative system requires a safety and functionality that is less apparent in the other systems.

Impediments to the activation of the affiliative motivational system

Impediments to the activation of the affiliative motivational system in a group therapy setting are as varied as the patients who enter our office. Although, group treatment is my preferred approach to dealing with affiliative difficulties, I am not suggesting that these issues cannot be addressed in individual treatment. Rather, I am saying that the dyad often does not focus on affiliation in a sustained way as does group treatment. Therefore, as I explore impediments, considering both patients' and therapists' potential issues, I have not ruled out the possibility of adequate focus on this motivational system in individual psychotherapy or psychoanalysis. Nor do I consider affiliative needs as separate from the remaining motivational systems.

Therapist impediments

Beginning with the manifestation of impediments, I will first consider the role of the therapist. Many therapists eschew group work, insisting that psychotherapy or psychoanalysis is sufficient to address any patient difficulties, feeling comfortable that all aspects of the seven motivational systems are available for exploration. As I said before, I do not generally disagree with this proposition. My experience in observing therapists has been informative in helping me formulate an opinion. Many analysts/ therapists have never received substantial training in group treatment. They lack basic theoretical and research information on the subject and therefore have not had the opportunity to observe a therapy group in action. This can therefore be a situation in which the therapist's sense of self may be threatened. Beyond this, looking at deeper issues, the therapist's difficulties with affiliation can interfere with their consideration of this treatment modality. Working individually, though often fraught is quite different from being with six to eight individuals, all with their own issues. If the clinician has had his own problems with affiliation, it is not likely that he/she will embrace group work. This hesitation can be reinforced by the daunting task of gathering patients to form a group as well as formulating how and why this particular group of people may work well together. While a full exploration of therapist impediments is an important topic for consideration, it is not the primary focus of this paper. Suffice it to say that it is a topic demanding fuller exploration at another time.

Patient impediments

As the field has expanded, we cannot deny the total embeddedness of all human activity in systems. Intersubjectivity, co-creation, and attachment research all demonstrate the inevitability of our intertwined lives. Therefore, focusing on affiliation needs become an even more important area of exploration as is considering the most effective ways in which to treat failures of affiliation.

The impediments we find in our work with our patients' affiliative motivations can be categorized in a variety of ways. Staying within the framework of self psychology offers a useful guideline for considering these impediments.

Kohut's selfobject theory (1984) provides a useful framework from which to consider these impediments. His conceptualization is that we all need healthy selfobject functions. Lichtenberg and colleagues conceptualized that the theory was better expressed in terms of selfobject experiences. This was explored in their 1992 book, *Self and Motivational Systems*. This conceptualization, selfobject experiences is what I use in considering this theoretical perception. Kohut considered the need for healthy selfobject functioning as embedded in the relationship with the other. It is in the holding and containing experiences that health self development occurs. The need for mirroring, idealizing, and twinship among other selfobject needs are apparent from birth manifesting developmentally. The failure to provide these selfobject needs impedes the development of a healthy self. It is in the therapeutic setting that these needs get reactivated and explored. Through a process evolving from empathic ruptures and repairs the self is gradually healed. It is in the transference that these selfobject experiences emerge leading to healthier functioning. Kohut did not, however, speak of the need for affiliative experiences in groups. When he referenced groups, he focused more on their destructive potential. It is in groups that my observation that the need for groupobject experiences is manifest, suggesting that our needs go well beyond the dyad and into the myriad groups in which we find ourselves. I suggested that groupobject needs or failures could be best addressed in a group setting. The affiliative system suggested by Lichtenberg *et al.* (2011) is an advance in considering our most basic need for groupobject experiences. That is, inherent in our need for others is that of social animals, the need for others in one's group. This basic experience can be called the groupobject experience, as basic as the need of the individual for selfobject experience. Both are needed to forge a strong sense of self.

Therefore, when someone in treatment manifests failures in attaining selfobject experiences, it is safe to assume that they will also have affiliative deficits impairing their ability to function in settings beyond the dyad. In other words, the more disrupted selfobject experiences are the more disrupted groupobject experiences will be. This view is important because of its implications about treatment.

Therefore, when I see someone in individual treatment, one of the first queries I have is about their functioning in complicated group settings, be it families, work, school, etc. It becomes apparent very quickly that affiliative functioning has been impeded. At this early stage, it is impossible to determine whether the improvement in functioning resulting from individual treatment has been effective not only in patient's dyadic encounters but also in larger settings. The addition of group therapy evolves out of failures in affiliation that emerge during treatment. It is then that the addition of group therapy can be instituted. The process of group placement is dependent upon a therapeutic fit. The transition will be successful through careful consideration about which group will be most effective in addressing affiliative failure. It is important to consider fit before placing a person in group.

Impediments can and will continue once the person is engaged in the group. It is here that we learn the most about what have been the most significant failures of affiliation. I have found that the traumatized person will have the most difficulty with group work. Often, however, it becomes apparent only after the person is actually in the group. It is in this setting, with all members present, that the person will begin to explore their fear about being with other people. This fear is often the opening into a trauma history, which has impeded all motivational systems, indicating the wide range of disorganization caused by trauma. All motivational systems are inevitably impacted by trauma, but I will focus primarily on affiliation and attachment.

Trauma in the last five decades has become a significant focus in the field. Our growing recognition of the role of trauma in human development has had a long evolution. Now, as we have learned more about the ubiquitous nature of trauma, we are quicker to explore trauma and its impact on motivational development. The significance of this recognition is particularly important when considering group placement for our patients for it is in group treatments that the fullest manifestation of trauma may be seen and probably activated. The failure of the therapist to recognize this can be the cause of reactivation of traumatic experiences. For example, if a patient has suffered in the nuclear family from a failure of empathy or understanding leading to destructive treatment by family members, the group can be both a place of reactivation of healthy affiliation as well as a source of further traumatization. It is imperative that the therapists have a full grasp of trauma history and is alert to the possible activation of trauma in this new setting. Even the most skilled group therapist can make costly errors in perhaps fostering this reactivation. It is in the working through of empathic injury that the patient gradually begins to feel safe enough to begin to form attachments to group members and to the group as a whole. That is, individual members may have difficulties with other group members as well as the therapist but still remain connected to the group as a whole.

Despite the possibility of these potential risks and further damage, it has been my observation that group treatments provides the something more that most patients require. It is also a recognition that we inevitably operate in systems and that healing takes place in systems.

From individual to group: a case

Robert entered my office in a frenzy. He looked terrified, his wild curly hair in disarray. I was struck by his anxiety that seemed to have an edge of terror. He began to tell the tale of the end of his marriage and his fear of being alone and losing everything in his impending divorce.

The story he told was of a wife with many demands and his inability to take them seriously. He described their life together; capturing how little time they spent together, reflecting few shared interests. A vivid example of the level of disconnection he described was apparent in his telling me about sitting on the couch in her presence, reading a book while masturbating. It was clear that he had little understanding that his engagement in this solitary behaviour while not engaging sexually with his wife would be upsetting for her. This detail was issued without any sense that he was able to consider that his behaviours could impact others, a mirror of his experiences with his own parents. This apparent lack of imagining himself into the other person's experience was a persistent theme in the early therapy years. I was, in Kohut's words, an archaic selfobject characterized by the sense of providing a function without a discernable sense of being experienced as a separate person. It became clear that Robert had suffered a profound disruption of his attachment motivational system. It was manifest in the above example as well as in many others. He had almost no friendships and his connection with his siblings was minimal. He did remain attached to his parents signalling a desperation increased by his wife's departure.

We met two to three times a week as divorce proceedings accelerated. During this period, experiencing severe anxiety attacks, Robert moved in with his parents. His anxiety became so unmanageable that at night he sometimes slept in bed with his parents. He delivered this information without any sense of how unusual it might appear. I was surprised by his retreat into his parent's bed. Little did I yet appreciate that his limited capacity for attachment as well as his early trauma had left him with few coping skills.

Our work progressed slowly as Robert tried to sort out how he was going to go forward in his life. He was calm enough to manage finding an apartment and moving into it. He continued to spend every weekend with his parents as he had when he was married to Barbara. The hallmark of this early therapy period was simply helping him get through each day. There was little room to explore his inner world. The real world was much too overwhelming to him. I did manage to get some early history that gave me a foundation to begin to formulate what had happened to this young man. During this early period his attachment to me was minimal despite the frequency of our sessions.

Robert was the eldest of two sons born to Russian immigrants who had fled Europe in the early nineteen-forties. He reported that as a child he was 'wild', describing incidents such as running around and around in the living room, purposefully running behind the television and getting his foot tangled in the wire, pulling the television off the stand, crashing it to the floor. He agreed that he was very angry but had little sense as to why. What he came to understand was that this and other desperate acts were designed to get attention from his parents, or for that matter, from anyone. Another incident he reported occurred when he was in second grade. He went into the classroom coat closet and stuck pins into the lunch bags of the other children. We talked about the meaning of these behaviours:

*

Robert: *I ran around the room knowing that I wanted to crash the television to the floor.*
Rosemary: *Sophisticated thinking for a four-year-old. As you look back, do you have any ideas about that behaviour?*
Robert: *Well, I remember feeling very, very angry . . .*
Rosemary: *And?*
Robert: *Nothing, I was just angry.*
Rosemary: *So, have you given any thought as to how strongly you were feeling back then?*
Robert: *Well, as I said, I was very angry.*
Rosemary: *I am curious as to why a four-year-old would be so angry and express it in such a dramatic way.*
Robert: *I wanted to vent I think. I can't really remember but I do remember how good it felt when I did it.*
Rosemary: *Consequences for feeling so good?*
Robert: *I don't remember anything else. I don't think I was spanked. I don't think anyone said much about it.*
Rosemary: *Too bad.*
Robert: *Why too bad? Do you think I should have been punished?*
Rosemary: *I meant too bad that no one got the message you were trying to convey.*
Robert: *Message?*
Rosemary: *Yes.*
Robert: *So you think I was trying to get some attention?*
Rosemary: *Desperately.*

*

This rather obvious interchange captures the tenor of the early years of our therapy work. Almost everything felt like a revelation to him. For a few years, he could not understand what would have made such a young boy so angry.

As his family history unfolded, it was clear how dysfunctional the family was. His mother was profoundly depressed and angry with his father. His father, an intellectual with an important government role in the Vietnam War, was absent for four to six months at a time. The boys were left with the mother who sank deeper into depression after begging his father not to leave on another work assignment. Often, there would be little food in the house and there was little monitoring of Robert or his younger siblings. He told these stories very matter-of-factly. This pattern persisted in our work: He would tell a story, often a gruesome tale, sometimes of a sexual nature regarding his mother. These tales were more like descriptions or little stories, but were absent of affect. This affective absence was also in the room between us. My efforts to explore feelings or feeling states were met with yet another description. He described that at fourteen he asked to go to an analyst. This story did have some affect. '*I told my mother I wanted to go and see someone. She said ok so I went to see this guy and he made me lie on the couch. He didn't say anything! He was worthless!*' I agreed that he didn't need any more silence in his life, his dad gone and his mother closed in her darkened bedroom. He was relieved to hear my agreement. These mirroring experiences were helpful but he did not seem concerned by his lack of attachment to me. I, on the other hand, was struck by how unconnected he seemed. This was also apparent in his lack of engagement in the larger world. He spent most of his time alone or in his graduate school classes, replicating his childhood isolation.

The first phase of the treatment was an effort to sooth him enough through his separation and divorce. There were some inroads made in that he began to consider the deprived family life as having consequences for him. He also began to exhibit affect in his stories. Perhaps of great significance was my experience of being two-dimensional. I had the fantasy that I could be a cardboard figure, sitting in my chair, and he wouldn't notice that the cardboard figure had been exchanged for me.

Robert gradually began to experience me as someone who was available to help him translate his early experiences in the family and how they were replicated in his current life and with me. He could engage somewhat more in the transference with me and I with him. At this time, I had become fully immersed in the work of Kohut using selfobject theory as a mainstay of my work. As a result, I was more attuned to subtle ruptures and the repair of these ruptures. With Robert, being able to detect these empathetic failures was quite difficult, reinforcing for me his continued difficulty with his emotions. It was during this time that he began his first group experience, giving me access to aspects of his character unavailable in individual work. He entered the group willingly enough but once there was unable to engage other members either about his or their issues. It was in the group that he experiences the most disruption with myself, my co-therapist, and group members, becoming quite contemptuous of our interpretations or other efforts made by group members to engage him. We began to clearly see his interpersonal difficulties. Rather than viewing these as his problems, he found the other members wanting. Using his intellect, he was able to dismiss people with a few well-chosen words. He then felt isolated and lonely in response to their withdrawal. I began to explore this contemptuousness in the individual work. What emerged was his pride in his identification with his intellectually accomplished father. He began to see that the only way to make contact with his father was by becoming engaged with him around his intellectual prowess. This technique allowed him to feel close to this distant man who supplied his son with marginal opportunities for healthy attachment. Robert remained detached from his equally detached mother who remained self-absorbed and disinterested for his entire life. We worked with his disconnection from her and what came to light was sexual excitement provoked by his mother's scanty nightgowns and her hiding out in her bed. His difficulty with his sexuality became a more significant part of our dialogues. As we worked on gaining trust he was able to explore his distance from me, understanding the safety of the disconnection: '*I don't know what to do with you – whether I should jump your bones or even trust you.*' This statement was a significant breakthrough for him and opened the way to deepened trust between us. By this time, Robert had remarried.

*

Robert: *Well, there was another big explosion over the weekend.*
Rosemary: *Oh?*
Robert: *Yes, Sara was furious because I forgot to make the hotel reservations.*
Rosemary: *Forgot?*
Robert: *Yes, we were supposed to go away for President's Day weekend.*
Rosemary: *Yes. But you forgot?*
Robert: *Well not exactly. I really hate to use the phone. I mean I never use it! When I do, I don't know what to say and besides, I really don't like to travel!* (This said with considerable energy.)

Rosemary: *You prefer to stay closer to home.*
Robert: *I do, I really do.*
Rosemary: *What does it mean to leave home; can you imagine yourself into that experience?*
Robert: *Yeah, it really upsets me. I guess the uncertainty is too overwhelming.*
Rosemary: *You seem to be experiencing something right now.*
Robert: *I'm remembering my mother threatening to leave us. It was while my dad was travelling.*
Rosemary: *Hmm.*
Robert: *Always, it was as if I would never be able to take care of myself. I really hate them both . . . I don't care if I ever see them again and Sara agrees!*

*

Robert launched into yet another story that was evidence of their disinterest and detachment. He and Sara had found a very special way to feel bonded. Both came from very difficult, dysfunctional families. They joined around their contempt and anger toward one or the other of the four parents. He relished these times, feeling like he was making great progress because he was 'feeling so much'. However, when he and Sara were not fighting the external enemy, their relationship erupted into rage attacks that left Robert tortured and unable to understand what had prompted Sara's attack. Despite his individual and group work, he only gradually came to see that his withdrawal, absence of affect and subtle contempt might have been part of the blow-up.

During this next phase of the work, Robert finally secured a strong bond with me. He became much less detached and was quite available in our work. He had finished his Ph.D., got a good job and he continues to grow professionally. His work in the group expanded in that he was able to develop interest in the other members, offering interpretations guided by his intellectual rather than his emotions. He never missed a session, either individual or group. I saw his growth and his efforts to understand his detachment.

His detachment became a primary focus when a major life event occurred: the birth of his first child. Robert rarely mentioned the baby or seemed particularly interested in him. His wife was furious with his self-removal. I was concerned that recent advances in his capacity for activation of the attachment motivational system had stalled. The threat the child posed was that he captured Sara's full attention. This appeared to be an enormous loss for Robert.

Our work returned once more to his early history. His brother was born when Robert was four years old. His birth marked the return of another major depression, again removing his mother from him. Now his own son was taking Sara away from him, prompting a traumatic reenactment of his early history. As we worked through this reactivation of loss, Robert made a decidedly quicker recovery and began to experience his child, now eighteen months old, in a much fuller way. The group provided encouragement to him through their understanding as well as challenging.

Robert had made a fuller commitment to both group and individual work. He was now lively, affectively available to himself, his therapists and group members. His relationship with his wife was solid as he learned to stand his ground, remaining engaged with her as they struggled with any issue that arose. His relationship with his son was one of shared interests and he worked at being available to him in a noncritical and engaged way, signalling his growth well beyond his own father's limitations. We were on solid ground and our sessions became more collaborative. He was comfortable challenging me in both the individual and group work – a significant advance for him. It was at this time that we discussed termination, agreeing that a step process would be effective. That is, he would stop his individual sessions and stay in group until he was ready to stop completely. Although his father was quite ill, he felt he had done good work with him in the last several years and did not feel that this should impede the termination process. The discussion of termination proceeded well and as we neared the date of our final individual session, I received a frantic call from Robert telling me that he had gone for a routine colonoscopy and it was discovered that he had cancer. Two days later, his father died.

This was a disrupted time for all of us. Robert was dealing with the death of his father and a cancer diagnosis. Needless to say, we did not stop his individual work. The group was stunned and upset by the news. Robert had become one of the 'old', loved and respected members, capable of both warm empathic engagement as well as confrontation and questioning.

Gradually, the group became a primary support system that held him through the worst of the chemotherapy and radiation necessary before surgery. During this period we increased his sessions that were essentially supportive as he worked through the diagnosis. The picture, however, became much more complicated when my co-therapist was diagnosed with cancer. By now, the group was rocked with anxiety. Robert and my co-therapist bonded around their shared experiences before my co-therapist left for eight months in order to pursue necessary treatment. The group was floundering; Robert was floundering after his cancer surgery, followed by several other medical emergencies. I can add, I was also floundering.

My co-therapist returned. The group began to re-solidify and Robert learned much about his capacity to be resilient as he recovered from blow after blow of serious medical diagnoses. Our relationship deepened further and my admiration of his courage became more and more apparent. The intersubjective field was alight with hope and hopefulness. We were collaborators in new and deeper ways. His capacity for attachment and affiliation blossomed.

During this time, with Robert solidifying his physical and emotional gains, forming deeper bonds with the group, Sally, another long-term group member was diagnosed and soon died from brain cancer. The group bonds deepened over the repeated traumas. Gathered in the cemetery, the group members participated in the shovelling of dirt on Sally's pine box on a cold, snowy day. This was a new kind of affiliation, addressing the full, final separation we all face.

Robert and I continue our individual and group work, characterized by a joint holding of the pain of this latest phase of treatment. Here is a portion of a recent group session in which conversation shifted to a review of current self experiences in the face of ongoing cancer treatment.

Rosemary: *You describe this treatment protocol so well. Have you thought about how you are progressing?*

Robert: *Yes, well I look back at all the bumps and how I would respond. It feels like I would shrink and turn inward, then deal with the situation and expand again – shrink and expand, shrink and expand, (using his hands to demonstrate).*

Rosemary: *Yes, like a rubber band that never loses its elasticity. Your resilience is remarkable.*

James: *I don't know how you do it. You are amazing.*

Robert:	*That is something all these battles have taught me. I can keep going on and do it while I remain optimistic. I never would have thought that I could have done this.*
Ruth Ann:	*Well, I feel like you have helped me see that we can really grow no matter what.*
Rosemary:	*Robert worked very hard to do it. It has been quite a journey! We all have learned more about coping with difficult, life threatening issues.*
Robert:	(Clearly feeling uncomfortable stirs in his chair) *Hmmm.*
Rosemary:	*You're uncomfortable?*
Robert:	*Yes, my grandmother would have said 'kanahara'* (said as he knocked on wood on the chest next to his chair).

The group laughed, everyone agreed.

James:	*I knock wood!*

More laughter.

Rosemary:	*All of these gains aren't just luck – you all know that.*
Robert:	*Yes, a lot of big changes. Can you imagine, I actually came up with the idea for a party to celebrate the five-year mark! I'm turning sixty, so I guess it will be a dual celebration.*
Rosemary:	*Terrific!*
Robert:	*I am not sure I could have done it without your help and the help of the group.*
Rosemary:	*Your capacity to recognize how much you have gained is important to all of us.*
Robert:	*Absolutely!*
James:	*I really admire you and wonder if I could handle things as you have* (James has had many losses and his efforts at attaching to group members has been inconsistent).
Robert:	*It took me a long time to get here!*
Ellie:	*I have been in group with you for a long time and your gains really impress me and encourage me to continue to try to attach in here. I think AA has helped some. I feel more connected to my woman's group.*

Focus shifts to Sally who has been dead for about a year:

Robert:	*I guess we all know that when we let ourselves get attached we also have to face the reality of loss. I still miss Sally. She did such a good job of maintaining her connections to us.*
Ruth Ann:	*Yeah, I was just thinking about her too! She really knew how to be part of the group. She kept us honest.*

Bill: *Honest? I don't see that, I think she was just better at being part of a group than I was. She always had a group of friends and she wasn't afraid to call them on their shit. I really learned from her to let people know what I was feeling.*

Robert: *She was a beacon for me. I was always so impressed by her capacity to go deep and find all the obscure, to me, connections between things. She was bored by surface stuff. I wonder if we can go deep without her.*

*

Robert's recognition of his gains as well as his concerns about the group's health were a significant gain. His concerns about the health of the affiliative process with Sally were a statement about the growth and sensitive affiliative advances he made.

Summary

Avoiding a focus or simply not appreciating the importance of affiliation denies therapists an important source of information about patients' functioning in the world. In the ongoing emphasis on the individual self within the dyad, we lose sight of how embedded we all are in systems more complicated and diverse than the dyad. Gergen captures this well:

> The long standing and much cherished tradition of the individual carries with it enormous costs . . . This tradition invites a sense of fundamental separation and loneliness; encourages narcissism at the expense of relationships; generates unending threats to one's person, and transforms the self into a marketable commodity
>
> (Gergen, 2009: 27)

We should not underemphasize the significance of living in communities. Not attending sufficiently to the impact of the larger environment can be a significant error for each of us. Close attention to the therapeutic group opens our awareness to larger cultural and global contexts.

The ongoingness of the process of making gains in both the capacity for attachment and affiliation is a useful place to end this chapter. It captures the never-ending, need for attachment and affiliation and how these motivations inevitably shift depending on the intersubjective field in which they occur. That is, we can assume that the struggle to maintain oneself is also very dependent upon the system in which we are operating. Therefore it remains important to reevaluate both attachment and affiliation depending on the context in which these needs occur.

Using the affiliative motivational system as a lens from which to view group behaviour provides a necessary and useful guideline when considering the functioning of the group as a whole as well as individual members of the group. It reminds us that the group context is constantly evolving within each person in each group and is dependent on the health and vitality of the affiliative motivational system in each group member thus giving us considerable information about the unfolding group process. Additionally, it reminds us to observe our own affiliative motivations, recognizing that in each intersubjective field of each group in which we work, we will respond differently based on our own attachment and affiliative needs and the make-up of each group.

Using motivational systems theory provides a lens from which to observe group action. Part of this action is the fact that, like all of the motivational systems, affiliation addresses our basic effort to maintain a homeostasis or equilibrium as we negotiate each group engagement. I am always amazed at the efforts groups make to continue to operate effectively. At times it can feel like the group is descending into chaos. With knowledge of complexity theory, we can sustain ourselves knowing that dipping into chaos can, through a tipping point, lead us to richer levels of group functioning. If the therapist can comfortably hold this idea, it is less likely that he/she will react with anxiety as a group goes through an often-extended period of struggle. Affiliation is basic to being a social being. Group treatment provides an environment from which to work toward a healthy level of affiliation with others.

References

Agrawal, H.R., Gunderson, J., Holmes, B.M. and Lyons-Ruth, K. (2004). Attachment studies with borderline patients: a review. *Harvard Reviews of Psychiatry*, 12: 94–104.

Ainsworth, M.D.S., Blehar, M.C., Waters, E. and Walls, S. (1978). *Pattern of Attachment: a psychological study of the strange situation.* Hillsdale: Elrlbaum.

Albasi C. (2006). *Attaccamenti Traumatici. I modelli Operativi Interni Dissociati.* Novara: Utet.

Albasi C. (2012). *Adolescenza e Trauma. Il caso di Sophie di In Treatment.* Milano: Franco Angeli.

Allen, J.G., Fonagy, P. and Bateman, A.W. (2008). *Mentalizing in clinical practice.* Arlington, USA: American Psychiatric Publishing.

American Psychiatric Association (APA) (1980), *Diagnostic and Statistical Manual of Mental Disorders* (3rd ed.), Washington, DC: American Psychiatric Association.

American Psychiatric Association (APA) (2000). *Diagnostic and statistical manual of mental disorders* (4th ed., text rev.). Washington, DC: American Psychiatric Association.

American Psychiatric Association (APA) (2013). *Diagnostic and statistical manual of mental disorders* (5th ed.). Washington, DC: American Psychiatric Association.

Ammaniti, M. and Gallese, V. (2014). *La Nascita dell'Intersoggettività. Lo Sviluppo del Sé tra Psicodinamica e Neurobiologia.* Milano: Raffaello Cortina.

Aron, L.A. (1996). A *Meeting of Minds: Mutuality in Psychoanalisys.* Hillsdale, NJ: Analytic Press.

Balint, M. (1952). *Primary Love and Psychoanalytic Technique.* London: The Hogarth Press.

Baron-Cohen, S., Tager-Flusberg, H. and Cohen, D.J. (1993). *Understanding other minds: Perspective from autism.* Oxford: Oxford University Press.

Bateman, A.W. (2012). Interpersonal psychotherapy for borderline personality disorder. *Clinical Psychologist Psychotherapist*, 19(2): 124–33.

Bateman, A.W. and Fonagy, P. (2000). Effectiveness of psychotherapeutic treatment of personality disorder. *British Journal of Psychiatry*, 177: 138–43.

Bateman, A.W. and Fonagy, P. (2006). *Mentalization-Based Treatment for Borderline Personality Disorder: A Practical Guide*. Oxford: Oxford University Press.

Bateman, A.W. and Fonagy, P. (2009). Randomized controlled trial of outpatient mentalization-based treatment versus structured clinical management for borderline personality disorder. *American Journal of Psychiatry*, 166(12): 1355–64.

Bateson, G. (1972). *Steps to an Ecology of Mind*. New York: Ballantine Book.

Battle, C.L., Shea, M.T., Johnson, D.M., Yen, S., Zlotnick, C., Zanarini, M.C., Sanislow, C.A., Skodol, A.E., Gunderson, J.G., Grilo, C.M., McGlashan, T.H. and Morey, L.C. (2004). Childhood maltreatment associated with adult personality disorders: findings from the Collaborative Longitudinal Personality Disorders Study. *Journal of Personality Disorders*, 18(2): 193–211.

Beatson, J. and Rao, S. (2014). Psychotherapy for borderline personality disorder. *Australasian Psychiatry*, 22(6): 529–32.

Beck, A., Freeman, A. and Davis, D. (2004). *Cognitive therapy of Personality disorders (2nd ed.)*. New York: Guilford Press.

Beebe, B. (1986). Mother-infant mutual influence and precursors of self-and object representations. In J. Masling (Ed.), *Empirical Studies of Psychoanalytic Theories*. Hillsdale, NJ: Lawrence Erlbaum Associates, pp. 27–48.

Beebe, B. (2000). Co-constructing mother-infant distress: The micro-synchrony of maternal impingement and infant avoidance in the face-to-face encounter. *Psychoanalytic Inquiry*, 20: 421–40.

Beebe, B. and Lachmann, F.M. (2002). *Infant research and Adult Treatment: Co-Constructing Interactions*. New York: Analytic Press.

Beebe, B., Jaffe, J., Chen, H., Buck, K., Cohen, P., Feldstein, S. and Andrews, H. (2008). Maternal depression at 6 weeks postpartum and mother– infant 4-month self- and interactive regulation. *Infant Mental Health Journal*, 29(5): 442–71.

Beebe, B., Jaffe, J., Feldstein, S., Mays, K. and Alson, D. (1985). Interpersonal timing: The application of an adult dialogue model to mother-infant vocal and kinesic interactions. In T. Field (Ed.), *Social perception in infants*. New York: Ablex.

Bellino, S., Rinaldi, C. and Bogetto, F. (2010). Adaptation of interpersonal psychotherapy to borderline personality disorder: a comparison of combined therapy and single pharmacotherapy. *Canadian Journal of Psychiatry*, 55(2): 74–81.

Benjamin, J. (1990). An outline of intersubjectivity: the development of recognition. *Psychoanalytic Psychology*, 7: 33–46.

Benjamin, J. (2002). The rhythm of recognition: Comment on the work of Louis Sander. *Psychoanalitic Dialogues*, 12(1): 43–5.

Berne, E. (1964). *Games People Play*. New York: Grove Press.

Berne, E. (1968). *Principless of Group Treatment*. New York: Oxford University Press.

Bion, W.R. (1959). *Experience with groups*. New York: Basic Books.

Blum, N., St John, D., Pfohl, B., Stuart, S., McCormick, B., Allen, J., Arndt, S. and Black, D.W. (2008). Systems Training for Emotional Predictability and Problem Solving (STEPPS) for outpatients with borderline personality disorder: a randomized controlled trial and 1-year follow-up. *American Journal of Psychiatry*, 165(4): 468–78.

Bohus, M., Haaf, B., Simms, T., Limberger, M.F., Schmahl, C., Unckel, C., Lieb, K. and Linehan, M.M. (2004). Effectiveness of inpatient dialectical behavioural therapy for borderline personality disorder: a controlled trial. *Behaviour Research and Therapy*, 42(5): 487–99.

Bos, E.H., van Wel, E.B., Appelo, M.T. and Verbraak, M.J. (2010). A randomized controlled trial of a Dutch version of systems training for emotional predictability and problem solving for borderline personality disorder. *Journal of Nervous and Mental Disease*, 198(4): 299–304.

Bowlby, J. (1969). *Attachment and loss (vol. 1), Attachment*. New York: Basic Books.

Bowlby, J. (1988). *A Secure Base*. London: Routledge.

Brady, K.T., Killeen, T.K., Brewerton, T. and Lucerini, S.(2000). Comorbidity of psychiatric disorders and posttraumatic stress disorder. *Journal of Clinical Psychiatry*, 61 Suppl 7: 22–32.

Bromberg, P.M. (1998). *Standing in the Spaces. Essays on Clinical Process, Trauma, and Dissociation*. Hillsdale: Analytic Press.

Bromberg, P.M. (2006). *Awakening the Dreamer: Clinical Journeys*. Mahwah, NJ: Analytic Press.

Brown, G.K., Newman, C.F., Charlesworth, S.E., Crits-Christoph, P. and Beck, A.T. (2004). An open clinical trial of cognitive therapy for borderline personality disorder. *Journal of Personality Disorders*, 18: 257–71.

Bucci, W. (1997). *Psychoanalysis and Cognitive Science*. New York: Guilford.

Bucci, W. (2005). Process research. In E.S. Person, A.M. Cooper and G.O. Gabbard (Eds.), *The American Psychiatric Publishing Textbook of Psychoanalysis*. Washington, DC: American Psychiatric Association, pp. 317–33.

Burrow, T. (1927). *The social basic of Consciousness*. London: Kegan Paul.

Cacioppo, J. T., & Patrick, B. (2008). *Loneliness: Human nature and the need for social connection*. New York: W. W. Norton & Company.

Carey, T.A. and Stiles, W.B. (2015). Some Problems with Randomized Controlled Trials and Some Viable Alternatives. *Clinical Psychology and Psychotherapy*.

Ceccarelli, M. (1998). Neurobiologia e multidimensionalità del comportamento umano. In C. Blundo and R. Stowe (Eds.). *I disturbi del comportamento tra neurologia e psichiatria*. Milano: Masson.

Ceccarelli, M. (2005). Teorie della mente, regolazione delle emozioni e coscienza: Per un modello biopsicosociale della coscienza. In F. Moser and A. Genovese (Eds.), *La Dimensione Relazionale in Psicoterapia cognitiva*. Trento: Curcu and Genovese Ed.

Clarke, S., Thomas, P. and James, K. (2013). Cognitive analytic therapy for personality disorder: randomised controlled trial. *British Journal of Psychiatry*, 202: 129–34.

Clarkin, J.F. (2012). An integrated approach to psychotherapy techniques for patients with personality disorder. *Journal of Personality Disorders*, 26(1): 43–62.

Clarkin, J.F., Levy, K.N., Lenzenweger, M.F. and Kernberg, O.F. (2007). Evaluating three treatments for borderline personality disorder: A multiwave study. *American Journal of Psychiatry*, 164: 922–8.

Cloitre, M., Garvert, D. W., Weiss, B., Carlson, E. B. and Bryant, R. A. (2014). Distinguishing PTSD, Complex PTSD, and Borderline Personality Disorder: A latent class analysis. *European Journal of Psychotraumatology*.

Cook, B.I., Miller R.L. and Seager R. (2009): Amplification of the North American 'Dust Bowl' drought through human induced land degradation. *Proceeding of National Academy of Sciences*, 106: 4997–5001.

Cottraux, J., Note, I., Boutitie, F., Milliery, M., Genouihlac, V., Yao, S. N., Note, B., Mollard, E., Bonasse, F., Gaillard, S., Djamoussian, D., Guillard Cde, M., Culem, A. and Gueyffier, F. (2009). Cognitive therapy versus Rogerian supportive therapy in borderline personality disorder: two-year follow-up of a controlled pilot study. *Psychotherapy Psychosom*, 78(5): 307–16.

Cowan, P.A. and MacHale, J.P. (1996). Coparenting in a Family Context: Emerging Achievements, Current Dilemmas, and Future Directions. In J.P. McHale and P.A. Cowan, Understanding How Family-Level Dynamics Affect Children's Development: Studies of Two-Parent Families. *New Directions for Child Development*, 74: 93–106. San Francisco: Jossey-Bass.

Damasio, A.R. (1994). *Descartes' Error*. New York: Grosset/Putnam.

Damasio, A.R. (1998). Emotion in the perspective of an integrated nervous system. *Brain Research Reviews*, 26: 83–6.

D'Andrea, W., Ford, J., Stolbach, B., Spinazzola, J. and van der Kolk, B.A. (2012). Understanding interpersonal trauma in children: why we need a developmentally appropriate trauma diagnosis. *American Journal of Orthopsychiatry*, 82(2): 187–200.

Darwin, C.R. (1872). *The expression of the emotions in man and animals*. London: John Murray.

Davidson, K., Norrie, J., Tyrer, P., Gumley, A., Tata, P., Murray, H. and Palmer, S. (2006). The effectiveness of cognitive behaviour therapy for borderline personality disorder: results from the borderline personality disorder study of cognitive therapy (BOSCOT) trial. *Journal of Personality Disorders*, 20(5): 450–65.

Dazzi, N. and De Coro, A. (1998). L'indagine sul processo nella psicoterapia psicoanalitica: per uno studio critico dei metodi di ricerca. In S. Di Nuovo e G. Lo Verso (Eds.), *Valutare le psicoterapie. La ricerca italiana*, Milano: Franco Angeli, pp. 126–40.

Dazzi, N., De Coro, A. and Andreassi, S. (2003, June). *CCRT and Motivational Systems in Case Formulation*. Paper presented at European Congress of SPR.

Dazzi, N., Lingiardi, V. and Colli, A. (2006). *La ricerca in psicoterapia. Modelli e strumenti*. Milano: Raffaello Cortina.

de Waal, F.B.M. (1982). *Chimpanzee Politics: Power and Sex Among Apes*. Baltimore, Md.: Johns Hopkins University Press.

Dennett, D.C. (1991). *Consciousness Explained*. Boston, MA: Little, Brown and Company.
Di Maggio, G. and Semerari, A. (2003). *I disturbi di personalità. Modello e trattamento*. Bari: Laterza.
Di Maria, F. and Lo Verso, G. (1995). *La psicodinamica dei gruppi*. Milano: Raffaello Cortina.
Diedrich, A. and Voderholzer, U. (2015). Obsessive-compulsive personality disorder: a current review. *Current Psychiatry Reports*, 17(2): 2.
Dixon-Gordon, K.L., Turner, B.J. and Chapman, A.L. (2011). Psychotherapy for personality disorders. *International Review of Psychiatry*, 23(3): 282–302.
Doering, S., Hörz, S., Rentrop, M., Fischer-Kern, M., Schuster, P., Benecke, C., Buchheim, A., Martius, P. and Buchheim, P. (2010). Transference-focused psychotherapy v. treatment by community psychotherapists for borderline personality disorder: randomised controlled trial. *British Journal of Psychiatry*, 196(5): 389–95.
Donald, M. (1991). *Origins of the Modern Mind: Three Stages in the Evolution of Culture and Cognition*. Cambridge, MA: Harvard University Press.
Eccles, J.C. (1989). *Evolution of the Brain: Creation of the Self*. London and New York: Routledge.
Edelman, G.M. (1989). *The Remembered Present. A Biological Theory of Consciousness*. New York: Basic Books.
Edelman, G.M. (1992). *Bright Air, Brilliant Fire. On the Matter of the Mind*. New York: Basic Books.
Elias, N. (1987). *The Society of Individuals*. Oxford: Blackwell, 1991.
Ellenberger, H. (1970). *The discovery of the Unconscious*. New York: Basic Books.
Emmelkamp, P.M., Benner, A., Kuipers, A., Feiertag, G.A., Koster, H.C. and van Apeldoorn, F.J. (2006). Comparison of brief dynamic and cognitive-behavioural therapies in avoidant personality disorder. *British Journal of* Psychiatry, 189: 60–4.
Ey, H. (1975). *Des idèes de Jackson à un modèle organo-dynamique en psychiatrie*. Toulouse: Edouard Privat.
Ey, H., Bernard, P. and Brisset, Ch. (1978). *Manuel de Psychiatrie*, 5th edn. Paris: Masson.
Fairbairn, W.R.D. (1952). *Psychoanalytic studies of the personality*. London: Tavistock.
Farrel, J.M., Shaw, I.A. and Webber, M.A. (2009). A schema focused approach to group psychotherapy for outpatients with borderline personality disorder: A randomized controlled trial. *Journal of Behaviour Therapy and Experimental Psychiatry*, 40(2): 317–28.
Fassone, G., Ivaldi, A. and Rocchi, M.T. (2003). Riduzione del drop-out nei pazienti con disturbi gravi di personalità: risultati preliminari di un modello di psicoterapia cognitivo-comportamentale integrata, individuale e di gruppo. *Rivista di Psichiatria*, 38: 241–6.
Fassone, G., Lo Reto, F., Foggetti, P., Santomassimo, C., D'Onofrio M.R., Ivaldi, A., Liotti, G., Trincia, V. and Picardi, A. (2015). A content validity study of AIMIT (Assessining Interpersonal Motivation in Transcripts). *Clinical Psychology and Psychotherapy*, doi: 10.1002/cpp. 1960

Fassone, G., Valcella, F., Pallini, S., Scarcella, F., Tombolini, L., Ivaldi, A., Prunetti, E., Manaresi, F. and Liotti, G. (2012). Assessment of interpersonal motivation in transcripts (AIMIT): an Inter and intra-rater reliability of a new method of detection of interpersonal motivationa systems in psychotherapy. *Clinical Psychology and Psychotherapy*, 19: 224–34.

Ferenczi, S. (1909). Introjection *and transference.* In S. Ferenczi, *Contributions to Psychoanalysis.* Boston: Badger, 1922.

Fink, G.R., Markowitsch, H.J., Reinkemeier, M., Bruckbauer, T., Kessler, J. and Heiss, W.D. (1996). Cerebral representation of one's own past: neural networks involved in autobiographical memory. *Journal of Neuroscience*, 16: 4275–82.

Fischer-Kern, M., Doering, S., Taubner, S., Hörz, S., Zimmermann, J., Rentrop, M., Schuster, P., Buchheim, P. and Buchheim, A. (2015). Transference-focused psychotherapy for borderline personality disorder: change in reflective function. *British Journal of Psychiatry*.

Fivaz-Depeursinge, E. and Corboz-Warnery, A. (1999). *The primary triangle. A developmental systems view of mothers, fathers and infants.* New York: Basic Books.

Fonagy, P. (1995). Playing with reality: the development of psychic reality and its malfunction in borderline patients. *International Journal of Psychoanalysis*, 76: 39–44.

Fonagy, P., Gergely, G., Jurist, E.L. and Target, M. (2002). *Affect Regulation, Mentalization, and the Development of the Self.* New York: Other Press.

Fonagy, P. and Target, M. (1996). Playing with reality. I. Theory of Mind and the normal development of psychic reality. *International Journal of Psychoanalysis*, 77: 217–333.

Foulkes, S.H. (1975). *Group-Analytic Psychoterapy. Method and Principles.* London: Gordon and Breach.

Frank, J.D. (1961). *Persuasion and Healing: A Comparative Study of Psychotherapy.* New York: Schocken Books.

Freud, S. (1953). Fragment of analysis of a case of hysteria [Dora]. In J. Strachey (Ed. and Trans.), *The standard edition of the complete psychological works of Sigmund Freud,* (vol. 7, pp. 7–122). London: W.W. Norton and Company. (Original work published 1905).

Freud, S. (1962). Heredity and the aetiology of the neuroses. In J. Strachey (Ed. and Trans.), *The standard edition of the complete psychological works of Sigmund Freud* (vol. 3, pp. 143–56). London: Hogarth Press. (Original work published 1896).

Freud, S. (1974). Group psychology and analysis of the ego. In J. Strakey (Ed. and Trans.), *The standard edition of the complete psychological works of Sigmund Freud,* (vol. XVIII; pp. 67–147). London: Hogarth Press. (Original work published 1921).

Frewen, P.A. and Lanius, R.A. (2014). Trauma-related altered states of consciousness: exploring the 4-D model. *Journal of Trauma and Dissociation*, 15(4): 436–56.

Gabbard, G.O. (2007). Do all roads lead to Rome? New findings on borderline personality disorder. *American Journal of Psychiatry*, 164(6): 853–5.

Gabbard, G.O., Schmahl, C., Siever, L.J. and Iskander, E.G. (2012). Personality disorders. *Handbook of Clinical Neurology*, 106: 463–75.

Gallese, V., Rochat, M., Cossu, G. and Sinigaglia, C. (2009). Motor cognition and its role in the phylogeny and ontogeny of intentional understanding. *Developmental Psychology*, 45, 103–13.

Gergen, R. (2009). Relational Being: Beyond self and community. New York: Oxford University Press.

Giesen-Bloo, J., van Dyck, R., Spinhoven, P., van Tilburg, W., Dirksen, C., van Asselt, T., Kremers, I., Nadort, M. and Arntz, A. (2006). Outpatient psychotherapy for borderline personality disorder: randomized trial of schema-focused therapy vs transference-focused psychotherapy. *Archives of General Psychiatry*, 63(6): 649–58.

Gilbert, P. (1989). *Human Nature and suffering*. London: Erlbaum.

Gill, M.M. (1994). *Psychoanalysis in Transition. A personal View*. Hillsdale London: Analytic Press.

Greenberg, J.R. and Mitchell, S.A. (1983). *Object Relations in Psychoanalytic Theory*. Cambridge, MA: Harvard University Press.

Gregory, R.J., DeLucia-Deranja, E. and Mogle, J.A. (2010). Dynamic deconstructive psychotherapy versus optimized community care for borderline personality disorder co-occurring with alcohol use disorders: a 30-month follow-up. *Journal of Nervous and Mental Disease*, 198(4): 292–8.

Guidano, V. and Liotti, G. (1983).*Cognitive Processes and emotional disorder*. New York: Guilford Press.

Henry, J.P. (1993). Psychological and physiological responses to stress: The right hemisphere and the hypothalamo- pituitary- adrenal axis, an inquiry into problems of human bonding. *Integrative Physiological and Behavioural Science*, 28: 369–87.

Herman, J.L. (1992a). Complex PTSD: A syndrome in survivors of prolonged and repeated trauma. *Journal of Traumatic Stress*, 5: 377–91.

Herman, J.L. (1992b). *Trauma and recovery: The aftermath of violence from domestic abuse to political terror*. New York: Basic Books.

Hertsgaard, L., Gunnar, M., Erickson, M.F. and Nachmias, M. (1995). Adrenocortical Responses to the Strange Situation in Infants with Disorganized/ Disoriented Attachment Relationships. *Child Development*, 66, 4: 1100–06.

Hoffman, I. Z., (1992). Some practical implications of a social constructivist view of the psychoanalytic situation. *Psychoanalytic Dialogues*, vol. 2, N. 2, Hillsdale, NJ: Analytic Press.

Holmes, E.A., Brown, R.J., Mansell, W., Fearon, R.P., Hunter, E.C., Frasquilho, F. and Oakley, D.A. (2005). Are there two qualitatively distinct forms of dissociation? A review and some clinical implications. *Clinical Psychology Review*, 25(1): 1–23.

Husserl, E. (1962). *Ideas: General Introduction to Pure Phenomenology*. London, New York: Collier, Macmillan. (Original work published 1913).

Intreccialagli, B. and Ivaldi, A. (2003). Matrici relazionali del processo terapeutico: una integrazione del setting individuale e di gruppo nella psicoterapia. *Rivista Psichiatria e Territorio*, vol. XX, n. 1.

Ito, Y., Teicher, M.H., Gold, C.A. and Ackerman, E. (1998). Preliminary evidence for aberrant cortical development in abused children: a quantitative EEG study. *Journal of Neuropsychiatry and Clinical Neurosciences*, 10: 298–307.
Ivaldi, A. (1998). *Psicoterapia di gruppo e psicoterapia individuale: contesti integrabili*. Comunicazione al simposio 'La psicoterapia del paziente grave: contesti interpersonali e integrazione dell'identità', Congresso SITCC, Torino, 12–15 novembre.
Ivaldi, A. (2004), Il Triangolo Drammatico: da strumento descrittivo a strumento terapeutico, *Rivista Cognitivismo clinico*, vol. 1, n. 2: 108–23.
Ivaldi, A. (2005). *Il modello di terapia integrata individuale e di gruppo per pazienti con disturbo di personalità borderline e/o comorbidità in Asse I/II*. Terapie integrate in Psichiatria. Scuola Cognitiva Firenze, 14 ottobre.
Ivaldi, A. (2006). *Cosa dicono i tuoi occhi*. Il caso clinico di Elsa. in 109 *Psicobiettivo*, vol. XXVI, 1.
Ivaldi, A. (2008). *Nel laboratorio dello psicoterapeuta. Un'esperienza critica per colmare il divario tra formazione teorica e pratica clinica*. Milano: Franco Angeli.
Ivaldi, A. (2009). Two session rooms for therapy: a combined outpatient psychotherapy, between the cognitive-evolutionary model and contemporary psychoanalysis. *GROUP: The Journal of the Eastern Group Psychotherapy Society*. MI,USA: Concord Editorial and Design Alto.
Ivaldi, A. and Foggetti, P. (2012). Schemi Interpersonali tipici di una personalità borderline e loro impatto sul transfert: un'ipotesi. Sesto Centro di Psicoterapia Cognitiva Roma. *Cognitivismo Clinico*, 9, 1: 15–25.
Ivaldi, A., Fassone, G. and Intreccialagli, B. (1998). *Psicoterapia individuale e psicoterapia di gruppo: contesti integrabili*. Comunicazione al simposio 'Psicoterapia del paziente grave: integrazione dell'identità', IX Congresso Nazionale Società italiana di Psicoterapia Comportamentale e Cognitiva, SITCC, Torino, 12–15 novembre.
Ivaldi, A., Fassone, G. and Intreccialagli, B. (2000). *Setting individuale e di gruppo: considerazioni critiche di un'esperienza terapeutica*. Comunicazione al simposio 'La psicoterapia fondata sulle evidenze: metodi, protocolli ed esiti', X Congresso Nazionale SITCC, Orvieto, 16–19 Novembre.
Ivaldi, A., Fassone, G., Mantione, M.G. and Rocchi, M.T. (2007). The integrated model (individual and group treatment) of cognitive-evolutionary Therapy for outpatients with BPD and Axis I/II comorbid disorders: outcome results and a single case report. *GROUP: The Journal of the Eastern Group Psychotherapy Society*, Concord Editorial and Design Alto, MI,USA.
Ivaldi, A., Fassone, G. and Rocchi, M.T. (2005). Ci vediamo al gruppo. Il modello cognitivo-evoluzionista di terapia integrata individuale e di gruppo. In G. Liotti, A. Rainone and B. Farina (Eds.), *Due terapeuti per un paziente*. Bari: Laterza.
Ivaldi, A., Foggetti, P. and Aringolo, K. (2009). *Disturbi di personalità e relazione, giochi polifonici tra le parti. Linee di sviluppo e modelli di intervento*. Milano: Franco Angeli.
Jackson, J.H. (1932). *Selected Writings of John Huglings Jackson* (editors: James Taylor, Gordon Holmes et F.M.R. Walshe), vol. II. London: Hodder and Stoughton, pp. 500–10.

Janet, P. (1889). *L'automatisme psychologique*. Paris: Felix Alcan.
Janet, P. (1898). Le traitement psychologique de l'hystérie. In A. Robin (Ed.), *Traité de térapeutique appliquée*. Paris: Rueff.
Karam, E.G., Friedman, M.J., Hill, E.D., Kessler, R.C., McLaughlin, K.A., Petukhova, M., Sampson, L., Shahly, V., Angermeyer, M.C., Bromet, E.J., de Girolamo, G., de Graaf, R., Demyttenaere, K., Ferry, F., Florescu, S.E., Haro, J.M., He, Y., Karam, A.N., Kawakami, N., Kovess-Masfety, V., Medina-Mora, M.E., Browne, M.A., Posada-Villa, J.A., Shalev, A.Y., Stein, D.J., Viana, M.C., Zarkov, Z. and Koenen, K.C. (2014). Cumulative traumas and risk thresholds: 12-month PTSD in the World Mental Health (WMH) surveys. *Depression and Anxiety*, 31(2): 130–42.
Kardiner, A. (1941). *The traumatic neuroses of war*. New York: Hoeber.
Kardiner, A. and Spiegel, H. (1947). *War, stress and neurotic illness: The traumatic neuroses of war*. New York: Hoeber.
Karpman, S. B. (1968). Fairy tales and script drama analysis. *Transactional Analysis Bullettin*, 7: 39–43.
Kernberg, O. (1984). *Severe personality disorders: Psychotherapeutic strategies*. New Haven, CT: Yale University Press.
Kessler, R.C., Sonnega, A., Bromet, E., Hughes, M. and Nelson, C.B. (1995). Posttraumatic stress disorder in the National Comorbidity Survey. Archives of General Psychiatry, 52(12): 1048–60.
Kohut, H. (1971). *The analysis of the self*. London: Hogarth Press.
Kohut, H. (1977). *The Restoration of the Self*, International Universites Press, New York.
Kohut, H. (1984). *How does analysis cure?* New York: International Universities Press.
Lanius, R.A., Williamson, P.C., Bluhm, R.L., Densmore, M., Boksman K, Neufeld R.W., Gati, J.S. and Menon, R.S. (2005). Functional connectivity of dissociative responses in posttraumatic stress disorder: A functional magnetic resonance imaging investigation. *Biological Psychiatry*, 57: 873–84.
LeDoux, J. (1996). *The Emotional Brain. The Mysterious Underpinnings of emotional life*. New York: Simon and Schuster.
Leichsenring, F. and Leibing, E. (2003). The effectiveness of psychodynamic therapy and cognitive behaviour therapy in the treatment of personality disorders: a meta-analysis. *American Journal of Psychiatry*, 160(7): 1223–32.
Levy, K.N., Meehan, K.B., Kelly, K.M., Reynoso, J.S., Weber, M., Clarkin, J.F. and Kernberg, O.F. (2006). Change in attachment patterns and reflective function in a randomized control trial of transference-focused psychotherapy for borderline personality disorder. *Journal of Consulting and Clinical Psychology*, 7 4(6): 1027–40.
Lewin, K. (1948). *Resolving social conflicts; selected papers on group dynamics*, G.W. Lewin (ed.). New York: Harper and Row.
Lichtenberg, J.D. (1981). The testing of reality from the standpoint of the body self. *Journal of American Psychoanalityc Association*, 26: 357–85.
Lichtenberg, J.D. (1983). *Psychoanalysis and Infant Research*. Hillsdale, NJ: Analytic Press.

Lichtenberg, J.D. (1989). *Psychoanalisys and Motivation*. Hillsdale, NJ: Analytic Press.
Lichtenberg, J.D. (2005). *Craft and Spirit: A Guide to the Exploratory Psychotherapies*. Hillsdale, NJ: The Analytic Press.
Lichtenberg, J.D. and Kindler, A.R. (1994). A motivational systems approach to the clinical experience. *Journal of the American Psychoanalytic Association*, 42: 405–20.
Lichtenberg, J.D., Lachmann, F.M. and Fosshage, J.L. (1992). *Self and Motivational Systems: Toward a Theory of Technique*. Hillsdale, NJ: Analytic Press.
Lichtenberg, J.D., Lachmann, F.M. and Fosshage, J.L. (1996). *The Clinical Excange: Techniques derived from self and motivational systems*. Hillsdale, NJ: Analytic Press.
Lichtenberg, J.D., Lachmann, F.M. and Fosshage, J. (2002). *A Spirit of Inquiry: Communication in Psychoanalysis*. Hillsdale, NJ: Analytic Press.
Lichtenberg, J.D., Lachmann, F.M. and Fosshage, J. (2011). *Psychoanalysis and motivational systems: A new look*. New York, NY: Routledge.
Linehan, M.M. (1993). *Cognitive behavioural treatment for borderline personality disorder*. New York: Guilford Press.
Lingiardi, V. (2002). *Alleanza terapeutica. Teoria, clinica, ricerca*. Milano: Raffaello Cortina. Da inserire nel testo.
Lingiardi, V., Amadei, G., Caviglia, G. and De Bei, F. (2011). *La svolta relazionale. Itinerari italiani*. Milano: Raffaello Cortina.
Lingiardi, V., Fassone, G., Gentile, D., Ivaldi, A. and Colli, A. (2014). Rotture e riparazioni dell'alleanza terapeutica e sistemi motivazionali interpersonali. I metodi CIS e AIMIT. In G. Liotti and F. Monticelli (Eds.), *Teoria e Clinica dell'Alleanza Terapeutica*. Milano: Raffaello Cortina.
Lingiardi, V., Filippucci, L. and Baiocco, R. (2005). Therapeutic alliance evaluation in personality disorders psychotherapy. Psychotherapy Research, 15(12): 45–53.
Lingiardi, V. and Gazzillo, F. (2014). *La personalità e i suoi disturbi. Valutazione clinica e diagnosi al servizio del trattamento*. Milano: Raffaello Cortina.
Lingiardi, V., Shedler, J. and Gazzillo, F. (2006). Assessing Personality Change in Psychotherapy with the SWAP-200: A Case Study. *Journal of Personality Assessment*, 86(1): 23–32.
Liotti, G. (1989). Attachment and cognition. In C. Perris, I. Blackburn and H. Perris (Eds.), *The Theory and practice of cognitive psychotherapy*. New York, Springer, pp. 71–99.
Liotti, G. (1993). Disorganized attachment and dissociative experiences: An illustration of the developmental-ethological approach to cognitive therapy. In K.T. Kuehlvein and H. Rosen (Eds.), *Cognitive therapies in action*. San Francisco: Jossey-Bass, pp. 213–39.
Liotti, G. (1994/2005). *La dimensione interpersonale della coscienza*. Roma: Caracci.
Liotti, G. (1995). La teoria della motivazione di Lichtenberg: un confronto con la prospettiva etologico-evoluzionista. *Psicoterapia*, 2: 104–12.

Liotti, G. (1999). Disorganized attachment and dissociative psychopathology: The contribution of attachment theory. In J. Solomon and C. George (Eds.), *Attachment Disorganization*. New York: Guilford.

Liotti, G. (2001). *Le opere della coscienza. Psicopatologia e psicoterapia nella prospettiva cognitivo-evoluzionista*. Milano: Raffaello Cortina.

Liotti, G. and Farina, B. (2011). *Sviluppi traumatici: Eziopatogenesi, clinica e terapia della dimensione dissociativa*. Milano: Raffaello Cortina.

Liotti, G. and Monticelli, F. (2008). Il manuale AIMIT: analisi degli indicatori motivazionali interpersonali nei trascritti. Milano: Raffaello Cortina.

Liotti, G., Pasquini, P. and The Italian Group for the Study of Dissociation (2000). Predictive factors for borderline personality disorder: Patients' early traumatic experiences and losses suffered by the attachment figure. *Acta Psychiatrica Scandinavica*, 102: 282–9.

Lorenz, K. (1941). Kant's doctrine of the a priori in the light of contemporary biology. In H. Plotkin (Ed.), *Learning, development and culture*, pp. 121–43. Chichester: John Wiley and Sons.

Luborsky, L. and Crits-Christoph, P. (1998). *Understanding transference: The core conflictual relationship theme method*. Washington, DC: American Psychological Association.

Luborsky, L., Diguer, L., Andrusyna, T., Friedman, S., Tarca Ch., Popp, C.A., Ermold, J. and Silberschatz, G. (2004). A method of choosing CCRT scorers. *Psychotherapy Research*, 14, 1: 127–34.

Luria, A.R. (1976). *The Working Brain. An Introduction to Neuropsychology*. Harmondsworth: Penguin.

Luxenberg, T., Spinazzola, J., van der Kolk, B.A. (2001). Complex trauma and disorder of extreme stress (DESNOS) diagnosis, part one: assessment. *Directions in Psychiatry*, 21: 373–90.

Lyons-Ruth, K. (2008). Contributions of the mother-infant relationship to dissociative, borderline, and conduct symptoms in young adulthood. *Infant Mental Health Journal*, 29(3): 203–18.

Lyons-Ruth, K., Dutra, L., Schuder, M.R. and Bianchi, I. (2006). From infant attachment disorganization to adult dissociation: relational adaptations or traumatic experiences? *Psychiatric Clinics of North America*, 29(1): 63–86, VIII.

Lyons-Ruth, K. and Jacobvitz, D. (1999). Attachment disorganization: Unresolved loss, relational violence, and lapses in behavioural and attentional strategies. In J. Cassidy and P.R. Shaver (Eds.), *Handbook of attachment: Theory, research, and clinical applications*, New York, NY: Guilford Press, pp. 520–54.

Lyons-Ruth, K., Yellin, C., Melnick, S. and Atwood, G. (2003). Childhood experiences of trauma and loss have different relations to maternal unresolved and hostile-helpless states of mind on the AAI. *Attachment and Human Development*, 5: 330–52.

Lyons-Ruth, K., Yellin, C., Melnick, S. and Atwood, G. (2005). Espanding the concept of unresolved mental states: Hostile/Helpness states of mind on the Adult Attachment Interview are associated with disrupted mother-infant communication and infant disorganization. *Development and Psychopathology*, 17: 1–23.

MacHale, J. (1997). Overt and Covert Coparenting Processes in the Family. *Family Process*, 36: 183–210.
MacHale, J. and Fivaz-Depeursinge, E. (1999). Understanding Triadic and Family Group Process during Infancy and Early Childhood. *Clinical Child and Family Psychology Review*, 2: 107–27.
MacLean, P.D. (1973). *A Triune Concept of the Brain and Behaviour*. Toronto: University of Toronto Press.
MacLean, P.D. (1982). On the origin and progressive evolution of the triune brain. In E. Armstrong and D. Falk (Eds.), *Primate Brain Evolution*. New York: Plenum Press, pp. 291–316.
MacLean, P.D. (1985). Brain evolution relating to family, play, and the separation call. *Archives of General Psychiatry*, 42: 405–17.
MacMain, S.F., Links, P.S., Gnam, W.H., Guimond, T., Cardish, R.J., Korman, L. and Streine, D.L. (2009). A randomized trial of dialectical behaviour therapy versus general psychiatric management for borderline personality disorder. *American Journal Psychiatry*, 166(12): 1365–74.
Maercker, A., Brewin, C.R., Bryant, R.A., Cloitre, M., Reed, G.M., van Ommeren, M., Humayun, A., Jones, L.M., Kagee, A., Llosa, A.E., Rousseau, C., Somasundaram, D.J., Souza, R., Suzuki, Y., Weissbecker, I., Wessely, S.C., First, M.B. and Saxena, S. (2013). Proposals for mental disorders specifically associated with stress in the International Classification of Diseases-11. *Lancet*, 381(9878): 1683–5.
Main, M. and Cassidy, J. (1988). Categories of response to reunion with the parent at age 6. Predicted from infant attachment classification and stable over a 1-month period. *Developmental Psychology*, 24: 415–26.
Main, M. and Hesse, E. (1990). Parents' unresolved traumatic experiences are related to infant disorganized attachment status: Is frightened and/or frightening parental behaviour the linking mechanism?. In M.T. Greenberg, D. Cicchetti and E.M. Cummings (Eds.), *Attachment in the preschool years*, Chicago: University of Chicago Press, pp. 161–82.
Main, M. and Solomon, J. (1990). Procedures for identifying infants as disorganized/disoriented during the Ainsworth Strange Situation. In M.T. Greenberg, D. Cicchetti and E.M. Cummings (Eds.), *Attachment in the preschool years: Theory, research and intervention*, Chicago: University of Chicago Press, pp. 121- 60.
Markowitz, J.C. (2005). Interpersonal therapy. In J.M. Oldham, A.E. Skodol and D. Bender (Eds). *The textbook of personality disorders*. Washington, DC: American Psychiatric Press.
Meares, R. (2012). *A dissociation model of borderline personality disorder*. New York: W.W. Norton and Company.
Meltzoff, A. (1990). Foundations for developing a concept of self: The role of imitation in relating self to other and the value of social mirroring, social modeling, and self practice in infancy. In D. Cicchetti and M. Beeghley (Eds.), *The Self in Transition: Infancy to Childhood*. Chicago: University of Chicago Press.

Meltzoff, A.N. and Moore, M. K. (1977). Imitation of facial and manual gestures by human neonates. *Science*, 198: 75–8.
Mitchell, S.A. (1988). *Relational Concepts in Psychoanalysis. An Integration*, Cambridge Mass: Harvard University Press.
Morin, E. (1990). *Introduction à la Pensée Complexe*. Edition du Seuil, Paris.
Morin, E. (1991). *La Méthode. IV. Les idèes, leur habitat, leur vie, leurs moeurs, leur organization*. Paris: Editions du Seuil.
Nijenhuis, E.R.S. (2008). *Somatoform dissociation, phenomena, measurement and theoretical issue*. New York: W.W. Norton and Company.
Noddings, N. (1984). *Caring, a feminine approach to ethics and moral education*. Berkeley: University of California Press.
Ogden, P., Minton, K. and Pain, C. (2006). *Trauma and the Body: A Sensorimotor Approach to Psychotherapy*. Norton Series on Interpersonal Neurobiology.
Oldham, J.M., Skodol, A.E., Kellman, H.D., Hyler, S.E., Doidge, N., Rosnick, L. and Gallaher, P.E. (1995). Comorbidity of axis I and axis II disorders. *American Journal of Psychiatry*, 152: 571–8.
Orange, D. (1995). *Emotional Understanding: Studies in Psychoanalytic Epistemology*. New York: Guilford.
Orange, D.M., Atwood, G. E. and Stolorow, R.D. (1997). *Working Intersubjectively: Contextualism in Psychoanalytic Practice*. Hillsdale, NJ: Analytic Press.
Panksepp, J. (1998). *Affective neuroscience: The foundations of human and animal emotions*. Oxford: Oxford University Press.
Paris, J. (1994). *Borderline Personality Disorder: a multidimensional approach*. Washington, DC: American Psychiatric Press.
Pasquini, P., Liotti, G., Mazzotti, E., Fassone, G., Picardi, A. and The Italian Group for the Study of Dissociation (2002). Risk factors in the early family life of patients suffering from dissociative disorders. *Acta Psichiatrica Scandinavica*, 105: 110–16.
Perry, B.D. (2001). The neurodevelopmental impact of violence in childhood. In D. Schetky and E. Benedek (Eds.), *Textbook of child and adolescent forensic psychiatry*. Washington, DC: American Psychiatric Press.
Perry, B.D. (2005). The neurosequential model of therapeutics: using principles of neurodevelopment to help traumatized and maltreated children. In N. Boyd Wedd (Ed.), *Working with Traumatized youth in Child Welfare*. New York, Guildford Press.
Popper, K. (1990). *A World of Propensities*. Bristol: Thoemmes Antiquarium Books.
Popper, K.R. (1959). *The Logic of Scientific Discovery*. London: Hutchinson.
Porges, S.W. (2001). The polyvagal theory: phylogenetic substrates of a social nervous system. *International Journal of Psychophysiology*, 42: 123–46.
Porges, S.W. (2003). The Polyvagal Theory: Phylogenetic Contributions to Social Behaviour. *Physiology and Behaviour*, 79: 503–13.
Porges, S.W. (2011). *The Polyvagal Theory*. New York, NY: W.W. Norton and Company.

Priebe, S., Bhatti, N., Barnicot, K., Bremner, S., Gaglia, A., Katsakou, C., Molosankwe, I., McCrone, P. and Zinkler, M. (2012). Effectiveness and cost-effectiveness of dialectical behaviour therapy for self-harming patients with personality disorder: a pragmatic randomised controlled trial. *Psychotherapy and Psychosomatics*, 81(6): 356–65.

Putnam, H. (1975). *Mind, language and reality. Philosophical papers, vol. 2*. Cambridge: Cambridge University Press.

Rafaeli, E. (2009). Cognitive-behavioural therapies for personality disorders. *Israel Journal of Psychiatry and Related Sciences*, 46(4): 290–7.

Reich, J. (2003). The effect of Axis II disorders on the outcome of treatment of anxiety and unipolar depressive disorders: a review. *Journal of Personality Disorders*, 17(5): 387–405.

Rizzolatti, G., Fogassi, L. and Gallese, V. (2001). Neurophysiological mechanisms underlying the understandingand imitation of action. *Nature Neuroscienze Rewieus*, 2: 661–70.

Rogers, C.R. (1957). *Client centreed Therapy*. Boston: Houghton-Mifflin.

Rosenvinge, J.H., Martinussen, M. and Ostensen, E. (2000). The comorbidity of eating disorders and personality disorders: a meta-analytic review of studies published between 1983 and 1998. *Eating Weight Disorderds*, 5: 52–61.

Ryle, A. and Kerr, I.B. (2002). *Introducing Cognitive Analytic Therapy: Principles and Practice*. Chichester: John Wiley and Sons.

Safran, J.D. and Muran, J.C. (2000). *Negotiating the therapeutic alliance: A relational treatment guide*. New York: The Guilford Press.

Sander, L.W. (1962). Issues in early mother child interaction. *Journal of the American Academy of base of text Child Psychiatry*, 1: 141–66.

Sander, L.W. (1969). The longitudinal course of early mother–child interaction-cross-case comparison in a sample of mother-infant pairs. In B.M. Foss (Ed.), *Determinants of infant behaviour*. London: Metthuen, vol. IV, pp. 189–227.

Sander, L.W. (1976). Issues in early mother–child interaction. In E. Rexford, L.W. Sander and T. Shapiro (Eds.), *Infant Psychiatry. A New Synthesis*. New Ilaven, CT: Yale University Press, pp. 127–47.

Sander, L.W. (1987). Awareness of inner experience: A system perspective on self-regulatory process in early development. *Child Abuse and Neglect*, 11: 339–46.

Şar, V. (2014). The many faces of dissociation: opportunities for innovative research in psychiatry. *Clinical Psychopharmacology and Neuroscience*, 12(3): 171–9.

Schore, A.N. (1994). *Affect regulation and the origin of the self: The neurobiology of emotional development*. Hillsdale: Erlbaum.

Schore, A.N. (2003a). *Affect dyseregulation and disorder of the self*. New York, NY: W.W. Norton and Company.

Schore, A.N. (2003b). *Affect Regulation and the Repair of the Self*. New York – London: W.W. Norton and Company.

Segalla, R. (1998). Motivational Systems and groupobject theory: implications for group therapy. In I. Harwood and M. Pines (Eds.), *Self Experiences in group: Intersubjective and self psychological pathways to human understanding*. London: Jessica Kingsley.

Shapiro, F. (1995). *Eye Movement Desensitization and Reprocessing, Basic Principles, Protocols and Procedures*, II Ed. New York: Guilfold Press;
Siegel, D.J. (1999). *The Developing Mind: toward a neurobiology of interpersonal experience.* New York: Guilford Press.
Simon, W. (2009). Follow-up psychotherapy outcome of patients with dependent, avoidant and obsessive – compulsive personality disorders: A meta-analytic review. *International Journal of Psychiatry in Clinical Practice*, 13: 153–65.
Soler, J., Pascual, J.C., Tiana, T., Cebrià, A., Barrachina, J., Campins, M.J., Gich, I., Alvarez, E. and Pérez, V. (2009). Dialectical behaviour therapy skills training compared to standard group therapy in borderline personality disorder: a 3-month randomised controlled clinical trial. *Behaviour Research Therapy*, 47(5): 353–8.
Solomon, J. and George, C. (1999). *Attachment Disorganization.* New York: Guilford Press.
Spangler, G. and Grossmann, K.E. (1999). Individual and physiological correlates of attachment disorganization in infancy. In J. Solomon and C. George (Eds.), *Attachment disorganization.* New York: Guilford Press, p. 95–124.
Stein, D.J., Koenen, K.C., Friedman, M.J., Hill, E., McLaughlin, K.A., Petukhova, M., Ruscio, A.M., Shahly, V., Spiegel, D., Borges, G., Bunting, B., Caldas-de-Almeida, J.M., de Girolamo, G., Demyttenaere, K., Florescu, S., Haro, J.M., Karam, E.G., Kovess-Masfety, V., Lee, S., Matschinger, H., Mladenova, M., Posada-Villa, J., Tachimori, H., Viana, M.C. and Kessler, R.C. (2013). Dissociation in posttraumatic stress disorder: evidence from the world mental health surveys. *Biological Psychiatry*, 73(4): 302–12.
Stern, D.N. (1971). A microanalysis of mother-infant interaction. *Journal of the American Academy of Child Psychiatry*, 19: 501–17.
Stern, D.N. (1985). *The Interpersonal World of the Infant.* New York: Basic Books.
Stern, D.N. (2004). *The Present Moment: in Psychotherapy and Everyday Life.* New York: W.W. Norton and Company.
Stoffers, J.M., Völlm, B.A., Rücker, G., Timmer, A., Huband, N. and Lieb, K. (2012). Psychological therapies for people with borderline personality disorder. *Cochrane Database of Systematic Reviews*, 8.
Stolorow, R.D. and Atwood, G.E. (1992). *Contexts of Being: The Intersubjective Foundations of Psychological Life.* Hillsdale, NJ: Analytic Press.
Sullivan, H.S. (1953). *The Interpersonal Theory of Psychiatry.* New York: W.W. Norton and Company.
Teicher, M.H., Tomoda, A. and Andersen, S.L. (2006). Neurobiological consequences of early stress and childhood maltreatment: are results from human and animal studies comparable?. *Annals of the New York Academy of Sciences*, 1071: 313–23.
Tomasello, M. (1999) *The Cultural Origins of Human Cognition.* Cambridge, Mass: Harvard University Press.
Trevarthen, C. (1974). The psychobiology of speech development. *Neurosciences Research Program Bulletin,* 12:570–85.
Trevarthen, C. (1979). Communication and cooperation in early infancy: a description of primary intersubjectivity. In M. Bullowa (Ed.), *Before speech.* Cambridge: Cambridge University Press, pp. 321–47.

Trevarthen, C. (1980). The foundations of intersubjectivity: development of interpersonal and cooperative understanding of infants. In D. Olson (Ed.), *The Social Foundations of Language and Thought: Essays in Honor of J.S. Bruner.* New York: W.W. Norton and Company, pp. 316–42.

Tronick, E.Z. (1989). Emotions and emotional communication in infants. *American Psychologist*, vol. 44(2): 112–19.

Tronick, E.Z., Als, H., Adamson, L., Wise, S. and Brazelton, T.B. (1978). Infants response to entrapment between contradictory messages in face-to-face interaction. *Journal of the American Academy of Child and Adolescent Psychiatry*, 17: 1–13.

Tronick, E.Z. and Weinberg, M.K. (1997). Depressed mothers and infants: failure to form dyadic states of consciousness. In L. Murray and P. Cooper (Eds.), *Post-partum depression and Child Development.* New York Guilford Press, pp. 54–81.

Tyrer, P., Reed, G.M. and Crawford, M.J. (2015). Classification, assessment, prevalence, and effect of personality disorder. *Lancet*, 385(9969): 717–26.

Tyrer, P., Thompson, S., Schmidt, U., Jones, V., Knapp, M., Davidson, K., Catalan, J., Airlie, J., Baxter, S., Byford, S., Byrne, G., Cameron, S., Caplan, R., Cooper, S., Ferguson, B., Freeman, C., Frost, S., Godley, J., Greenshields, J., Henderson, J., Holden, N., Keech, P., Kim, L., Logan, K., Manley, C., MacLeod, A., Murphy, R., Patience, L., Ramsay, L., De Munroz, S., Scott, J., Seivewright, H., Sivakumar, K., Tata, P., Thornton, S., Ukoumunne, O.C. and Wessely, S. (2003). Randomized controlled trial of brief cognitive behaviour therapy versus treatment as usual in recurrent deliberate self-harm: the POPMACT study. *Psychological Medicine.* 33(6): 969–76.

Valent, P. (1998). *From Survival to Fulfillment.* Philadelphia, PA: Brunner/Mazel.

Van der Hart, O., Nijenhuis, E.R.S. and Steele, K. (2006). *The Haunted Self. Structural Dissociation and the Treatment of Chronic Traumatization.* New York: W.W. Norton and Company.

Van der Kolk, B.A. (2005). Il Disturbo Traumatico dello Sviluppo: verso una diagnosi razionale per i bambini cronicamente traumatizzati In V. Caretti and G. Craparo (Ed.), *Trauma e Psicopatologia. Un approccio evolutivo-relazionale.* Roma, Astrolabio, 2008, pp. 81–93.

Van Dijke, A., Ford, J.D., Frank, L.E. and van der Hart, O. (2015). Association of Childhood Complex Trauma and Dissociation with Complex PTSD Symptoms in Adulthood. *Journal of Trauma and Dissociation*, 16(4): 428–41.

Verheul, R., van den Bosch, L.M.C., Koeter, M.W.J., De Ridder, M.A.J., Stijnen, T. and Van Den Brink, W. (2003). Dialectical behaviour therapy for women with borderline personality disorder: 12-month, randomized clinical trial in The Netherlands. *British Journal Psychiatry*, 182:135–40.

Vygotskij, L.S. (1962). Thought and language (E. Hanfmann and G. Vakar, Eds. and Trans.). Cambridge, MA: MIT Press (Original work published 1934).

Wachtel, P. L. (1997). *Psychoanalysis, behavior therapy, and the relational world.* Washington, DC: American Psychological Association.

Wallerstein, R.S. (1986). *Forty-two Lives in Treatment: A Study of Psychoanalysis and Psychotherapy.* New York: Guilford Press.

Watzlawick, P., Beavin, J. and Jackson, D.D. (1967). *Pragmatics of human communication. A Study of Interactional Patterns, Pathologies, and Paradoxes.* New York: W.W. Norton and Company.
Weinberg, I., Gunderson, J.G., Hennen, J., Cutter, C.J. Jr. (2006). Manual assisted cognitive treatment for deliberate self-harm in borderline personality disorder patients. *Journal of Personality Disorders*, 20(5): 482–92.
Weinberg, I., Ronningstam, E., Goldblatt, M.J., Schechter, M. and Maltsberger, J.T. (2011). Common factors in empirically supported treatments of borderline personality disorder. *Current Psychiatry Report*, 13(1): 60–8.
Weiss, J., Sampson, H. and The Mount Zion Psychotherapy Research Group (1986). *The Psychoanalytic process: Theory, clinical observation, and empirical research,* New York: Guilford Press.
Williams, R. and Dazzi, N. (2006). Il concetto di empatia tra clinica e ricerca empirica. In N. Dazzi, V. Lingiardi and A. Colli (Eds.), *La ricerca in psicoterapia: strumenti e modelli.* Milan: Raffaello Cortina, pp. 389–436.
Wilson, E.O. (2012). *The Social Conquest of Earth.* New York: Liveright Publishing Corporation.
Winnicott, D.W. (1965). *The Maturational Processes and the Facilitating Environment.* London: Hogarth Press (Reprinted London: Karnac Books, 1990).
Yalom, I.D. (1995). *The theory and practice of group psychotherapy* (4th ed.). New York: Basic Books.
Yen, S., Shea, M.T., Battle, C.L., Johnson, D.M., Zlotnick, C., Dolan-Sewell, R., Skodol, A.E., Grilo, C.M., Gunderson, J.G., Sanislow, C.A., Zanarini, M.C., Bender, D.S., Rettew, J.B. and McGlashan, T.H. (2002). Traumatic exposure and posttraumatic stress disorder in borderline, schizotypal, avoidant, and obsessive-compulsive personality disorders: findings from the collaborative longitudinal personality disorders study. *Journal of Nervous and Mental Disease*, 190(8): 510–18.
Yeomans, F.E., Levy, K.N. and Caligor, E. (2013). Transference-focused psychotherapy. *Psychotherapy (Chic)*, 50(3): 449–53.
Young, J.E. (2003). *Young Parenting Inventory.* New York: Cognitive Therapy Centre.
Young, J.E., Klosko, J.S. and Weishaar, M.E. (2003). *Schema Therapy: A practitioner's guide.* New York: The Guilford Press.
Zambrano, M. (2007). *Filosofía y Educación.* Manuscritos. Málaga, Fundación María Zambrano (trad. it.: *Per l'amore e per la Libertà: scritti sulla filosofia e sull'educazione.* Genova: Marietti, 2008).
Zanarini, M.C., Frankenburg, F.R., Dubo, E.D., Sickel, A.E., Trikha, A., Levin, A. and Reynolds, V. (1998). Axis I comorbidity of borderline personality disorder. *American Journal of Psychiatry*, 155: 1733–9.
Zorn, P., Roder, V., Soravia, L. and Tschacher, W. (2008). Evaluation of the 'Schema-focused Emotive Behavioural Therapy' (SET) for patients with personality disorders: results of a randomised controlled trial. *Psychotherapie, Psychosomatik, Medizinische Psychol*ogie, 58(9–10): 371–8.

Index

Locators in *italics* refer to figures and tables.

Abbreviations used in subheadings:
BPD = borderline personality disorder
RCTs = randomized controlled trials
REMOTA = relational/
  multi-motivational therapeutic
  approach

4-D model, diagnostic criteria 106

abuse, childhood: *see* childhood
  abuse
acting out: *see* enactment
actualization 124, 196
adolescence 9, 29; affiliation system
  34; clinical examples 45, 194;
  diagnostic criteria 103; REMOTA
  approach 151; *see also* childhood
Adult Attachment Interview 51
Aetiology of Hysteria (Freud) 68
affective attunement: *see* attunement
affect regulation: childhood trauma
  88–9; clinical examples 95–101,
  156–8, 165; discussion at La
  Sapienza 40, 58, 60; effectiveness
  of differing treatment models 113;
  and empathy 160; insecure-
  disorganized attachment 64, 66;
  polyvagal theory 92–5; REMOTA
  approach 118

affiliation/affiliative motivational
  system 174–5, 217, 218, 239, 240;
  group therapy 217–25; impediments
  to activation 225–8; REMOTA
  approach 171–6, *173*, 186, 196;
  theoretical perspectives 9, 26, 29,
  30, 33–5; *see also* attachment-
  affiliation system
agency: *see* intentional agency
aggressive instinctual drives 7; *see
  also* dual drives theory
agitation: *Anna* 64, 65, 66, 75, 80;
  Lucia 138, 139; *Enrico* 96, 97;
  Rita 90; *Sofia* 155
agonistic system *27*, 34; *see also*
  aversive motivational system
AIMIT (Assessment of Interpersonal
  Motivation in Transcripts) 25
alcohol/substance abuse: clinical
  example 143, 147, 166; diagnostic
  criteria 102; naturalistic study
  213
allegiance effect, research 204
alliance: *see* therapeutic alliance
altered consciousness: *see* dissociative
  disorders/states
ambivalent attachment 6, 22
American Women's Liberation
  Movement 69

amitriptyline 203
amygdalohypothalamic brain circuits 89
analysts: *see* therapists
Angie (clinical example) 11–12
Anna (clinical example) 63–6, 75–6, 80, 91, 150–1
antidepressants 203
anxiety/anxiety disorders: clinical examples 47, 48, 95–7, 228, 229, 235; diagnostic criteria 102, 104; group therapy *173*, 184, 224, 240; naturalistic study *211*; therapist 132; treatment 107, 108
archaic self objects, therapist as 229
Aron, L. A. 20
arousal dysregulation: clinical examples 66, 95–101, 140, 186; diagnostic criteria 102, 106; polyvagal theory 92–5; treatment 114; *see also* affect regulation
art 170
aspecific factors 15
Assessment of Interpersonal Motivation in Transcripts (AIMIT) 25
assessment of trauma-related disorders: *see* diagnostic criteria
Association for Research on the Psychopathology of the Attachment System (ARPAS) 25
Associazione di Psicoterapia Cognitiva 117
attachment-affiliation system 26, *27*, 29, 33, 217; dysregulation 40, 45; infant research 29
attachment system 52, 53, 55, 218; and childhood trauma 74–6, 79; clinical examples 49, 229, 233; discussion at La Sapienza 39, 58, 60; group therapy 217, 218; REMOTA approach 118, 175; theoretical perspectives *27*, 28, 30, 33; treatment 108
attachment theory/styles 2, 3, 19, 24, 57, 239; actualization 196; insecure 63–4, 95, 219; mind-body issue 18; neo-dissociationist theories 67; polyvagal theory 94, 95; secure 40, 95; traumatic 71, 74, 78–80; treatment models 108, 109, 114; *see also* disorganized attachment
attention disorders, childhood trauma 78
attention-seeking, clinical example 230
attitude, analytic 125–6
attunement 30, 36n1; child–caregiver 28, 29, 74, 79, 91, 159; therapeutic 21, 124, 138, 170
authenticity: analytic 85, 86, 87, 125, 133, 156; data 197
autonomic nervous system, polyvagal theory 92–5
aversive motivational system 34, 35, 217; clinical examples 41, 43–4, 49; discussion at La Sapienza 39, 60; dysregulation 40; infant research 29
avoidance responses: BPD 40; polyvagal theory 95; *see also* dissociative disorders/states

Bateman, A. P. 1, 3, 22, 26, 109
Beebe, B. 120, 160
beginning therapy: naturalistic study 210; REMOTA approach 135, 136–7
Behavioural and Symptom Identification Scale-32 (BASIS-32) 208, 212–13, *213*
belonging, sense of 29, 33, 96: REMOTA approach 175, 182, *182*, 183, 184, 189, 196; *see also* affiliation/affiliative motivational system; group therapy
benchmarking practice 206
Benjamin, J. 21, 22
Berne, E. 140
biological multidimensional theories 17, 18, 25, 31; *see also* evolutionism

Bion, W. R. 174
biopsychosocial consciousness model 187–9
body dysmorphic disorder 53, 104
body, role in therapy 18, 120, 167, 170; *see also* mind-body issue
borderline personality disorder (BPD) 13; diagnostic criteria 104; dysregulation of motivational systems 40; effectiveness of differing treatment models 112–13; empirically supported treatments 106–8; REMOTA approach 118; *see also* naturalistic study
Boston Psychotherapy Research Group 159
bottom up approaches 120, 170
bottom up theories 56; *see also* infant research
boundaries, therapeutic relationship 3, 64, 114; naturalistic study 209; REMOTA approach 137, 140, 141, 161; *see also* contract, therapeutic
Bowlby, J. 2, 18, 19, 24, 25, 57, 74, 79
BPD: *see* borderline personality disorder
brain function: and childhood trauma 88–9; polyvagal theory 15, 92–5, 96, 99; *see also* hierarchical model of mental functioning
Bromberg, P. M. 82, 84, 87, 105, 144
burn-out, therapist 216
Burrow, T. 174

cancer diagnoses: clinical examples 205, 234–5; research issues 198
caregiving system 217; complex trauma 76, 77, 78; discussion at La Sapienza 52, 54, 55, 56, 57; theoretical perspectives 9, 26, 27, 30, 34, 35; *see also* controlling-caregiving strategy
case studies: *see* clinical examples
Cassidy, J. 76

CAT (cognitive analytic therapy) 107, 111
categorization of information 126, 187–8
catharsis 68
CBT (cognitive behavioural therapy) 107
Ceccarelli, M. 18
central nervous system 24, 92–5, 96, 99; *see also* brain function
Chiara (clinical example), REMOTA approach 167–70
child–caregiver attunement 28, 29, 74, 79, 91, 159
childhood abuse: physical 72–3, 81, 87, 88–9; sexual 53–4, 68 69, 70; *see also* infant research; trauma
clinical examples: *Angie* 11–12; *Anna* 63–6, 75–6, 80, 91, 150–1; *Chiara* 167–70; *Diana* 53–4; *Dora* 68; *Egidio* 152; *Elsa* 136, 143–8, 163–6, 176–8, 193–6; *Enrico* 95–101; *Lucia* 138–42, 205; *Marco* 71–5, 77–88; *Monica* 179–80; *Mr. T.* 6–7; *Rita* 89–91; *Robert* 228–37; *Sister Mary* 35, 41–4, 50, 59–62; *Tom* 8; *Veronica* 35, 44–9, 50; *see also Sofia*
clinical exchange 21; *see also* therapeutic relationship
clinical process approach, motivational systems theory 40
Cluster A disorders 106–7, 111, *211*
Cluster C disorders 107, 110, *211*
co-constructions of reality 21, 23
cognitive analytic therapy (CAT) 107, 111
cognitive behavioural therapy (CBT) 107
cognitive-evolutionary intersubjective therapy (CEIT): *see* naturalistic study
cognitive-evolutionary perspective xiii–xiv, 1, 2, 3, 4n1, 24, 25–7; affiliation 175; comparison with psychoanalytic theories 30–6;

importance of research 15; relational turn 19; traumatic attachment 71; *see also* evolutionism; Liotti
Cognitive Processes and Emotional Disorders (Liotti and Guidano) 25
cohesion 28, 31; REMOTA approach 182–3, 186
combat neurosis 69
combined individual and group therapy: *see* dual setting
communication: *see* explicit communication; implicit communication
compartmentalization 103, 105, 125
complex posttraumatic stress disorder (C-PTSD) 70, 103, 104, 105
complex trauma disorder 70; *see also* difficult patients; trauma
conference (University of Rome 2007): *see* La Sapienza conference
conflict management, group therapy 183–5, 187
consciousness, altered: *see* dissociative disorders/states
constructivism, relational turn 22
container function 7, 182
context of therapy 148–51, *149*, *160*, 160, 161
contract, therapeutic: naturalistic study 208; REMOTA approach 137–8, 140–4, 146, 151
controlling-caregiving strategy: discussion at La Sapienza 52, 54; trauma 76, *77*; REMOTA approach 142
controlling interpersonal strategies 34, 51–3, 76–7, *77*, 78
controlling-punitive strategy: discussion at La Sapienza 51–2; trauma 76, *77*, 87; REMOTA approach 142
controlling-submissive strategy, discussion at La Sapienza 52
control treatments, randomized clinical trials 203

cooperation/cooperative systems 26, *27*, 36; discussion at La Sapienza 60–1; group therapy 183–5; therapeutic relationship 59, 137
cortisol 74, 76
cost-effective treatments 215
countertransference: *see* transference-countertransference
C-PTSD (complex posttraumatic stress disorder) 70, 103, 104, 105
criticism: group therapy 223; narcissistic personality disorders 40
cultural affiliation, analytic attitude 126
Cultural Origins of Human Cognition, The (Tomasello) 175
cumulative cultural evolution 175

Darwinian perspectives 17, 24; *see also* evolutionism
data authenticity, RCTs 197
Dazzi, N. 159
DBT (dialectical behaviour therapy) 107–8, 111–12
DDP (dynamic deconstructive psychotherapy) 107, 110
deadness: *see* dissociative disorders/states
death instinct 7; *see also* dual drives theory
defensive mechanisms: BPD 109; childhood trauma 74–5; clinical examples 65, 80; discussion at La Sapienza 55; dissociation as 105
defensive exclusion, childhood memories 79
depersonalization: clinical examples 53, 99; diagnostic criteria 103, 105, 106; polyvagal theory 93
depression: clinical example 153, 189; diagnostic criteria 102, 105; polyvagal theory 93; *see also* affect regulation
derealization 93, 99, 103, 105
Descartes, René 16

DESNOS (disorders of extreme stress not otherwise specified) 103, 104
detachment 12, *27*; clinical examples 49, 65, 233; diagnostic criteria 105; therapeutic relationship 12–13; *see also* dissociative disorders/states
developmental approaches 40; *see also* infant research
diagnostic criteria 102–6, 117; naturalistic study 208, 214, 215; *see also* DSM
dialectical behaviour therapy (DBT) 107–8, 111–12
Diana (clinical example) 53–4
difficult patients 1, 3, 63, 66, 91; attachment 114; REMOTA approach 119, 135, 152, 170, 194; naturalistic study 197; *see also* trauma
disorders of extreme stress not otherwise specified (DESNOS) 103, 104
disorganized attachment: brain function 88–9; childhood trauma 74, 76, 77, 88–9; discussion at La Sapienza 51–3, 54; group therapy 181; model of traumatic development *77*; REMOTA approach 142; working hypothesis 118
dissociative disorders/states: BPD 40; childhood trauma 66–71, 77, *77*, 78, 88–9, 170; clinical examples 45–7, 49, 54, 98, 99, 100, 151; diagnostic criteria 103, 104, 105; dysregulation of motivational systems 40–1; neo-dissociationist theories 66–7; as normal mental function 84–5, 105; polyvagal theory 95; theoretical perspectives 6–7; *see also* detachment
DIWMs (dysfunctional internal working models) 79–80, 81
Dodo metaphor, effectiveness of differing treatment models 112
dogma, psychoanalytic 14, 16, 30
domination-submission 26, 40, 59

Donald, M. 18
Dora (patient of Freud) 68
dorsovagal complex 92–3, 95, 147
double-blind approach, RCTs 200, 201
drama triangles 139–41, 145, 146
dreams, clinical example 48
drop-out rates: *see* patient drop-out
DSM (Diagnostic and Statistical Manual of Disorders) 102–3; naturalistic study 208; post-traumatic stress disorder 69, 70
dual drives theory xiii, 2, 7, 20–1, 24
dualist paradigm 16, 17; *see also* mind-body issue
dual setting (individual and group therapy) 2, 3, 108, 109, 114; REMOTA approach 116, 119–20, 154, 176–7, 182, 187–93; *see also* naturalistic study
dynamic deconstructive psychotherapy (DDP) 107, 110
dysfunctional internal working models (DIWMs) 79–80, 81
dysregulation of emotion: *see* affect regulation
dysregulation of motivational systems 40–4, 49; and childhood trauma 75, 79; polyvagal theory 95; *see also* motivational systems theory

eating disorders 41, 104, 151
Edelman, G. M. 1, 16, 17–18, 36, 187
Egidio (clinical example), REMOTA approach 152
efficacy of treatment: differing models 1, 2, 15, 111–14, 204–5; empirically supported treatments 106–11; importance of research 15; individual therapist characteristics/X factor 84, 129–30
egalitarian cooperative system 26, *27*, 33, 55
ego psychology 20
Elias, N. 183

Elsa (clinical example), REMOTA approach 136, 143–8, 163–6, 176–8, 193–6
embodiment of therapy 18, 120, 167, 170; *see also* mind-body issue
emotional detachment: *see* detachment
emotional regulation: *see* affect regulation
empathy xv, 7, 8, 9, 22, 30, 31; affiliative motivational system 228; analytic attitude 125; clinical example 231; discussion at La Sapienza 49–50; effectiveness of differing treatment models 129; relational turn 22; REMOTA approach 124, 158–61, *160*, 163, 170; theoretical perspectives 7, 8–9, 14
empirically supported treatments 106–11
empirical observation 57
enactment 7; and childhood trauma 82, 85; clinical example 44; resolving 88; *see also* transference-countertransference
Enrico (clinical example), complex trauma 95–101
epidemiological studies 102; *see also* prevalence rates
episodic memories 79
epistemic motivational systems 26–7
Eros 7; *see also* dual drives theory
ethological perspectives 33–6, 57, 175
etiopathogenic continuum 64, 117–18
etiopathogenic models 67, 71, 115
evolutionary epistemology 31
evolutionism 2, 4n1, 19, 22, 23, 25, 30–2; affiliative motivational system 218; discussion at La Sapienza 55, 56, 57, 58, 59; dual settings 187–9; empathy 159; hierarchical architecture of mental functioning 66–7, 92; *see also* cognitive-evolutionary perspective; phylogenetics

examples, clinical: *see* clinical examples
existentialist approach 17, 18, 22
expectations, positive/negative, discussion at La Sapienza 39, 50, 61
explicit communication 5, 73, 101; REMOTA approach 147, 164, 166, 169, 171, 179
exploratory-assertive system 217; clinical example 43; discussion at La Sapienza 39; dysregulation 40; infant research 29, 32
Ey, H. 67

facial expressions 88, 164
Fairbairn, W. R. D. 20–1
family system: affiliative motivational system 225; clinical example 154, 156, 157; group therapy 179
Farina, B. 77, 104
feminism, relational turn 20, 21–2
field, concept of 18; *see also* intersubjective field
fight-or-flight response: childhood trauma 75; clinical examples 98, 186; comparison of cognitive with psychoanalytic theories 34; effectiveness of differing treatment models 114; infant research 29; polyvagal theory 93; reptilian brain 26
flashbulb memories 89
fog: *see* dissociative disorders/states
Fonagy, P. 1, 3, 22, 26, 88, 109, 160
Foulkes, S. H. 174
4-D model, diagnostic criteria 106
free zones 146, 176, 208
Freudian theory 2, 7, 20, 22, 24; dissociative disorders/states 68; dual drives theory xiii, 2, 7, 20–1, 24; groups 174–5; sexual abuse in childhood 68, 69
Frewen, P. A. 106
frightened–frightening (FF) caregivers 74, *77*, 77

fright without solution 74–5, *77*, 140
functionalism 17
functional magnetic resonance imaging (fMRI) 15

Games People Play (Berne) 140
Gergen, R. 239
Gilbert, P. 19, 24, 25
Global Assessment Functioning (GAF) 208, 212–13, *213*
gold standard, RCTs 199–201
gorilla metaphor 82, 144
grandiosity, narcissistic personality disorders 40
Greenberg, J. R. 21
group therapy 2, 3, 217–19, 239, 240; affiliation 223–8; clinical example 228–37; cohesion 182–3; conflict management 183–5; functioning in groups 220–1; group membership 218, 221–2; REMOTA approach 119, 150, 171–6, *172*, *173*, 179–85; therapeutic relationship 181–2; *see also* dual setting
Guidano, V. 25

here and now 20, 23, 120, 142: group therapy 179; naturalistic study 210; therapeutic relationship *160*, 161, 163
Herman, J. L. 70
hic et nunc: *see* here and now
hierarchical model of mental functioning 23, 25–7, *27*, 31–3; and childhood trauma 75; evolutionism 66–7; polyvagal theory 92–5; REMOTA approach 126, 170
holistic perspectives, mind-body issue 15
homeostatic motivational systems 26, 31–2, 94, 240; *see also* physiological regulation system
Homo sapiens 55; ultrasociality 175; unique nature of 59, 60
hope, discussion at La Sapienza 61
hostile–helpless attachment figures 74

hostile–helpless (HH) caregivers 77, *77*
human beings 55; ultrasociality 175; unique nature of 59, 60
human factors, therapist characteristics 84, 129–30, 203–4
humility 14, 30, 88
hypervigilance 100
hypnosis 68, 69
hypothalamic circuits, limbic system 89
hysteria 68, 69

identity diffusion 109; *see also* mental integration
implicit communication 5, 7, 21; body in 167; clinical examples 73, 166; group therapy 184; REMOTA approach 120, 147, 164, 170, 171; therapeutic relationship 83, 84, 85
implicit memory 28, 90
impulsive behaviours: and childhood trauma 89, 91, 92; clinical example 190; insecure-disorganized attachment 64; REMOTA approach 138
IMS: *see* interpersonal motivational systems
inadequacy feelings 40
incest: *see* sexual abuse in childhood
individual therapy, REMOTA approach 135, 136–7; *see also* dual setting; naturalistic study
infant research 1, 2; discussion at La Sapienza 39, 57; empathy 159; non-verbal communication 167; polyvagal theory 94; REMOTA approach 120; sensual–sexual system 29; theoretical perspectives 21–2, 28–33, 36n1
inferences 5, 8–9, 61
information processing, sub-symbolic/symbolic 81, 88
insecure attachment 63–4, 95, 219
Institute of Child and Adolescent Neuropsychiatry 2

Institute of Self Psychology and Relational Psychoanalysis of Rome (ISIPS) 3
integrated teamwork 1, 23, 113, 118; *see also* multidisciplinary approaches
integration, mental: *see* mental integration
integration, theoretical 30–6
intentional agency/intentionality 17, 36, 55; complex trauma 79, 80; discussion at La Sapienza 59, 60; group therapy 175; implicit/explicit communication 164; infant research 36, 37n2
interdisciplinary approaches: *see* multidisciplinary approaches
internalization behaviours 76
internal working models (IWMs) 74, 161; childhood trauma 77, *77*, 78, 79–80, 81, 87; clinical examples 164, 185; discussion at La Sapienza 51; effectiveness of differing treatment models 114; empathy *160*; group therapy 171, 174, 178, 179, 180; REMOTA approach 137, 140, 143, 145, 146, 157–8, 167
international conference: *see* La Sapienza conference
interpersonal motivational systems (IMS) 3, 4n1, 77, 175; naturalistic study 210; REMOTA approach 158; theoretical perspectives 26, *27*, 35, 35; *see also* motivational systems theory
interpersonal psychotherapy for BPD (IPT-BPD) 107, 108
interpersonal theory, relational turn 20
interruption of therapy 118, 131, 141, 148, 208
intersubjective field 21, 82, 220, 224, 240
intersubjective school 2, 19, 26, 31, 36, 37n2; affiliative motivational system 218; comparison of cognitive with psychoanalytic theories 32–3; discussion at La Sapienza 58, 60; implicit/explicit communication 164; naturalistic study 210; primary and secondary intersubjectivity 94; relational turn 21, 22, 23; *see also* psychoanalytic perspective
intrapsychic dynamics 7
isolated mind, myth of 22
isolation, psychotherapist 222
IWMs: *see* internal working models

Jackson, J. H. 66, 67
Janet, P. 66, 67, 68, 69, 103
judgementalism, group therapy *172*, 178, 182, 185, 186

Kant, I. 16–17
Kardiner, A. 69
Karpman, S. B. 140
Kohut, H. 22, 58, 158, 176, 226, 229, 231

La Sapienza conference (University of Rome 2007) 38, 49–50; clinical examples 41–50, 59–62; Lichtenberg's contribution 39–41, 56, 60–2; Liotti's contribution 49, 50–5, 57–60; motivational systems theory 39–41, 54–5
La Svolta Relazionale (Lingiardi) 20
Lachmann, F. M. 160
Lanius, R. A. 106
letter to *Angie* 11–12
libidinal drives 7; *see also* dual drives theory
Lichtenberg, Joseph xiii–xv, 1, 3, 227; affiliation 174–5; comparison of cognitive with psychoanalytic theories 30–6; discussion at La Sapienza 39–41, 56, 60–2; groups 174, 175; mind-body issue 18; motivational systems theory 24, 27–30, 39–41, 217, 219; relational turn 19; *see also* psychoanalytic perspective

limbic system (paleomammalian complex) 25, 26–7, 32, 33, 89
limits, analyst 14, 114, 127, 133, 134, 222
linear causality, RCTs 199
Lingiardi, Vittorio 20
linguistic symbolization 88
Liotti, G. xiii–xv, 1, 3, 24, 25–7, 77; comparison of cognitive with psychoanalytic theories 30–6; diagnostic criteria 104; discussion at La Sapienza 49, 50–5, 57–60; mind-body issue 18; relational turn 19; *see also* cognitive-evolutionary perspective
Lucia (clinical example), REMOTA approach 138–42, 205

MacLean, P. 25, 31, 36, 67, 92
Main, M. and Cassidy, J. 76
Marco (clinical example), complex trauma 71–5, 77–88
Mary: see Sister Mary
MBT (mentalization-based therapy) 107, 108–9
meaning construction 26, 80
Meares, R. 105
medication: *see* pharmacological treatment
meditation 134
Meeting of Minds, A (Aron) 20
memory: childhood 43, 44, 79; implicit 28, 90
mental integration 84–5; and childhood trauma 74–5; identity diffusion 109; psychopathology as dissolution of 67; REMOTA approach 138
mentalization 3, 26–7, 88; analytic attitude 125; difficult patients 64; dual setting 188; empathy 161; implicit/explicit communication 164; REMOTA approach 137, 142, 154; relational turn 22; treatment models 113–14, 118, 129

mentalization-based therapy (MBT) 107, 108–9
mental regulation: *see* affect regulation; physiological regulation system
Mental Research Institute 18
Merleau-Ponty, M. 17
meta-cognition 188; *see also* mentalization
metacontext of therapy 148–51, *149*, *160*, 160, 161
metaphor, theoretical perspectives 5, 9–10
meta-theory of human relatedness 1, 2
mind: *see* brain function; mental integration
mind-body issue 15, 16–18
mindfulness 107, 113, 134
Minton, K. 170
mirroring 40, 97, 226, 231
mirror neurons 15, 159
Mitchell, S.A. 20, 21
model of traumatic development 77
models, as distinct from theories 14
model scene 180
moment-to-moment shifts 39–40
Monica (clinical example), REMOTA approach 179–80
monist paradigm, mind-body issue 16, 17
mother–child interaction 21–2, 167; *see also* infant research; implicit communication
motivational systems theory xiii–xv, 1–2, 4n1, 7, 9–10, 23–5, 240; comparison of cognitive with psychoanalytic theories 30–6; complex trauma 71; discussion at La Sapienza 39–41, 51–5; effectiveness of differing treatment models 111–14; group therapy 217, 219, 220, 221, 223, 224; neo-dissociationist theories 67; polyvagal theory 94; *see also* attachment-affiliation system; aversive motivational system;

cognitive-evolutionary perspective; exploratory-assertive system; interpersonal motivational systems; physiological regulation system; psychoanalytic perspective; sensual–sexual system; relational/multi-motivational therapeutic approach (REMOTA)
Mr. T. (clinical example) 6–7
multidimensional theories 16, 18 , 25, 67
multidisciplinary approaches 15, 17, 18, 19; *see also* integrated teamwork
multi-motivational theories xiii–xiv, 1, 67, 71, 187; *see also* motivational systems theory
mutuality: clinical exchange 21; therapeutic relationship 82, 123
myelinization, neurons 94
myth of the isolated mind 22

narcissistic personality disorders 40
National Institute of Health study 56
naturalistic study 197, 206: discussion 214–16; methodology 207–10; results 210–13, *211*, *213*
neglect, childhood 70, 74, 88, 100
negotiation: discussion at La Sapienza 60–1, 62; therapeutic relationship 84, 137, 139
neocortex (neomammalian complex) 25, 26–7, 32–3
neo-dissociationist theories 66–7
nervous system 24, 92–5, 96, 97, 99; *see also* brain function
networks, therapeutic: clinical example 143; group therapy 183
neuroscientific perspective 1, 2, 4n1, 7, 19; empathy 159; importance of research 15; relational turn 22, 23
night time panics, clinical example 46
Nijenhuis, E. R. S. 105
non-verbal communication 167; *see also* implicit communication

Object Relations in Psychoanalytic Theory (Greenberg and Mitchell) 21
object relations theory 7, 20, 21, 22
obsessive-compulsive disorder, diagnostic criteria 104
Oedipus complex 52
Ogden, P. 170
one-dimensional theories, mind-body issue 17
open-mindedness xiv, 5
openness, therapeutic relationship 86, 88
organic-genetic-dynamic theory of the mind 67
outcome studies 207; methodological issues 197–9; naturalistic study 212–13, 214; *see also* research
outpatients, REMOTA approach 148–9
oxytocin 55, 94

Pain, C. 170
paleomammalian complex (limbic system) 25, 26–7, 32, 33, 89
Palo Alto School 18
panic disorders: clinical example 95, 98–100; polyvagal theory 93; *see also* affect regulation
parataxic distortions 20
patient drop-out: clinical examples 130–1; dual setting 187; naturalistic study 212, 216; outpatients 149; REMOTA approach 118
patients: receptivity 5–6; sociodemographics, naturalistic study *211*
Personalities and relationships conference: *see* La Sapienza conference
personality organization 109, 159–60
pharmacological treatment: *Anna* 64; antidepressants 203; *Elsa* 143, 147, 165; REMOTA approach 119; *Sofia* 128, 154, 155, 157, 189, 191

phenomenological-existentialist approach 17, 18, 22
phylogenetics 23, 25–7, *27*, 31–3, 66–7; polyvagal theory 92–5; *see also* evolutionism; hierarchical model of mental functioning
physical childhood abuse 72–3, 81, 87, 88–9
physiological regulation system (physiological self) 28, 31–2, 217; discussion at La Sapienza 39, 40, 41; dysregulation 40, 66; *see also* homeostatic motivational systems
Plato 16
pleasure 35; relational turn 20–1; *see also* dual drives theory
polyvagal theory 15, 92–5, 96, 99
Porges, Stephen 15, 92, 94, 95
pornography 82, 87
postmodernism, relational turn 20, 22
post-traumatic stress disorder (PTSD) 69, 70–1; diagnostic criteria 102–3, 104; *see also* trauma
prayer 134
Present Moment, The (Stern) 58; *see also* here and now
prevalence rates, personality disorders 106; *see also* epidemiological studies
pride, healthy/normal 40
primary consciousness, analytic attitude 126
primary intersubjectivity 37n2, 94
primary triangle (mother-father-child) 33, 36n1, 39
protoreptilian complex (reptilian brain) 25, 26, 31–2, 75
proximal development zones 141
Psychoanalysis and Motivational Systems: A New Look (Lichtenberg, Lachmann and Fosshage) 217, 219
psychoanalytic perspective xiii–xiv, 1, 2, 3, 9, 27–30; comparison of cognitive with psychoanalytic theories 30–6; importance of research 15; mind-body issue 17;

motivational systems theory 24, 27–30; relational turn 19; *see also* intersubjective school; Lichtenberg
psychodynamic model 17
psychophysiology of trauma 88–9
psychotherapy: empirically supported treatments 106–11; importance of research 14, 15; randomized clinical trials 199–201; relational turn 19; *see also* efficacy of treatment; relational/multi-motivational therapeutic approach; therapists
PTSD: *see* post-traumatic stress disorder

Quality of Life Index (QoL-I) 208, 212–13, *213*

rage 40; *see also* affect regulation
randomized clinical trials (RCTs) 106, 199–207, 216
receptivity, patients 5–6
reciprocity, clinical 21, 22, 123; *see also* therapeutic relationship
recording of sessions, REMOTA approach 119–20
reductionism, mind-body issue 17
reflective functioning: analytic attitude 126; empirically supported treatments 108, 109
Relational Concepts in Psychoanalysis (Mitchell) 20
relational/multi-motivational therapeutic approach (REMOTA) 115; analytic attitude of therapist 125–7; *Anna* 150–1; body, role in therapy 167, 170; *Chiara* 167–70; cohesion 182–3; contract, therapeutic 137–8, 140–4, 146, 151; dual setting 119–20, 154, 176–7, 182, 187–93; *Egidio* 152; *Elsa* 136, 143–8, 163–6, 176–8, 193–6; empathy 124, 158–61, *160*, 163, 170; group therapy 150, 171–6, *172*, *173*, 179–85; implicit/explicit communication 164, 166, 167, 170,

171; individual therapy 135, 136–7; *Lucia* 138–42; *Monica* 179–80; metacontexts 148–51, *149*, 151, *160*, 160, 161; therapist training 127, 129, 133; working contexts 116–17; working hypothesis 117–19; *see also Sofia*; therapeutic relationship in context of REMOTA approach
relational psychoanalysis xv, 2, 3, 7, 17, 187; theoretical perspectives 18–23; traumatic attachment 78–80; *see also* therapeutic relationship
reparation of interaction errors: childhood trauma 74, 79, 88; effectiveness of differing treatment models 112; therapeutic relationship 59, 87, 226, 231
reptilian brain 25, 26, 31–2, 75
research: gold standard 199–201; importance of 14–16; methodological issues 197–9; traumatic attachment 78–9; *see also* naturalistic study; RCTs
residential treatment models 114
reversed attachment 76
Rita (clinical example), complex trauma 89–91
Robert (clinical example), group psychotherapy 228–37
Romanian orphanages 58
rules, defiance of 42, 43
ruptures, repairing: *see* reparation of interaction errors

sample populations: naturalistic study 207–8; RCTs 202–3
sampling bias, RCTs 203
schema-focused therapy (SFT) 107, 110–11
schemas 8, 39, 40
secondary consciousness, biopsychosocial consciousness model 188
secondary intersubjectivity 37n2, 94

secure-agentic self 34; *see also* intentional agency
secure attachment 40, 95
Segalla, R. 3
Self and Motivational Systems (Kohut) 226
self-confidence 28, 31
self-consciousness, analytic attitude 126
self-destructive behaviour 12; *Anna* 63–6, 75–6, 80; *Elsa* 136, 143–8, 178, 195; naturalistic study *213*; *Rita* 90
self-disclosure, therapeutic alliance 59, 87–8
selfobject theory 7; clinical example 229, 231; group therapy 223, 226–7; transference 176
self-other distinctions, infants 28, 32
self, physiological: *see* physiological regulation system
self psychology 3, 158; motivational systems theory 28, 225; relational turn 22
self-worth, healthy/normal 40
semantic memories 79
sensual–sexual system 29–30, 34, 35, 217; discussion at La Sapienza 39, 40, 42–3
separation anxiety 78
separation cries 31, 57, 155
sexual abuse in childhood 53–4, 68 69, 70
sexualized controlling strategies 52
sexual system, phylogenetic levels of functioning 26, *27*, 35
SFT (schema-focused therapy) 107, 110–11
shame: healthy/normal 40; therapist 132; *see also* affect regulation; aversive motivational system
Sister Mary (clinical example), discussion at La Sapienza 35, 41–4, 50, 59–62
sleeping problems 41, 46, 47

Social Conquest of Earth, The (Wilson) 218, 221
social engagement system, polyvagal theory 94, 94
social interaction, polyvagal theory 94, 95
social operational theories 8
social play, phylogenetic levels of functioning 26
sociodemographic patient variables, naturalistic study *211*
Sofia (clinical example), REMOTA approach: group therapy 185–6, 189–92; individual therapy 121–2, 124–5, 127–32; pregnancy/abortion 152–7, 162–3; suicide attempts 134–5, 155, 157, 191–2; working with emotions 156–7
splitting, BPD 109
SSRIs (selective serotonin-reuptake inhibitors) 203
Steele, K. 105
Stern, D. N. 22, 24, 44, 53–4, 58
still face experiment 83
strange situation procedure 89
stress: disorders 103, 104; hormones 74, 76; regulation 88–9; *see also* trauma
study populations: naturalistic study 207–8; RCTs 202–3
submissive hero-worship, narcissistic personality disorders 40
sub-symbolic information processing 81
substance abuse: *see* alcohol/substance abuse
suicidal ideation/suicide: clinical example 135, 155, 157, 191–2; empirically supported treatments 106, 108, 109
Sullivan, H. S. 9, 20
support networks, complex trauma 64
symbolic representations: discussion at La Sapienza 60; implicit communication 167; information processing 81, 88

sympathetic-adrenal system, polyvagal theory 93, 95, 96, 99
systems training for emotional predictability and problem solving (STEPPS) 107, 111

T., Mr. (clinical example) 6–7
teamwork 1, 23, 113, 118; *see also* multidisciplinary approaches
telephone contact, naturalistic study 208–9
templates/schemas 8, 39, 40
tension, muscular 93, 100
termination of therapy: *Elsa* 147–8, 163–4; *Robert* 234
terrible twos 59
TFP (transference-focused psychotherapy) 107, 108, 109
theoretical perspectives 5–10, 11–18; difficult patients 66–7; discussion at La Sapienza 39–41, 57–9; group therapy 220; importance of research 14–16; integration 30–6; naturalistic study 210; relational turn 18–23; *see also* motivational systems theory
theory of mind: *see* mentalization
therapeutic alliance 21, 24–5, 59, 110, 113; complex trauma 84, 85; REMOTA approach 119, 125, 137–8, 141, 161, 182; *see also* therapeutic relationship
therapeutic continuum 161
therapeutic contract: *see* contract, therapeutic
therapeutic frame 85
therapeutic networks: clinical example 143; group therapy 183
therapeutic relationship 3, 24–5, 38; arousal regulation 95–101; authenticity 85, 86, 87; boundaries 64; clinical examples 53, 233; effectiveness of differing treatment models 112–14; emotional detachment 12–13; empathy 124, 159–61, 163; implicit

communication 83, 84, 85, 170; importance of research 15; mirroring 97; mutuality 82; negotiation 84; openness 88; relational turn 20, 21; self-disclosure 87–8; *see also below*

therapeutic relationship in context of REMOTA approach 118–19, 130, 132, 134; analytic attitude 126; complexity 120–1; dual setting 120–1, 176–7; *Elsa* 143, 146, 164, 166; empathy 124, 159–61, 163; group therapy 181–2; metacontexts *149*; negotiation/therapeutic contract 137–8, 140; and relationships in general 123–4; *Sofia* 157; training for 127; X factor 129–30

therapeutic space i, 64, 114

therapists: analytic attitude 125–7; characteristics, RCTs 203–4; effectiveness 84, 129–30; experience 14, 22–3; responses 44; training 127, 129, 133; vulnerability 129, 132, 133, 134

Tom (clinical example) 8

Tomasello, M. 33, 36, 37n2, 160, 175

tornado dream, *Veronica* 48

training, therapist 127, 129, 133

trances: *see* dissociative disorders/states

transference-countertransference 3, 5, 7; clinical examples 43–4, 130–1; effectiveness of differing treatment models 112–13; REMOTA approach 130–1, 176

transference-focused psychotherapy (TFP) 107, 108, 109

trauma xiii, 1, 66–71; *Anna* 63–6, 75–6, 80, 91, 150–1; attachment 71, 78–80; bottom up approaches 170; controlling interpersonal strategies 76–7; diagnostic criteria 102–4; discussion at La Sapienza 51; dissociative disorders/states 68–71; *Elsa* 145; *Enrico* 95–101; group therapy 181; *Marco* 71–5, 77–88; model of traumatic development *77*; motivational systems theory 227–8; polyvagal theory 92–5; psychophysiology 88–9; REMOTA approach 119, 135, 147; *Rita* 89–91; *Robert* 229, 231, 233, 234; sexual abuse in childhood 68; *Veronica* 49; war veterans 69

trauma-related altered states of consciousness (TRASC) 106

traumatic attachment 71, 78–80

travelling companions, group therapy 196

treatment models: comparison of cognitive with psychoanalytic 34; empirically supported 106–11; research 16; *see also* efficacy; RCTs

tricyclic antidepressants 203

tripartite brain 92; *see also* hierarchical model of mental functioning

Tronick, E. Z. 83

two-dimensional theories, mind-body issue 17

uncontrolled variables, RCTs 200–1

unspecified dissociative disorder 105

values 23

Van der Hart, O. 105

Van Dijke, A. 104

vengeance, narcissistic personality disorders 40

ventrovagal complex, polyvagal theory 93–5, 96, 101

Veronica (clinical example), discussion at La Sapienza 35, 44–9, 50

Vietnam War 69

vulnerability, therapist 129, 132, 133, 134

Vygotskij, L. S. 18, 111, 117, 141

war trauma 69
Williams, R. 159
Wilson, E. O. 218, 221
withdrawal: *see* dissociative
  disorders/states
working models: *see* internal working
  models

World Health Organization, diagnostic
  criteria 102–3
World Wars I and II 69

X factor, REMOTA approach 129–30

Taylor & Francis eBooks

Helping you to choose the right eBooks for your Library

Add Routledge titles to your library's digital collection today. Taylor and Francis ebooks contains over 50,000 titles in the Humanities, Social Sciences, Behavioural Sciences, Built Environment and Law.

Choose from a range of subject packages or create your own!

Benefits for you
- Free MARC records
- COUNTER-compliant usage statistics
- Flexible purchase and pricing options
- All titles DRM-free.

Benefits for your user
- Off-site, anytime access via Athens or referring URL
- Print or copy pages or chapters
- Full content search
- Bookmark, highlight and annotate text
- Access to thousands of pages of quality research at the click of a button.

REQUEST YOUR FREE INSTITUTIONAL TRIAL TODAY

Free Trials Available
We offer free trials to qualifying academic, corporate and government customers.

eCollections – Choose from over 30 subject eCollections, including:

Archaeology	Language Learning
Architecture	Law
Asian Studies	Literature
Business & Management	Media & Communication
Classical Studies	Middle East Studies
Construction	Music
Creative & Media Arts	Philosophy
Criminology & Criminal Justice	Planning
Economics	Politics
Education	Psychology & Mental Health
Energy	Religion
Engineering	Security
English Language & Linguistics	Social Work
Environment & Sustainability	Sociology
Geography	Sport
Health Studies	Theatre & Performance
History	Tourism, Hospitality & Events

For more information, pricing enquiries or to order a free trial, please contact your local sales team:
www.tandfebooks.com/page/sales

The home of Routledge books

www.tandfebooks.com